A JOURNAL OF CONTEMPORARY WRITING

IRISH PAGES
DUILLÍ ÉIREANN

IRISH PAGES is a biannual journal, edited in Belfast and publishing, in equal measure, writing from Ireland and overseas. It appears at the end of each six month period.

Its policy is to publish poetry, short fiction, essays, creative non-fiction, memoir, essay reviews, nature-writing, translated work, literary journalism, and other autobiographical, historical, religious and scientific writing of literary distinction. There are no standard reviews or narrowly academic articles. Irish-language and Scots writing are published in the original, with English translations or glosses. IRISH PAGES is a non-partisan, non-sectarian, culturally ecumenical, and wholly independent journal. It endorses no political outlook or cultural tradition, and has no editorial position on the constitutional question. Its title refers to the island of Ireland in a purely apolitical and geographic sense, in the same manner of The Church of Ireland or the Irish Sea.

The sole criteria for inclusion in the journal are the distinction of the writing and the integrity of the individual voice. Equal editorial attention will be given to established, emergent and new writers.

The views expressed in IRISH PAGES are not necessarily those of the Editors. The journal is published by Irish Pages Ltd, a non-profit organization.

Submissions, by post only, are welcome but must be accompanied by return postage or an international reply coupon. No self-addressed envelope is required. Reporting time is nine months. If work is accepted, an electronic copy may be requested.

Your subscription is essential to the independence and survival of the journal. Subscription rates are £24stg/€36/$72 for one year. Visit our website at www.irishpages.org for a subscription form or to order online.

IRISH PAGES
129 Ormeau Road
Belfast BT7 1SH

Advisory Board
William Crawley
Darragh Mac Intyre
Manfred McDowell
Ruth Carr
Bernard O'Donoghue
Noel Russell
Daniel Tobin

Legal Advice: Elliott Duffy Garrett, Belfast

IRISH PAGES is set in 12/14.5 Monotype Perpetua and printed in Glasgow by Bell & Bain.

This issue has been generously asssisted by the Arts Councils of Northern and Southern Ireland.

ISBN 978-1-7393537-9-7

PRINCIPAL FUNDER

IRISH PAGES

ASKOLD MELNYCZUK, *Guest Editor*

CHRIS AGEE, *Editor*

KATHLEEN JAMIE, *Scottish Editor*

RÓISÍN COSTELLO, *Irish Language Editor*

MEG BATEMAN, *Scottish Gaelic Editor*

MILENA WILLIAMSON & JACOB AGEE, *Managing Editors*

RUTH CARR, STEPHEN DORNAN & RUTH PADEL, *Contributing Editors*

ALANNAH MILLAR (Scotland)
CASSIA BLONDELOT (Ireland)
Editorial Assistants

EDITED IN BELFAST
VOLUME 12, NUMBER 1

"Against barbarity, poetry can resist only by confirming its attachment to human fragility, like a blade of grass growing on a wall when armies march by."

Mahmoud Darwish *(from the Arabic)*

———

"Desolate, despairing,
I walk through high tide,
scrambling for a poem
in what it leaves behind.

The dark time is on us
that has been foretold.
The empty shore, as daylight
diminishes, is cold, cold."

Cathal Ó Searcaigh *(from the Irish)*

———

"Let all those who hold up the moon
above this red-hot August have enough strength, enough love.
Let's not forget the sparkling rays of dawn.
Still, we speak about rain, as if it were
the wedding of loved ones.
We talk about autumn like
faith that will not fail."

Serhiy Zhadan *(from the Ukrainian)*

IRISH PAGES
DUILLÍ ÉIREANN

VOLUME 12, NUMBER 1

CONTENTS

War in Europe

PORTFOLIO

FROM THE IMPERIALISM ARCHIVE

The Patron of This Issue

ARROWSMITH PRESS

FRIENDS AND SUPPORTERS OF *IRISH PAGES*

Anonymous (Glasgow)
Gerry Bell
Graham Benson
Lucy Brennan
Vincent Browne
Paddy and Feena Bushe
John Cassidy
Manus Charleton
Jenny Cleland
Charles Coventry
Maggie Dalton
Joan Dargan
Donnell and Alison Deeny
Joe and Geradline Duffy
Jeannie Farr
Gandolfi Fish (Glasgow)
Brendan Flynn
Elliot Duffy Garrett
Jack Gillespie
André Gumuchdjian
Joseph M Hassett
Philip Haughey
Marie Heaney
Kenneth Irvine

Celeste King
John Liddy
Brian Mac Call
Celine Mac Intyre
Enda McDonough
Manfred McDowell
Robert McDowell
John McGinley
John McMahon
Colette Ní Ghallchóir
Patricia Ní Ivor
Gordon Peake
Peter Power-Hynes
Joe Prendergast
Gillian Reynolds
William Reynolds
Carolyn Richardson
Tony Skelton
Anne Smith
Alex Stafford
Timothy Vignoles
Bret Walker
David Woods

Subscribe / donate online at www.irishpages.org

Carpathians
Western Ukraine, 1997
Patrick Breslin

GUEST EDITOR'S FOREWORD

—

Askold Melnyczuk

An anti-colonial battle.

When Chris Agee invited me to edit this special issue of *Irish Pages* I seized the opportunity. Ireland is the natural ally of all countries engaged in anti-colonial battles. The very title Chris proposed, "War in Europe", immediately set the right tone. Without waiting on Brussels, Chris granted Ukraine the wish that has cost it so dearly in blood and treasure: membership in the European Union. It was for this Ukrainians rebelled against their former president, Viktor Yanukovych, and it's for this they are being punished by Russia today. Hundreds of thousands have died; cities have been leveled. And I've just learned that Ukraine's most celebrated poet, Serhiy Zhadan, plans, at the age of 50, to enlist in the National Guard.

The poetry of Yeats had long provided me with a model of verse which manages to argue both with itself and the world without lapsing into jingoism or rhetoric. I was also fortunate enough to count Seamus Heaney a friend in the years of Ireland's "Troubles" and to witness how skillfully he managed to weave responses to public dramas with more intimate and personal reflections, to speak to issues relating to the polis without sounding "political". For some of us, the personal is political, whether we like it or not.

These days my mornings begin with a quick read of the *Kyiv Independent*, even before *The New York Times* or *The Guardian*. Editing this from the safety of Boston, Massachusetts, I'm acutely aware of how far I am from Europe, and further still from the hot war in Ukraine. Surely one of the central tasks for those of us "in between" is communicating the urgency of the situation.

My abiding gratitude to Chris, Jacob Agee, and Milena Williamson. Working with them has been a joy.

FOUR POEMS

—

Serhiy Zhadan

Autumn faith.

MAYBE IT'S TIME TO START (2022)

Maybe it's time to start.
I try to convince myself that it's not time,
that it's not right to blindly pronounce words
that haven't been spoken yet,
that haven't been printed,
no matter how much I choked
on the air this spring,
empty, wordless
no matter how much I choked
on the air this summer,
burning, without language
language is stronger than the fear of silence,
language should fill the breast pockets of life,
language should envelop places where people gather,
where they need to talk about themselves,
so that
they'll be recognized for their own voice.
Language sat in our lungs like a cold in March,
weighing us down like the clothes of fugitives
trying to cross a freezing river.
Deprived of a voice,
we weren't more honest with ourselves in silence.
We gave up our right to sing in the global choir,
afraid we'd sing a false note, afraid we'd miss the beat.
Silence stands behind us like an unsown field.
Speechless like wells filled with stones.
Maybe this – our fear, our despair,
explains the desperate silence of embittered witnesses

who saw it all, who should testify,
sing out and name the killers,
call for justice.
Sound must be sown at midnight
to create the mist of morning song.
All this carries anxiety.
All this carries consequences.

15 June 2022

There will be a moment when you dare to stand up,
break out of the silence that surrounds and oppresses you.
What makes you angry or smile these days?
My voice lit by the summer sun.

What gives you the strength to pull sounds out of language
at times when whispers betray our weariness and despair?
Feeling this is ours, feeling a hand that leads you
to the light in the center of the city.

We talk about distance
measured by stubborn waiting.
We sing of skies full of sorrow
and hills where the army stops.
Let me have the patience to listen to your silence,
listen as you ignore random questions.

Let all those who hold up the moon
above this red-hot August have enough strength, enough love.
Let's not forget the sparkling rays of dawn.
Still, we speak about rain, as if it were
the wedding of loved ones.
We talk about autumn like
faith that will not fail.

1 September 2022

A glow from a twig pulled out of the dark
by the first frost of autumn,
a breath from the heavens held by the pines,
cools, and settles as
dewy beads on a goose feather,
glistening in the sun —

it's time to talk about how we've all changed,
to notice the weariness in our eyes, the joy of our singing,
it's important now, in this dark moment
to appreciate what we've left behind
the right to enjoy silence, to enjoy a voice,
to smile at animals, who don't lose their sense of trust
even in the dark.

What changed in my language? You appeared in it.
Your presence appeared in it.
Like in a building, full of sleepers, when a light appears in window,
and now you can't help but notice how the darkness
is filled with meaning and fire.

The twig, a source of light,
stands firm through the first rains,
the luxury of rereading, the luxury of returning —
everything has changed, nothing will be the same,
everything takes courage —
courage to name something
and say it out loud.

Don't be afraid, language will not betray you,
when you try to explain
why you and I have no chance,
don't be afraid, language will explain, why we wander in the dark,
unable to tear ourselves away from each other,
why our mutual dependency frightens us,
why our mutual distance torments us.

Black beasts of love break free from the leash at the voices of children.
Who will challenge submission and stasis?
Twig, fight the wind, sing despite the approaching darkness.
Language needs those
who speak softly
and are silent, but convincing.

19 October 2022

It feels like every year
in November
a forest surrounds poets –
a forest of firing squads,
a forest of the condemned, who kept letters
in their pockets like yesterday's bread crumbs.

This is the seasonal trauma for a literature hounded
out of cities, as the greatest threat.
Writers were fished out of editorial offices,
like trout from streams,
leaving behind only ripples
for young authors orphaned and unprepared.

The fall sharpens our perception of an unfinished poem,
a manuscript that fell sick like a tree
in an urban space that lacked freedom.

This forest surrounds poets with lungs
burnt by the gas of the Great War.
It surrounds actors whose movements
recreate a cabaret dance of agony.
It surrounds priests, it surrounds teachers and editors.

This quiet community is so steeped in books
that even in their final movements, they call out, O, Death!
The tall bright pines are all that's left of justice.
The fog in the throat, a substitute for emptiness and despair.

The weight of this forest, like the weight of a rhythm,
that alarms the acoustics of libraries and quarries.
It sheds light on the clear cuts hacked into
the autumn forests of our continuity.
The continuity of our writing, the continuity of our song.
Invisible burial mounds mark every great literature.
The sand under our feet, filled with their broken teeth, is our language.

27 November 2022

Translated, from the Ukrainian, by Virlana Tkacz and Wanda Phipps.

Serhiy Zhadan is an internationally renowned Ukrainian poet and novelist. He was born 1974 in the Luhansk Region of Ukraine and educated in Kharkiv, where he lives today. He currently helps organize local artists and musicians as volunteers delivering humanitarian aid in Kharkiv. He is the award-winning author of seventeen books of poetry as well as numerous prose works, and his books have been translated into over thirty languages. In 2022, Zhadan was awarded the Hannah Arendt Prize for Political Thought, as well as the Peace Prize of the German Book Trade for his "outstanding artistic work and his humanitarian stance with which he turns to the people suffering from war and helps them at the risk of his own life." He is the front man for the band Zhadan and the Dogs.

Virlana Tkacz was born in Newark, NJ in 1952 and graduated from Columbia University with an MFA in theatre directing. She heads Yara Arts Group and has directed forty original shows at La MaMa Experimental Theatre in New York, as well as in Kyiv, Lviv, Kharkiv, Bishkek, Ulaanbaatar, and Ulan Ude. She received an NEA Poetry Translation Fellowship for her translations with Wanda Phipps of Serhiy Zhadan's poetry. She is the author of the bilingual catalogue Kurbas: New World *(Kyiv, 2019) and a book of poems* Three Wooden Trunks *(Lost Horse Press, 2022).*

Wanda Phipps was born in Washington, DC in 1960 and now lives in Brooklyn, NY. She studied theater and the arts at Barnard College of Columbia University in New York City, acting at American Conservatory Theater in San Francisco, and poetry at Naropa University in Colorado. She is the author of the books: Mind Honey *(Autonomedia, 2021);* Field of Wanting: Poems of Desire *(BlazeVOX, 2008); and* Wake-Up Calls: 66 Morning Poems *(Soft Skull Press, 2004). Her poems have been translated into Ukrainian, Hungarian,*

Arabic, Galician and Bangla and appeared in over one hundred literary magazines as well as numerous anthologies. She is the recipient of a New York Foundation for the Arts Poetry Fellowship and a founding member of Yara Arts Group.

Together Virlana Tkacz and Wanda Phipps have received the Agni Poetry Translation Prize, the National Theatre Translation Fund Award, and numerous translation grants from the New York State Council on the Arts. Yale University Press has published two books of their translations: What We Live For, What We Die For: Selected Poems by Serhiy Zhadan in 2019, and How Fire Descends: New and Selected Poems by Serhiy Zhadan in 2023, which was a Finalist for the PEN America Poetry in Translation Award. Their translations have also appeared in many literary journals and anthologies and are integral to the theater pieces created by Yara Arts Group.

WAR STAYS FOR DINNER

———

Askold Melnyczuk

Grace, justice, power and freedom

James Joyce was right: History was the nightmare I was trying to escape when I fled New Jersey for Boston. It wasn't easy. A garrulous guest, History had been joining us for dinner for as long as I could remember. Sitting down at 4:00 p.m., so that my father could eat with us before heading to work second shift at the Anheuser-Busch plant in Newark, my sister and I would listen to tales of a lost world. Presiding silently at the head of the table, wearing a jacket and tie, my grandfather, would wink at us, acknowledging our bewilderment without interrupting our parents' rehearsal of all that had been lost to war – friends, family, home, a country. Occasionally he would add a story of his own.

We knew, for example, that, after serving in the Austro-Hungarian army during the First World War, for which he'd interrupted his graduate studies in Byzantine Art and Art History at the University of Vienna, he'd returned to Ukraine to do archeological field work documenting the Scythian presence around Odesa. There he was arrested by the Bolsheviks. One morning he was lined up with other Ukrainian prisoners before a firing squad. When he heard the guns go off, he dropped to the ground. His would-be executioners were drunk, he explained. After discharging their rifles, they walked away, leaving the bodies where they fell. My grandfather escaped. He made his way to St. Petersburg where, the story goes, he met with Trotsky who permitted him to ride with the Bolsheviks to make sure the most precious icons weren't damaged as they looted Ukraine's churches. Did this really happen? I know this last detail only from a funeral oration delivered after my grandfather's death by one of his students.

History loves the dead.

———

My grandfather eventually returned to Peremyshl, an ancient city with a mixed Polish, Ukrainian, and Jewish population. Its roots dated back to the eighth century, with evidence of a Christian monastic settlement on the site by the ninth century – a hundred years before the baptism of Kyiv. My grandfather's mother was Polish – a member of what was known as "mala shlachta", petty gentry, a fact on which my mother prided herself, lording it over my father, a lowly member of the business class from Czernivtsi. My grandfather and his brother assumed Ukrainian identities; their sister Sabina identified as Polish – as was the common practice at that time. They were indeed prominent citizens in a city central to Ukrainian cultural evolution. "The signs of growing interest in the cultural aspects of nationhood", writes the historian Orest Subtelny, "appeared in the early 19th century in the ancient city of Peremyshl, the seat of the Greek Catholic eparchy, site of a lyceum and rich libraries, and the homes of some of the most sophisticated members of the Ukrainian clergy."

My grandfather, who never finished his thesis on Byzantine Art, began teaching in one of the city's two Ukrainian-language high schools. There he advised his students to study rather than waste time politicking.

Grandfather's stories were hardly unique. Every older member of our large extended family had similarly harrowing briefs. One uncle had spent a couple of years in Siberia before being released so that he could join in the fight against Hitler after the collapse of the Soviet/German alliance.

Hearing these stories in the disjunctive calm of suburban New Jersey, my sister and I were unsure of how to relate to this terrible lost world. It sounded like a good place to leave. Yet, given how badly our parents wanted to return, there was clearly more to it. Attachment to childhood memories was surely part of it, of course. My mother loved recalling the summers she spent on her grandfather's farm in Laskivci where she would arrive from the train station in a "britchka" – a small, horse-drawn carriage. But, over time, I understood that what they really missed was the richness of the culture which had shaped them: music, ranging from folk songs to the classical compositions of Lysenko and Lyudkevich; poetry, not only Shevchenko and Franko (with whom my grandfather studied) but also of the writers of the 1930s, most of whom who died violent deaths during Stalin's reign of terror and who constitute a group known collectively as "the executed renaissance". Then came the poets and fiction writers of the sixties – many of whom were so-called dissidents – whose works my parents bought and my mother read: Vasyl Stus, Ivan Drach, Lina Kostenko, Oles Honchar, Mykola Rudenko, Ivan Dziuba, and many others. Whenever one of them was arrested my sister and I would join our parents at protest marches in front of the UN or outside the Soviet embassy in New York or Washington.

The vivid and at times overwhelming histories we heard at home had little resonance in the outside world. There, Ukraine did not exist except as a subset of Russia. Our schoolteachers didn't care to hear our stories. The cultural sensitivity so widespread (if endangered) today was still decades away. We were expected to assimilate and join the consumer culture – or so it appeared. Watching the Cosby Show, I longed for the normalcy evinced by that model African-American household.

I had not yet absorbed one of literature's primary lessons: appearances deceive.

At the height of the Cold War, public perceptions were fueled by a well-funded Soviet disinformation apparatus, and supported by the animus of many red-diaper babies. I was repeatedly told that Ukraine didn't exist and, at the same time, that all Ukrainians were Nazis. This state of affairs lasted well-into the nineties and only began shifting gradually after Ukraine declared independence.

Having to persuade others that one exists, and is not the child of Nazis, grows old fast.

One evening in the fall of 1994 I was watching the popular television news program *Sixty Minutes* alongside my wife when Morley Safer, one of the program's hosts, floated the idea that perhaps all Ukrainians (who didn't really exist) were genetically antisemitic.

I couldn't help recalling my mother's stories – not only the ones rehearsed over the dinner table but the more detailed ones I had translated myself back in the seventies so she could read them out at synagogues, where she was a regular invited speaker.

In her talks, she described how her life changed in 1939, when the Germans advanced east: "In the early days of the war, when the Germans began bombing the city center, my mother took her children to wait out the attack at the home of the Sheflers, who lived on the outskirts of the city. When the presence of military barracks nearby made even that area into a target, Mother gathered up the family and, in the company of Mrs. Shefler and her children, moved to a neighboring village where they passed the critical period in the home of an acquaintance. When the fighting subsided, both families returned to their respective homes."

She goes on to describe the two families' relationship in warm detail. From 1923 to 1929 the families were neighbors: "We normally spent the holidays (Rosh Hashanah, Yom Kippur, Purim) with the Sheflers. The older Sheflers were orthodox and adhered to the law. Their sons, on the other hand, entertained more modern opinions – which their parents tolerated only grudgingly. All four of the boys – Samyk, Vilyk, Mundek, and Edek (Izydor), attended the Ukrainian high school ... After we moved, Mrs. Shefler and my mother continued visiting each other. Mrs. Shefler often complained that Edek, who was very handsome, was always dating Ukrainian girls. Because the Sheflers were people of modest means, Edek wasn't able to attend university. Instead, he too went to work. Moreover, in 1936, his father died, after which his two older brothers married and moved to other cities while he and his brother Samyk stayed to care for their mother."

She goes on to describe the brutality of the Soviet regime. There wasn't a Ukrainian family who didn't have at least one of its members arrested or deported. A cousin, as well as her father's brother-in-law, were both killed by the Bolsheviks. Her younger brother was arrested and disappeared. Among the Polish intelligentsia, too, many judges and high-ranking military officers had been murdered or exiled to Siberia.

In 1942 my mother dropped out of university to attend to her dying mother, as well as to care for her six-year-old sister (my aunt, who witnessed all this, is 87, and lives just outside Washington D.C.). By then one part of the city had been partitioned with barbed wire and turned into a ghetto. Jews were forced to wear armbands emblazoned with the Star of David.

Then the Germans began transporting the older people out of the ghetto. My mother recounts stories about friends who came seeking help. Among them were the Koestlers, who'd obtained two forged IDs and wanted to get to Warsaw but feared someone at the train station might recognize them as they were buying tickets. They stayed the night and the next day my mother and uncle bought their tickets and escorted them to the train: "Eventually we received a coded telegram from Warsaw: 'Aunt is well.' We later learned they survived the war." There was Dr. Kuba-Reinbach, who hid with them for three weeks before being spirited out of the city by friends. And then there were the Sheflers.

———

These memories, this ancient history, flares up now of course because of Putin's mad nonsense about "denazification". Eight million Ukrainians were killed in World War II (among them, 600,000 Ukrainian Jews). This was on the heels of Stalin's genocidal famine of 1932-33 which had cost some five million lives. An additional two and a half million Ukrainians were deported to work camps in Germany. The combined losses of France, Italy, the UK, and the US in that war totaled around two million. And Putin's canard about Ukraine as a nation of Nazis deserves to be answered.

———

My mother's story continues:

"One evening, around curfew, we were all home except for Father, who always arrived late from his committee meetings, when the doorbell rang. 'Who's there?' I asked. A voice at once strange and familiar whispered: 'Helen, hand me the key to the cellar. It's me, Edek. I'm with my wife' (we hadn't heard that he'd gotten married while in the ghetto). I opened the door and in the dim light spilling out of the hallway I saw a horrifyingly pale face which in no way resembled the handsome man I knew so well. I froze. 'It's me alright. Give me the key.' I took a deep breath, turned and went to get the key. I told my brother Orest who was at the door. Orest led the Sheflers to the cellar. When Father returned, we explained what had happened. He told Orest to bring them up at once."

The Germans had begun killing the ghetto's residents then transporting the bodies out at night and dumping them in the Jewish cemetery. Edek and his new wife, Esther, pretended they'd been shot. They were thrown onto a truck full of corpses and dumped into a mass grave out of which they later crawled.

Their mother had already been deported (they learned later that she'd been killed). Samyk was still in the ghetto. Edek didn't know the whereabouts of his two older brothers. My mother recalled Edek saying: "Professor, you are our father now. You must decide what to do with us. This is my young wife, Esther. We were married not long ago and haven't begun to live yet and now it seems it's time for us to die."

My uncle set about creating a secret space in the pantry by blocking a part of it off with a bookcase. There the Sheflers hid and slept.

Maintaining silence about their presence posed a challenge. In fact, my mother did tell her closest friends so that they understood the risk they took visiting. Only my aunt Christine, six years old at the time, managed to keep the secret.

The police station was directly across the street.

At one point Maria, the housekeeper, threatened to turn the family in, relenting only after my uncle pointed out that the Germans would see her as complicitous and would surely execute her as well. Then there was

"Captain Violin", a Gestapo officer who came to play the violin, accompanied by my mother on the piano. He and my grandfather had served together in the Austro-Hungarian Army. The Captain had no idea that the Sheflers were among his audience. My mother always credited her father's deep faith for protecting them.

As the Bolsheviks approached, my grandfather learned that his name was on the list of those scheduled for deportation, or worse: "We had to leave before the Bolsheviks returned. We packed the most valuable among Father's books and brought them to the Bishop's Palace for safekeeping. We gathered a few necessary items and left on the last civilian train from Peremyshl to Krakow, where Father's brother lived. We were sorry to say goodbye to the Sheflers and we were uncertain whether we would ever see each other again."

"...The Sheflers live in Israel now ... We maintained a correspondence and they always assured us we were their only family. It's the kind of feeling that springs up between people not bound by blood but whose fates twined in difficult times, in the days when man was wolf to man."

The families were reunited in the seventies when my mother and uncle traveled to Israel to plant a tree at Yad Vashem. Such are the fascists Putin has set out to murder, because today, again, man is wolf to man.

—

"History is a nightmare during which I'm trying to get a good night's sleep", quipped Delmore Schwartz. I would have far preferred these stories remain the faint memories of a bad dream, but Russia's assault on Ukraine has reminded me of history's grim continuities. That genocidal violence should surface in Europe in the early decades of the 21st century, and then be echoed in Israel's equally genocidal revenge against Gaza, must give us all pause.

The central problem of the nineteenth century, wrote Albert Camus, was how to live in a world abandoned by grace. With God gone missing, the solution turned on humans creating their own earthly paradise, a utopia founded on the principle of justice. But justice according to whom? Lenin? Hitler? By the middle of the twentieth century the question became: how do we live in a world ruled by neither grace nor justice? In fact, events had already provided the answer. Into the vacuum marched the will to power. Maintaining a grip on power for its own sake has become the authoritarian's goal. Cue Putin, Trump, Netanyahu, Lukashenko, Orban – the list grows longer by the day. Unlike its predecessors, however, power appears unwilling to yield the floor. Even formulating the next question is difficult. Where do we go once we admit that neither grace, nor justice, not even the will to power have, will, or can succeed in bringing the social forces tearing us apart into some kind of equilibrium?

Can we imagine a value strong enough to displace the pursuit of power? Is freedom a value? The dictionary definition suggests it is: "the power or right to act, speak, or think as one wants without hindrance or restraint." Freedom is precisely what the citizens of Russia and other totalitarian countries sacrifice. Their speech and behavior are monitored. Individuals are punished for stepping out of line, for thinking for themselves, for attempting to define their own identities. Having tasted freedom, Ukrainians would rather die than revert to the status of an occupied territory. The God of Freedom is worthy of worship. For Ukrainians, freedom means Europe and the US. But as James Baldwin reminded us: "Freedom is not something that anybody can be given. Freedom is something people take, and people are as free as they want to be."

During the Maidan Revolution in 2014 I asked Oksana Zabuzhko why she kept running from the barricades to the lecture hall. Her reply was clarifying. "Because if I'm not on the barricades, there won't be a hall in which to lecture; and if I'm not in the lecture hall, then what are the barricades for?" Ukraine's existential battle for cultural self-preservation has been going on for a long time. I'm confident that, this time, Ukraine will prevail. To which I'd only add these words from Benjamin Franklin: "Those who would give up essential liberty to purchase a little temporary safety deserve neither liberty nor safety." Slava Ukraini.

15 April 2024 (Patriot's Day)
Medford, Massachusetts

A novelist, poet and essayist, Askold Melnyczuk was born in 1954, grew up in New Jersey, and received a BA from Antioch College and MA from Boston University. His debut novel, What Is Told (1994), a "New York Times Notable Book" — which Seamus Heaney described as "a great novel of unresentful sorrow and half-requited grief" — was the first commercially-published novel to treat the Ukrainian-American experience. His second, The Ambassador of the Dead (2001), was selected as one of the "Best Books of the Year" by the Los Angeles Times, which noted: "Melnyczuk's Ambassador is an eloquent meditation on the human need for a rooted historical perspective. His ambassador, Adriana, invites comparison to one of the tempestuous Karamazovs. With her, he has brought the great tradition of Russian literature to American soil in a transplant that is a work of art." The House of Widows *(2008) was chosen by the American Libraries Association's "Booklist" as an Editor's Choice. His most recent book is a story collection,* The Man Who Would Not Bow *(2021). A book of poems,* The Venus of Odesa, *will appear in 2025.*

His work has appeared in The New Yorker, The Paris Review, The Nation, The New York Times, Glimmer Train, The Antioch Review, Ploughshares, Harvard Review, Words Without Borders *and* Irish Pages. *He co-edited* From Three Worlds: The New Writing from Ukraine. *Currently a Professor in the MFA Program at the University of Massachusetts, he has also taught at the Bennington Writing Seminars, Boston University, and Harvard. He is Founding Editor of* AGNI *(1973) and the Arrowsmith Press (2006), and his work has been translated into German, Polish, Russian and Ukrainian.*

THE FALL OF THE PAN-RUSSIAN UTOPIA[1]

———

Serhii Plokhy

On the "Russia idea".

In the fall of 2008, Vladimir Putin, then the prime minister of Russia, who had just left the office of the president, asked Aleksei Venediktov, the editor in chief of the radio station Echo of Moscow, which was liberal but still tolerated by the authorities, what aspects of his two presidential terms would make it into school history textbooks.

Venediktov, who had begun his career as a history teacher, responded that it would be Putin's initiative leading to the reunification of the Moscow Patriarchate with the Russian Orthodox Church abroad – an émigré institution that had remained anti-Bolshevik and loyal to the Romanov dynasty after the Revolution of 1917. Surprised, Putin asked, "And is that all?" In 2015, seven years after their original conversation and one year after the annexation of the Crimea, Putin asked Venediktov the same question. "Putin knows perfectly well", remarked Venediktov in an interview, "that history books for both Russian and Ukrainian schools will say that 'Khrushchev returned the Crimea, and Putin took it back.'"[2]

Putin compared himself not only to the Soviet leaders like Khruschev but also to the Russian emperors Peter I, Catherine II, and Alexander II. Their busts and portraits made their way into Putin's antechamber in the Kremlin, and his press secretary, Dmitrii Peskov, attested to his superior's interest in history. "Putin reads all the time", confided Peskov on one occasion, "mostly about the history of Russia. He reads memoirs, the memoirs of Russian historical state figures."[3]

In May 2009, less than a year after the invasion of Georgia, he made a public show of his admiration for imperial Russian thinkers. Despite rainy weather, he showed up in the company of numerous reporters at the cemetery of the Donskoi Monastery in Moscow to lay flowers on the graves of General Denikin and his wife, along with the grave of Ivan Ilyin and that of Ivan Shmelev, another Russian émigré writer whose remains had been returned to Russia. Putin also laid flowers on the grave of Aleksandr Solzhenitsyn, who had died in Moscow the previous year.[4]

Referring to General Denikin, whose grave he honored first, Putin encouraged one of the reporters accompanying him at the ceremony to read Denikin's memoirs. "Denikin discusses Great and Little Russia, Ukraine", said Putin. "He writes that no one may meddle in relations between us; that has always been the business of Russia itself." Denikin was in fact following Aleksandr Pushkin, who had attacked the West for criticizing Russia's assault on Poland after it rebelled against the empire in 1830. If Pushkin referred to Russo-Polish relations, Denikin referred to those between Russia and Ukraine. In Putin's view, it was up to Russia to decide how to conduct its relations with a weaker neighbor. The Slavic roots of the two peoples became his excuse to condemn any Western support for Ukraine.[5]

Archimandrite Tikhon, who was rumored to be Putin's spiritual adviser at the time, confided to the assembled reporters that Putin had personally paid for the tombstones of the Denikins, Ilyin, and Shmelev. The archimandrite also told them of Putin's admiration for Solzhenitsyn, whom he called "an organic and committed statist." Solzhenitsyn was not only a believer in a strong Russian state but also a promoter of Russia as an East Slavic state based on the Pan-Russian, imperial model of the Russian nation, including Russia, Ukraine, and Belarus.[6]

Solzhenitsyn was the key figure who linked the imperial thinking of the past with a plan for dealing with post-Soviet Russian challenges and realities. In his essay of 1990, *Rebuilding Russia: Reflections and Tentative Proposals*, Solzhenitsyn called for the separation of the Eastern Slavs from the non-Slavic republics of the Soviet Union and the formation of a "Russian Union" consisting of Russia, Ukraine, Belarus, and northern Kazakhstan. This was an awkward compromise between the Soviet and imperial visions of Russian national identity. In the Soviet tradition, Solzhenitsyn, who was half-Ukrainian, referred to the Ukrainians as a separate nation, but, according to imperial tradition, he considered them one and the same people as the Russians.

If one followed Ernest Gellner's definition of nationalism as the establishment of congruence between political and ethnonational borders, then Solzhenitsyn's "reconstructed" Russia was to become quadripartite. But his plan never materialized, and several years later Solzhenitsyn went on to question the legitimacy of the Ukrainian borders. In his essay *Russia in Collapse* (1998), Solzhenitsyn argued for the annexation of eastern and southern Ukraine, denouncing its "inordinate expansion onto territory that was never Ukraine until Lenin: the two Donets provinces, and the whole southern belt of New Russia (Melitopol-Kherson-Odesa) and the Crimea."[7]

Putin shared Solzhenitsyn's belief that parts of eastern and southern Ukraine were not its historical territories but, as he told President George Bush in 2008, were a gift from the Russian Bolsheviks. As for Solzhenitsyn's compromise view, that was not a major issue for Putin as long as the political project of Russo-Ukrainian unity and the imperial model of a tripartite Russian nation were realized. Like Solzhenitsyn, Putin accepted the Soviet division of the Russian nation into Russians, Ukrainians, and Belarusians, but continued to think of them as representatives of essentially one people. Solzhenitsyn's vision of Russia served as a bridge between imperial notions of Russian language, culture, and identity and views that began to become popular in Russian political circles with the arrival of Vladimir Putin in the Kremlin.

Russia was ready to move beyond the Soviet legacy when it came to its vision of itself and relations with its neighbors, but the movement was backward in history. Putin emerged as its leader. At his disposal he had the ideas of the Eurasianists, who offered justification for Russian control of the former imperial space; the proponents of a big Russian nation, who wanted a common East Slavic state; and, finally, the views of those who, in case other integrationist projects failed, were prepared to settle for a Greater Russia annexing historically or ethnically Russian enclaves.

———

Where Russia begins and ends, and what territories the historical "gathering of the Russian lands" should encompass, are old questions that have preoccupied Russian thinkers and statesmen for generations.

Most Russians believe today, as they have believed for centuries, that their state and nation originated in Kyiv (in the Russian version, "Kiev"), the center of the medieval polity that historians call Kyivan Rus'. Centered on today's Ukrainian capital, it encompassed a good part of what is now Ukraine, Belarus, and European Russia. Kyivan Rus', formed in the tenth century, fell under the blows of the Mongols in the thirteenth century, but not before giving birth to numerous semi-independent polities. The most powerful of them were Galicia-Volhynia in present-day Ukraine and southern Belarus; Great Novgorod or the Novgorodian republic in the northwestern lands of the former Kyivan realm; and the principality of Vladimir – later Moscow in its northeastern part – the historical core of modern Russia.[8]

The Russians can indeed trace back to Kyiv the origins of their religion, written language, literature, arts, law code, and – extremely important in the premodern era – their ruling dynasty. Their attempts to claim Kyiv as the source of their ethnicity, language, and popular culture turned out to be more problematic. Travelers from Moscow and St. Petersburg found that the locals in Kyiv and environs spoke a language different from theirs, sang different songs, and had a distinct culture. But that did not matter too much, as the myth of Russia's Kyivan origins had already embedded itself in the consciousness of the Russian elites by the late fifteenth century.[9]

The origins of that myth go back to the mid-fifteenth century, the earliest years of the Grand Principality of Moscow, later known as Muscovy, as an independent state. Its founder was Ivan the Great, the ruler of Moscow and one of the many descendants of the Kyivan princes who established Moscow's rule over a huge realm extending from Nizhnii Novgorod in the east to Great Novgorod, or simply Novgorod, in the west. It was in the midst of Ivan's war against Novgorod, one of the heirs of Kyivan Rus', that the myth of Russia's Kyivan origins was born, originally as a dynastic claim. Ivan declared himself the heir of the Kyivan princes, claiming the right to rule Novgorod on that basis. He defeated the Novgorodians at the Battle of Shelon in 1471 and absorbed the republic into his realm in 1478. The independent Russian state, born of the struggle between Moscow and Novgorod, resulted from the victory of authoritarianism over democracy.

No element of the reunification saga was considered more important by the imperial historians than the establishment of Muscovy's control over eastern Ukraine in the mid-seventeenth century. Their Soviet successors hailed it as the "reunification of Ukraine with Russia" – in effect, the culmination of Ukrainian history with its complete assimilation by Russia. Many Ukrainian historians, for their part, referred to the "reunification" as a military alliance, personal union, or even outright subjugation.

In the nineteenth century the Russian historians, including the most influential of them, Vasilii Kliuchevsky, claimed that the "gathering of the Russian lands", or the "reunification of Rus" after the Mongol invasion by the Moscow princes and then the tsars was the quintessential feature of the Russian historical process. That interpretation of history, rooted in the myth of Russia's Kyivan origins, was supposed to culminate in the triumphal reunification of the Rus' lands in one Russian state, or "Russia, one and indivisible." According to Kliuchevsky, that process had been largely completed by the mid-nineteenth century.[10]

Ironically, it was exactly in the mid-nineteenth century that the imperial "gathering of the Russian lands" project encountered an enemy that it could not defeat. The name of the enemy was nationalism. It came first in two Polish uprisings that rocked the Russian Empire. In the long run, however, it was Ukrainian nationalism, awakened by the imperial campaigns to suppress Polish mobilization, that posed the main threat to imperial Russian statehood. If the Poles resisted imperial rule, the Ukrainians threatened the unity of the "reunified" Catherinian empire by claiming an identity distinct from the Russian.[11]

The empire struck back by forging a model of Russian nationalism closely allied with its empire. In 1832, in the aftermath of the first Polish uprising, the newly appointed deputy minister of education, Count Sergei Uvarov, proposed a tripartite formula to Emperor Nicholas I that could serve as the keystone of a new Russian identity to be forged by the educational system. It consisted of three concepts to which a loyal subject of the tsar would have to subscribe: Orthodoxy, Autocracy, and Nationality. In the past, Russian subjects had been obliged to be loyal to God, the Sovereign, and the Fatherland. Nationality, which replaced the "fatherland", was as much a reaction to rising Polish nationalism as it was an attempt to emulate German nation-building. Uvarov was particularly influenced by the ideas of the German historian and philologist Karl Wilhelm Friedrich Schlegel, a follower of Johann Gottfried von Herder, who envisioned a unified German state to be based on the German nation united by language and customs.[12]

For Uvarov, the envisioned nationality was to be indisputably Russian, but it would include the other East Slavic heirs of Kyivan Rus', the Ukrainians and Belarusians. The population of the two lesser branches was mainly Orthodox in religion, but a significant minority belonged to the Uniate Church, which had been established in the late sixteenth century. Its adherents, who lived in the eastern borderlands of partitioned Poland, followed Orthodox ritual but acknowledged the supremacy of the Roman pope. In Uvarov's eyes they were Russian but not Orthodox, and many believed them susceptible to Polish insurgent propaganda. The "problem" was solved before the end of the 1830s, when the Uniates were forcibly "reunited" with the Russian Orthodox Church. The Russian nation, integrated by loyalty to the tsar, was now united by religion as well.

The history textbooks written under Uvarov's supervision legitimized the creation of one Russian nation, now united within imperial borders and subject to the scepter of the tsar. The imperial narrative envisioned the origins of the Russian nation in medieval Kyiv of the princely era. That nation had been divided by foreign invaders ranging from the Mongols to the Poles but reunited by the Russian tsars to become once again consolidated and invincible.[13]

The model of a united Russian nation did not remain unchallenged for long. Taking a cue from the Poles, the Ukrainians soon raised the banner of their own national movement. The empire encountered a challenge from the ranks of the Russian nation that it was trying to build in opposition to Poland. In the 1840s, Kyivan intellectuals led by a professor of history at the local university, Mykola Kostomarov, and a drawing instructor at the same university, Taras Shevchenko, formed a clandestine organization that claimed the existence of a distinct Ukrainian nation. Drawing on traditions of Cossack history and historical chronicles, they were fascinated with the Ukrainian language and the lore and culture of the common people. According to Herder and his followers, that was the taproot of national identity.

The modern Ukrainian national project was born, and it was much more threatening to the Russian Empire than the Polish revolt. Kostomarov envisioned a Slavic federation to replace the Romanov and Habsburg monarchies and empires. The empire felt compelled to adjust the model of the unified Russian nation. It did so in the aftermath of the second Polish uprising (1863-64), which once again put the loyalty not only of the Poles but also of the Ukrainians and Belarusians into question. The new model of the unified Russian nation was tripartite, postulating the existence of separate "tribes" of Great Russians, Little Russians (Ukrainians), and White Russians (Belarusians). They spoke different "dialects" of Russian, went the argument, put forward by the conservative Russian journalist Mikhail Katkov, among others, but that was no reason to doubt the unity of the tripartite nation.[14]

To ensure that it would remain united, the authorities decided to arrest the development of distinct Ukrainian and Belarusian languages. The first ban on the publication in Ukrainian of anything other than folklore — including the Bible, religious texts, and language primers, along with school textbooks — was introduced in 1863 and remained in effect, with some modifications, until the first decade of the twentieth century. It was then abolished in the turmoil caused by the Revolution of 1905 in the Russian Empire. The ban on Ukrainian-language publications delayed the development of the modern Ukrainian national project but failed to suppress it. The Ukrainians of Galicia, a part of Ukraine taken over by Austria as a result of the partitions of Poland, continued to publish in Ukrainian not only their own works but also the writings of their counterparts from Russian-ruled Ukraine.[15]

The model of a tripartite Russian nation, which the Russian historian Alexei Miller calls a "big Russian nation", was adopted by the imperial elites in the second half of the nineteenth century and became part of the ideological credo and personal belief, as well as identity, of many of the country's political, religious, and military leaders. The Russian Revolution put an end to the dominance of the tripartite nation in Russian political and ethnonational thought. Ukraine created its own statehood in 1917 and declared its independence in 1918. The same year the Austro-Hungarian parts of Ukraine declared their independence and in 1919 formed one unified Ukrainian state. It lost the fight against the Poles, the White Russians and the Bolsheviks, and disappeared from the map of Europe. But the idea of Ukrainian independence would live on.

By the time the Bolsheviks established their rule in Ukraine, in 1920, Vladimir Lenin concluded that Ukrainian aspirations to independence were so strong, not only among Ukrainians in general but even among the Ukrainian Bolsheviks themselves, as to require the granting of a degree of autonomy and a status equal to that of Russia. Not only were the Ukrainians recognized as a distinct nationality (as were the Belarusians), no longer a "tribe" of a tripartite Russian nation as in tsarist times, but pro-forma recognition of independence was given to a puppet Soviet Ukrainian state, and Ukrainian became its official language.

Realizing that the national movements brought to power by the effects of World War I and the Revolution of 1917 would have to be accommodated, the Bolsheviks strove to gain their cooperation. This accommodation eventually went beyond issues of language, culture, and the recruitment of local cadres into de-facto occupation administrations. It also included the creation of state institutions and recognition of the formal independence of the Bolshevik-controlled puppet states formed to delegitimize the new truly independent states and governments established by the national minorities in the borderlands of the former empire.[16]

In 1922, Lenin resisted Joseph Stalin's attempts to incorporate non-Russian republics into the Russian Federation and insisted on the creation of a Union state in which those republics would be distinct polities with rights equal to those of Russia. Vladimir Lenin's main contribution to the history of Russo-Ukrainian relations was the endowment of Russia, or the Russian Federation – the name under which it entered the Soviet Union – with a territory and institutions of its own, distinct for the first time in centuries from the territory and institutions of the empire that the Bolsheviks were seeking to preserve. If anything, Lenin laid the foundations for the formation of modern Russia, not Ukraine.[17]

The idea of a big Russian nation went into the Russian emigration along with the White Guard generals defeated by the Bolshevik Red Army and the intellectuals who supported their vision of Russia, one and indivisible. Among the émigrés was General Anton Denikin, whose memoirs would make a strong impression on Vladimir Putin, and the philosopher Ivan Ilyin, an admirer of fascism, whose article, "What the Dismemberment of Russia Promises the World", would become a frequently quoted source in the speeches and pronouncements of Putin and other Russian officials at the start of the new millennium. Ilyin argued that one day Russia would gather its lands back under its tutelage.[18]

———

The dissolution of the Soviet Union by the leaders of Russia, Ukraine, and Belarus one week after the Ukrainian referendum for independence on December 1, 1991, put questions about the territorial boundaries of Russia and nature of Russian national identity back on the political agenda with unprecedented urgency.

The new state borders of the former Soviet republics left approximately 30 million ethnic Russians and Russian-speaking members of other nationalities that associated themselves mainly with Russia beyond the borders of the Russian Federation. The leading Russian nationalist writer Aleksandr Solzhenitsyn, who returned to Russia from Cold War exile in the United States in 1992, decried the division of the "Russian people" by the post-Soviet borders, identifying it as the essence of the new Russian question. For the same reason, Putin called the Soviet collapse the greatest geopolitical tragedy of the twentieth century.[19]

Boris Yeltsin and his advisers faced a major challenge of transforming the post-Soviet Russia into a European nation-state according to the model established over the previous two centuries by the French Revolution and its successors. It was based on the definition of nationalism by the Czech-British philosopher Ernest Gellner as the "political principle which holds that political and national units should be congruent." Given the millions of non-Russians and non-Slavs within the borders of the Russian Federation and the tens of millions of "Russians" and Soviets of different stripes beyond those borders, the task of Russian nation-building was all but impossible without a major war, which had been the main instrument used to create the European system of nation-states. In the 1990s, the latest example was the Greater Serbia project of Slobodan Milošević.[20]

Yeltsin and his government could not afford such a war, nor did they want one. In fact, Moscow went to war with the non-Slavic and non-Christian Chechnya in defense of a different principle – the inviolability of the borders of the Russian Federation, challenged by Chechen separatism. The two ferocious Chechen wars brutalized Russian politics and society, strengthening the imperial model of Russian identity as transethnic and transcultural. They did so in part on the foundations but also at the expense of the Soviet identity developed in communist times. The new leaders in Moscow, who had come to power in opposition to communism and largely contributed to the collapse of the Soviet Union, now faced communist opposition to their rule. They rejected Soviet identity as an instrument of Russian nation-building or a means of maintaining Russian control over the post-Soviet space. They looked instead for an alternative, and Yeltsin even called for a new model of the Russia idea.[21]

In the course of the 1990s there emerged a number of political, cultural, and ideological concepts not based on the Soviet model. They competed with that model as possible means of uniting the political components of the Russian Federation and the post-Soviet republics no longer subject to Moscow's rule. One such concept was Eurasianism, which gave its name to a number of reintegrationist projects and institutions in the post-Soviet space. Rooted in the writings of Russian intellectuals including Prince Nikolay Trubetzkoy and Petr Savitsky, who found themselves in exile after the Bolshevik Revolution, Eurasianism sought to recreate the former Russian imperial and now post-Soviet space on the basis of Russia's imperial heritage, Russian culture, and Orthodox Christianity, which might integrate the non-Russian parts of the former empire into the present-day Russian Federation.

The old Eurasianism of the Russian émigrés captured the imagination of part of the intellectual elite that was dissatisfied with the liberal-democratic discourse embraced by Yeltsin's advisers, and some of its supporters and interpreters made their way into the Kremlin's orbit after Vladimir Putin's rise to power. Aleksandr Dugin, a neo-Eurasianist who advocated the creation of a Eurasian empire and has been considered an ideologue of Russian fascism, became an adviser to Sergei Naryshkin. He served at that time as chief of the presidential staff, would go on to serve as the speaker of the Duma, and then the head of the foreign intelligence service, Putin's old institutional home.[22]

Putin adopted many elements of traditional and revived Eurasianism as parts of his world view. In his official pronouncements he spoke repeatedly of

Russia as a unique multiethnic civilization not only different from the West but opposed to it in history, culture, and values. But he also embraced with equal if not greater enthusiasm the ideas of a different group of Russian thinkers who juxtaposed Russia to the West predominantly as a Eurasian Slavic or Russian civilization. That trend of thought, represented by such figures as Aleksei Khomiakov, Ivan Kirievsky, and Konstantin Aksakov, pre-dated Eurasianism, going back to the first decades of the nineteenth century, which produced one of the most consequential schisms in Russian intellectual history, that between Westernizers and Slavophiles. The former insisted that Russia's destiny lay with the West, while the latter emphasized Russian uniqueness, rooted in history, language, culture, and nationality.

Putin first publicly subscribed to the imperial idea of a big Russian nation and declared that Russians and Ukrainians were one and the same people in the course of his visit to Kyiv in the summer of 2013. He was there with Patriarch Kirill of the Russian Orthodox Church to mark the supposed 1025th anniversary of the baptism of Kyivan Rus'. "We understand today's realities", declared Putin, speaking to the friendly audience of conference participants in an address appropriately entitled "Orthodox Slavic Values: The Basis of Ukraine's Civilizational Choice." "We have the Ukrainian people and the Belarusian people and other peoples, and we are respectful of that whole legacy, but at the foundation there lie, unquestionably, our common spiritual values, which make us one people."[23]

Next year, in late February 2014, Vladimir Putin invaded Ukraine by annexing the Crimea and starting the hybrid warfare in Ukraine's Donbas. The Russo-Ukrainian war had begun.

———

On March 18, 2014, Vladimir Putin delivered one of the most consequential speeches of his career, trying to explain why he annexed the Crimea and what that was supposed to mean for Russia and Russian-Ukrainian relations.

Addressing a joint session of the lower and upper houses of the Russian parliament – the deputies of the State Duma and the members of the Federation Council, joined by regional leaders and representatives of Kremlin-controlled civic organizations – Putin asked the deputies to approve a law annexing the Ukrainian Crimea and the city of Sevastopol to the Russian Federation. Two days after the referendum, Putin was ending the Crimea's short-lived independence by annexing the peninsula – the first annexation of a sovereign nation's territory in Europe by a foreign state since World War II.[24]

In his speech, Putin declared that the Crimean self-defense units had taken the initiative to bring about reunification, and the people of the Crimea had decided their fate, preventing Sevastopol from being turned into a NATO military base. He took advantage of the opportunity to remind NATO and the West of all the injustices allegedly committed against international law and Russia, from the bombing of Serbia to the recognition of Kosovo's independence, as putative justification for Russia's actions in the Crimea, and denounced the "color revolutions" as coups engineered by the West.

Putin made an unprecedented appeal to Russian nationalism. This was a marked departure from his earlier statements and pronouncements, in which his main addressee and point of reference was the multiethnic Russian political nation embodied by the citizens of the Russian Federation, referred to as *rossiiane* rather than ethnic *russkie*. Now he claimed that Russia and the Russians were the greatest divided nation in the world. After the fall of the USSR, said Putin, when "Crimea ended up as part of a different country...Russia realized that it was not simply robbed, it was plundered." "All these years", he declared, "citizens and many public figures have come back to this issue, saying that Crimea is historically Russian land and Sevastopol is a Russian city."

There were also elements of the speech that appealed to Russo-Ukrainian unity, despite Putin's attack on Ukraine and annexation of part of its territory. "Orthodoxy", claimed Putin, "predetermined the overall basis of the culture, civilization, and human values that unite the peoples of Russia, Ukraine, and Belarus." He even declared that Russia was taking the Crimea on behalf of both Russians and Ukrainians to prevent its loss to a third party. "Crimea is our common historical legacy and a very important factor in regional stability", Putin went on. "And this strategic territory should be part of a strong and stable sovereignty, which today can only be Russian. Otherwise, dear friends (I am addressing both Ukraine and Russia), you and we – Russians and Ukrainians – could lose Crimea completely, and that could happen in the near historical perspective."

Putin made a hybrid argument for the annexation: appealing to Russian history, territory, and identity, he invoked the legacy of empire to claim the Crimea under the banner of Russian ethnic nationalism, while also maintaining that Russians and Ukrainians were Slavic brethren. The latter was meant to exploit the sense of Russo-Ukrainian unity to which many citizens of Russia and Ukraine subscribed. Putin assured Ukrainians that Crimea was a unique case – a part of Ukraine historically, culturally, and ethnically belonging to Russia. The rest of Ukraine was safe. "Do not believe those who want you to fear Russia, shouting that other regions will follow Crimea", declared Putin. "We do not want to divide Ukraine; we do not need that."[25]

In fact, the division of Ukraine was exactly what Putin undertook in the weeks and months following his Crimean speech. In the second half of March, soon after Russia's annexation of the Crimea, the governments of Poland, Romania, and Hungary received a proposal signed by Vladimir Zhirinovsky, the leader of the ultranationalist Liberal Democratic Party and head of its faction in the Russian parliament. Zhirinovsky invited the governments of those countries, which had controlled or occupied parts of Ukraine during the interwar period and World War II, to conduct referendums on the "return" of such territories to themselves. He offered to reestablish European borders existing prior to the signing of the Molotov-Ribbentrop Pact between Nazi Germany and the USSR in 1939. "It is never too late to correct historical errors", read the letter. It was not clear whether Zhirinovsky was writing on behalf of the Kremlin.[26]

A Polish Foreign Ministry spokesperson dismissed Zhirinovsky's letter as a "complete oddity", while his superior, Radosław Sikorski, revealed a few months later that he had heard the same proposal from Putin himself. The offer had been made during the visit of an official Polish delegation to Moscow in February 2008, just as Ukraine was applying for a NATO Membership Action Plan. Neither Poland nor any other central European country showed interest in the Russian proposal. But what would have happened if they had been prepared to consider it? At about the same time as Putin made his offer to the Polish delegation, "some not entirely academic quarters in Moscow" – to quote the source of that report, the Russian political scientist Dmitri Trenin – had discussed the idea of creating a buffer state to be called "New Russia" out of parts of southern Ukraine and Moldova. Its name was borrowed from that of the imperial province established by Catherine II in the northern Black Sea region in the last decades of the eighteenth century.[27]

During the Moscow discussions of 2008, it had been proposed that Transnistria, a separatist enclave of Moldova, become part of the new state, but by the spring of 2014 the geography of the imagined region had changed. In early April a British reporter heard anti-Kyiv protesters in the city of Donetsk, far away from Catherine II's historical province, chanting "New Russia". In mid-April Putin took it upon himself to define the geographic scope of the area that he called "New Russia". Answering questions during a televised marathon phone-in, Putin defined "New Russia" as the Ukrainian oblasts of Kharkiv, Luhansk, Donetsk, Kherson, Mykolaiv, and Odesa – the entire east and south of Ukraine. "These are all the territories that were transferred to Ukraine in the [19]20s by the Soviet government. Why they did it, God knows. All this happened after the corresponding victories of Potemkin and Catherine II in the well-known wars centered in Novorossiisk. Hence [the Russian name] Novorossiia ['New Russia']. Then, for various reasons, these territories left [Soviet Russia], but the people remained there."[28]

Putin's geographic definition of "New Russia" was ahistorical, as the eighteenth-century province had been limited to the Pontic steppes north of the Black Sea and did not extend to Kharkiv, Luhansk, or Donetsk. But that definition corresponded to Solzhenitsyn's list of historically and linguistically Russian lands that had been included in Ukraine but did not properly belong to it. Solzhenitsyn's historical excursus was as misguided as Putin's: after the Bolshevik Revolution, Russians constituted only 17 percent of the population of the lands that Catherine II had designated as a province and that Putin was now claiming, allegedly for historical reasons, as the "New Russia" province of the Russian Federation. The Ukrainian majority in those regions was the reason why they had been allotted to the Ukrainian SSR in the 1920s. Putin, for his part, was now referring to imperial Russia's annexation of the Crimea and southern Ukraine in the late nineteenth century to make not only a historical but also an ethnonational claim to a much larger region.[29]

The "New Russia" of Putin and Russian nationalists now found its new geographic boundaries in the Ukrainian Donbas. Russian and separatist propaganda exploited the Odesa tragedy of early May to mobilize votes for the independence of the Donetsk and Luhansk oblasts. The referendums that took place in the same month were organized even more hastily than the one in the Crimea, and the organizers predictably declared victory for the pro-independence side. Those who showed up for the referendums voted for the independence not of Putin's "New Russia" but of the two separate "people's republics" of Donetsk and Luhansk. The idea of such republics harked back not to imperial but to early Soviet times, in particular to the short-lived Donets-Kryvyi Rih Bolshevik-controlled polity during the Russian Revolution. Soviet mythology resonated with the locals much more strongly than distant memories of empire.

The war in Donbas started the next month after Putin's Crimea speech, would continue through more or less active phases for eight years, claiming 14,000 lives in Ukraine alone. "New Russia" would disappear from Putin's lexicon after the signing of the Minsk Agreements of 2013, but it would become a badge of identity and a battle cry for the numerous groups of Russian Eurasianists, Russian nationalists, Orthodox monarchists, and neo-Nazis who flocked to the area in hopes of building the polity of their dreams. One of the major supporters of "New Russia", the leader of neo-Eurasianism, Aleksandr Dugin, even adjusted his theories to allow for the existence of a "Big Russia" as part of Eurasia, producing a curious mélange of Eurasian and Russian nationalist ideas. Backed by Russian money and instructed and directed by the Russian intelligence services, the Russian nationalists and Eurasianists soon took control of the newly proclaimed republics.[30]

———

In July 2021, Putin had surprised Russia watchers throughout the world by releasing a long historical essay, which to all appearances he had written himself, with some assistance. Putin's reading of history clearly intensified during the COVID lockdown of 2020-2021. This time around he was not just reading but also writing.

The essay, titled "On the Historical Unity of Russians and Ukrainians", reflected his already well-known views, elaborated with a long excursus into history. After the failure of his Eurasian integration project in Kyiv and the implementation of his Greater Russia scenario by the annexation of the Crimea, Putin was returning to the imperial vision of a big Russian nation, a Pan-Russian project endorsed by Aleksandr Solzhenitsyn, among others. "I said that Russians and Ukrainians were one people – a single whole", wrote Putin in the opening statement of the lengthy essay. "These words were not driven by some short-term considerations or prompted by the current political context. It is what I have said on numerous occasions and what I firmly believe."[31]

What followed was an extended discussion of the history of Russia and Ukraine whose basic premises followed the line established in the nineteenth century by Count Sergei Uvarov and his favorite historian, whom he had commissioned to write school textbooks on Russian history, Nikolai Ustrialov. Like Ustrialov, Putin dwelled on what he regarded as the original unity of the big Russian nation, established in medieval times, when the Russian people were not only ruled by the same princes and belonged to the same Orthodox Church but also allegedly spoke the same language. Kyivan Rus' had in fact been a multiethnic polity whose territory spanned thousands of kilometers. But Putin, like Ustrialov and many others who followed the historian's lead, attributed the loss of presumed Russian unity to bad rulers and foreign enemies.[32]

"The wall that has emerged in recent years between Russia and Ukraine, between the parts of what is essentially the same historical and spiritual space, to my mind is our great common misfortune and tragedy", wrote Putin. "These are, first and foremost, the consequences of our own mistakes made at different periods of time. But these are also the result of deliberate efforts by those forces that have always sought to undermine our unity." When it came to "our own mistakes", Putin pointed first and foremost to those allegedly committed by the Bolsheviks, Vladimir Lenin in particular. The list of Russia's historical enemies was long, from the thirteenth-century Mongols to the Poles of the fifteenth and sixteenth centuries, then the Austro-Hungarians and again the Poles in the nineteenth century, as well as the Germans in the twentieth century.

The Poles played a special role as the nation responsible for the breakup of the united Russian people in all imperial Russian narratives, and Putin's version did not depart from that long-established tradition. "The idea of the Ukrainian people as a nation separate from the Russians started to form and gain ground among the Polish elite and part of the Malorussian ['little Russian', an imperial term for Ukrainian] intelligentsia", wrote Putin, all but following the argument put forward by the imperial authorities in 1863 as grounds for prohibiting Ukrainian-language publications. He then tried to explain the Russian Empire's prosecution of leaders of the Ukrainian movement, and especially its prohibitions on Ukrainian-language publications, by blaming the Poles once again. "These decisions were taken against the backdrop of dramatic events in Poland and the desire of the leaders of the Polish national movement to exploit the 'Ukrainian issue' to their own advantage", wrote Putin.[33]

Putin's contribution to his predecessors' historical schemas was the notion of Ukraine as an anti-Russia or, as he described it, "a barrier between Europe and Russia, a springboard against Russia." It was allegedly a concoction of evil Western forces. "Inevitably, there came a time when the concept of 'Ukraine is not Russia' was no longer an option", wrote Putin. "There was a need for an 'anti-Russia' concept, which we will never accept. The owners of this project took as a basis the old groundwork of the Polish-Austrian ideologists to create an 'anti-Moscow Russia.'" Putin pledged action: "we will never allow our historical territories and people close to us living there to be used against Russia."

Putin was clearly upset with the Ukrainian democracy that kept generating political leaders dedicated to the idea of the independence of Ukraine. He complained that "presidents, members of parliament, and ministers would change, but the attitude of separation from and enmity toward Russia would remain." That was allegedly the result of the political system established by the "Western authors of the anti-Russia project". Without naming the new Ukrainian president Volodymyr Zelensky, Putin accused him of lying to his electorate. "Reaching peace was the main election slogan of the incumbent president", wrote Putin. "He came to power with this. The promises turned out to be lies. Nothing has changed. And in some ways the situation in Ukraine and around Donbas has even degenerated."[34]

In late 2021, as rumors about Putin's failing health started to circulate with new intensity in Russia and abroad, observers began to notice changes in his appearance, including his puffy face – possibly an effect of medication. And it was impossible to ignore Putin's desire to protect himself from COVID-19 or other infections by seating foreign dignitaries who came to see him at the opposite end of a ridiculously long table. This led Russian political commentators to concern themselves with the question of Putin's legacy, in which the Crimea and Ukraine featured prominently. The political consultant and expert on Ukraine Sergei Markov, who was close to the Kremlin, suggested that "Putin cannot step down leaving Ukraine occupied, given that Russians there are being turned into anti-Russians by means of terror." He then explained his thought in terms of the Pan-Russian project: "Because Ukraine is in fact part of Rus.'"[35]

But there were also those in the Russian nationalist camp who did not believe that the war between the Russians and Ukrainians was a good idea. The head of the All-Russian Officer Assembly, Colonel General Leonid Ivashov, published an open letter to Putin opposing the war on the grounds of Russian national interest and Slavic unity. "The use of military force against Ukraine will, in the first place, put into question the existence of Russia itself as a state", wrote Ivashov. "Secondly, it will make Russians and Ukrainians mortal enemies forever. Thirdly, thousands (tens of thousands) of healthy young men will perish on both sides, and that will unquestionably affect the future demographic situation in our countries, which are dying out."[36]

—

Putin made the formal decision to go to war at the February 21 meeting of the Russian Security Council, which approved the de facto denunciation of the Minsk Agreements and supported the proposal to recognize the "independence" of the two puppet statelets in the Ukrainian Donbas. As Putin suggested in front of cameras, he had not discussed his decision to denounce the agreements and recognize the independence of the Donbas "republics" with the members of the council beforehand. What he wanted was to hear their opinion. Heavily edited television footage of the meeting left little doubt that they had no opinions of their own. They did their best to provide arguments in favor of a decision that had already been made, and the head of foreign intelligence, Sergei Naryshkin, even incurred reprimands from Putin, first for vacillating about recognition of the two "people's republics" and then for overshooting the target by proposing to annex them to Russia.[37]

The footage strongly suggested that the decision to go to war was Putin's own. The rest were there merely to voice support. Among those present was the Russian foreign minister Sergei Lavrov, whom Putin, according to the investigative journalist Christo Grozev, allegedly never consulted on the issue of going to war with Ukraine. According to the anecdote shared by the Western Russia watchers, when asked who Putin's advisers were, Lavrov allegedly answered: Peter the Great, Catherine the Great, and Alexander II – Russian emperors of the eighteenth and nineteenth centuries, whose busts decorated Putin's quarters in the Kremlin.[38]

After Russian television showed the footage of the Security Council meeting, it broadcast a lengthy speech by Putin explaining his decision to denounce the Minsk Agreements of 2015. The speech indicated that Putin was not about to limit himself to the Donbas, whether the statelets were to be declared formally independent or annexed outright, as Naryshkin had suggested. Putin was after Ukraine as a whole. He returned to the main themes of his historical essays of July 2021 in an attempt to delegitimize the existence of Ukraine as both state and nation.

"Modern Ukraine was entirely created by Russia or, to be more precise, by Bolshevik, Communist Russia", declared the Russian president. "This process started practically right after the 1917 revolution, and Lenin and his associates did it in a way that was extremely harsh on Russia – by separating, severing what is historically Russian land." That theme was deeply rooted in the writings of Russian White Guard émigrés such as General Anton Denikin and was a prominent thread in Solzhenitsyn's thinking and writing. Putin decided to add weight to his argument by pointing out that he had studied the topic on the basis of archival documents.[39]

In Ukrainian social media, the reaction to Putin's statement was ridicule. Within a few hours, Facebook was flooded with images of Vladimir Lenin surprised to learn that he had created Ukraine. Another montage inserted Lenin into the monument to the legendary founders of Kyiv, the brothers Kyi, Shchek, and Khoryv and their sister, Lybid. Lenin replaced Lybid at the prow of the boat carrying the founders of the Ukrainian capital. The monument expresses popular Ukrainian belief that their country's roots go back to the Middle Ages. Putin had scant interest in the Ukrainian reaction – his decision had already been made.[40]

On February 21, the day of the Security Council meeting, Putin recorded another address, this one to be released on the morning of the Russian attack. In it he justified the coming aggression as a response to what he called "genocide" committed by "the forces that staged the coup in Ukraine in 2014: against the millions of inhabitants of the Donbas." He argued that the actions of the Kyiv authorities left Russia no choice but to act. "In these circumstances", declared Putin, "we have to take bold and immediate action. The people's republics of the Donbas have asked Russia for help." The reference was to a request made by the leaders of the puppet states in the Russian-occupied part of the Donbas, recently recognized by Moscow as independent. Their request gave Putin a formal *casus belli*, set the minimum goal of Russian aggression – the takeover of the entire Donbas – and misled the Ukrainian side into thinking that the war might be limited to the Donbas alone.

Other parts of the address suggested that the Donbas was a mere pretext. Although Putin called his aggression a "special military operation", he characterized it as a global struggle, in the tradition of Stalin's Great Patriotic War, against the hostile West and the Ukrainian fascism that it supported. "Focused on their own goals, the leading NATO countries are supporting the far-right nationalists and neo-Nazis in Ukraine, those who will never forgive the people of the Crimea and Sevastopol for freely making a choice to reunite with Russia", claimed Putin. "They will undoubtedly try to bring war to the Crimea just as they have done in the Donbas, to kill innocent people just as members of the punitive units of Ukrainian nationalists and Hitler's accomplices did during the Great Patriotic War. They have also openly laid claim to several other Russian regions."[41]

Putin formulated the goal of his "special military operation" as follows: "demilitarize and denazify Ukraine, as well as bring to trial those who perpetrated numerous bloody crimes against civilians, including against citizens of the Russian Federation." The meaning of demilitarization was quite clear: Ukraine was to be left defenseless, at the mercy of Moscow. But what did "denazification" mean? Putin's propaganda had spent years portraying some of the Ukrainian volunteer military formations of 2014 as Nazi. But more was at stake than those battalions. A few days earlier, the United States had warned the United Nations that Russian intelligence services were compiling lists of people "to be killed or sent to camps". They included "Russian and Belarusian dissidents in exile in Ukraine, journalists and anti-corruption activists, and vulnerable populations such as religious and ethnic minorities and LGBTQI+ persons." There was also little doubt that anyone resisting the invasion would be killed or put on trial. Putin called on the Ukrainian military "immediately to lay down arms and go home".[42]

Russian spies, especially the special directorate of the Federal Security Service (Russian acronym FSB), which was charged with clandestine operations in Ukraine, were feeding Putin descriptions of the attitude of the Ukrainian population toward its own government and Russia that conformed to his historical fantasies. The FSB reported that Ukrainians would greet their Russian liberators. A vast network of agents was recruited in Ukraine not only to spy on the Ukrainian government, military, and people, but also to organize mass demonstrations in support of liberating Russian troops and take over key government installations as they approached, replicating the takeover of the Ukrainian Crimea and Donbas in the spring of 2014.[43]

Putin expected Ukrainians to welcome with flowers the Russian forces sent to liberate them from Nazism and nationalism. Instead, they met the Russians with Javelins, Stingers, and Ukraine's own Skif (Scythian) or Stuhna anti-tank guided missiles. Faced with stiff resistance, the "liberation army" was frightened, confused, and disoriented. If Putin was the victim of his own delusions, historical and otherwise, his troops became victims of his propaganda efforts.

By claiming that Russians and Ukrainians were one and the same people, Putin left his soldiers unprepared for a war in which the entire population would oppose the invading army and support its own armed forces. In Ukraine, the Russian invasion destroyed the last vestiges of the belief that Ukrainians and Russians were fraternal peoples, to say nothing about their being one and the same people. That was true even of those features of common heritage to which Putin had sought to appeal in his articles and speeches, including historical roots, religious tradition, and joint resistance to the Nazi occupation.

In the city of Pereiaslav in the Kyiv region, where Hetman Bohdan Khmelnytsky had sworn allegiance to the Russian tsar in 1654, the city authorities removed the monument to the "reunification of Russia and Ukraine", the centerpiece of propaganda about Russo-Ukrainian unity. The Kyiv monument to the "Motherland" defending the city against Nazi aggression, a sword raised in one hand and a shield in the other, built by the Soviets in the 1980s and known as a symbol of Kyiv, remained intact but changed its meaning. It was now considered a symbol of resistance to the Russian invasion. There was also a new attitude toward the lyrics of one of the most popular Soviet songs, which began with lines known to every schoolchild in the USSR: "On June the twenty-second / Precisely at four in the morning / Kyiv was bombed / And we were told that the war had begun." The lines referred to the German bombardment of Kyiv in June 1941, but now the invaders bombing the city were Russians.[44]

It was a sad irony that Russian bombardment was killing Russian speakers and destroying landmarks and locations claimed by Russian imperial and then Soviet culture. Andrei Krasniashchikh, a professor at Kharkiv University and an author who had been writing and publishing in Russian, decried the demolition of Kharkiv by Russian bombardment as destruction of pre-Soviet and Soviet Russian culture in Ukraine by those who had allegedly come to protect it.[45]

"I don't know what has become of the homes of Shulzhenko, Bunin, and Khlebnikov", continued Krasniashchikh, listing the names of other famous residents of Kharkiv, the Soviet singer Klavdiia Shulzhenko and the Russian writers Ivan Bunin and Velimir Khlebnikov. "His house", wrote Krasniashchikh about Khlebnikov's old place, "is next to the oblast police department, which was bombed on March 2, and a bomb fell on the art museum with works by Aivazovsky, Repin, and Levitan." All three painters mentioned by Krasniashchikh were considered the pride of Russian culture.

"The home of [Isaak] Dunaevsky", he continued, referring to the famous Soviet composer and conductor, "on Yaroslav the Wise Street, there was bombing there as well. They are bombing everywhere. 2,055 buildings. The fine university campus has shattered windows. Our department is on the sixth floor opposite." Krasniashchikh then reported on the news from Bucha: "In the rucksack of a Russian soldier killed in Ukraine they found a book by Bulgakov, a little gold cross, a child's earrings with ladybird ornaments, and gold teeth." He titled his article "How Russian Culture Is Burning under Bombardment."[46]

In the first week of May a Russian missile destroyed the museum of Hryhorii Skovoroda, a famous eighteenth-century philosopher who has been considered the founder not only of Ukrainian but also of Russian religious philosophy – a major influence on Vladimir Soloviev and Nikolai Berdiaev. The museum was located fifty kilometers northeast of Kharkiv in the village of Ivanivka, renamed Skovorodynivka after the philosopher, who had died there. The Ukrainian minister of culture, Oleksandr Tkachenko, believed that the destruction of the museum had been deliberate. "Skovorodynivka is distant from other villages and infrastructure; in fact, there are only fields in the vicinity", said the minister. "I have no doubt that they were aiming at Skovoroda in particular. I think that he himself once said, 'Don't fraternize with those hiding evil intentions.'"[47]

Also under attack were monuments of Kyiv's princely era – a heritage that Putin and Russian nationalists of all stripes considered their own. That was the case in the city of Chernihiv, one of the princely capitals of Kyivan Rus' claimed by Russian writers, thinkers, and politicians of every persuasion as the cradle of their civilization. First mentioned in the Kyivan Chronicle under the year 907, Chernihiv was the site of a number of architectural monuments of the medieval era, including the eleventh-century Holy Savior Cathedral and the Dormition Cathedral, the Yelets Monastery and the Church of St. Elijah, all dating from the twelfth century. There were also buildings of the early modern era, built in what has been known in Ukraine as the Cossack baroque style.[48]

On March 6, the bombardment was particularly intense. Forty-seven people were killed, and bombs hit the building of the literary and art museums. The twelfth-century Yelets Monastery was damaged on the following day. The bombardment of the surrounded city continued through the rest of March, claiming hundreds of additional civilian victims and destroying more of the city's museums, libraries, and university buildings. The siege came to an end on March 31, when the Ukrainian army recaptured the strategic highway connecting Kyiv and Chernihiv. The city, partly ruined, with half its population turned into refugees, began to return to some semblance of normality and count its losses –human, physical, and emotional.[49]

Russian bombs cracked open not only church buildings but also the edifice of the Moscow Patriarchate. The Ukrainian Orthodox Church under the jurisdiction of Moscow rebelled against Patriarch Kirill, who had issued a statement at the beginning of the war calling on "all parties to the conflict to do everything possible to avoid civilian casualties" and invoked the tenth-century baptism of Kyivan Rus', a state from which both Ukrainians and Russians trace their origins, as part of a tradition that should help to overcome "the divisions and contradictions that have arisen and have led to the current conflict".[50]

Kirill's formal subordinate and ally in Ukraine, Metropolitan Onuphry, the head of the Ukrainian Orthodox Church subject to the Moscow Patriarchate, had little tolerance for his superior's refusal to name and condemn the aggressor. "Russia has launched military actions against Ukraine, and at this fateful time I urge you not to panic, to be courageous, and to show love for your homeland and for one another", stated the Metropolitan, who had been considered a staunch supporter of Ukraine's ties with Moscow, in an address to his flock. He then appealed to the Russian president, all but accusing him of the "sin of Cain" by offering a very different interpretation of the common baptism of Rus' in 988 by Prince Volodymyr of Kyiv, to which Patriarch Kirill had alluded.

"Defending the sovereignty and integrity of Ukraine", continued Onuphry, "we appeal to the President of Russia and ask him immediately to stop the fratricidal war. The Ukrainian and Russian peoples came out of the Dnieper baptismal font, and the war between these peoples is a repetition of the sin of Cain, who killed his own brother out of envy. Such a war has no justification either from God or from people." Metropolitan Onuphry's statement was one of many similar pronouncements, public and private, issued in Kyiv and other cities of Ukraine after the Russian attack. In June Bishop Lonhyn, who was close to Onuphry, challenged Kirill by "thanking" him during a church service for the bloodshed that he had *endorsed*. "Your Holiness, we thank you for your blessing. For the fact that people are dying, and blood is being shed. For having bombed our monasteries, our churches. For continuing to kill our monks, our priests. We thank you, Your Holiness, for your great blessing of bloodshed."[51]

The council of the Ukrainian Orthodox Church subordinate to the Moscow Patriarchate, convened in late May 2022, registered its "disagreement" with Patriarch Kirill and made a step toward independence from Moscow, allowing its eparchies not to pray for the patriarch and its churches to use consecrated oil supplied by Kyiv rather than Moscow — a major step toward full autocephaly according to Orthodox practice. The Moscow Patriarchate responded when one of its eparchies in the "Donetsk People's Republic" refused to pray for Metropolitan Onuphry. Despite the war, Kyiv still maintained formal control over parts of its former eparchies on the territory of the Donetsk and Luhansk "republics". But now, with those statelets recognized by Moscow as independent, and Kyivan bishops rebelling against Patriarch Kirill's endorsement of the war, all bets were off. The parishes of the Moscow Patriarchate in Ukraine were splitting as well, while the Ukrainian government moved to evict the Moscow patriarchate from the premises of Ukraine's oldest and most revered Kyiv Caves monastery.[52]

———

In June 2022, Russia celebrated the 350th anniversary of Peter I, the first Russian tsar also to be called an emperor. The anniversary was marked with academic conferences and meetings as well as public events, not only in Moscow and St. Petersburg but also in regional centers. In Moscow, on the premises of the VDNKh – the Russian Exhibition of Achievements of the National Economy – the authorities organized a multimedia exhibition dedicated to Peter and his legacy. Titled "Peter I. The Birth of the Empire", the exhibition covered his role in state-building, diplomacy, and the creation of a "civic society", as well as reforms of education and development of culture.[53]

On June 9, Peter's official birthday, Vladimir Putin arrived at the VDNKh to open the exhibition in person. He also met with young Russian entrepreneurs, engineers, and scientists. Peter did a great deal for the development of Russian entrepreneurship and science, founding the Russian Academy of Sciences, and a meeting of that kind in conjunction with the exhibition seemed appropriate. But when Putin addressed the young entrepreneurs and scholars, his emphasis was not so much on Peter's contribution to Russian science and technology – Putin mentioned in passing his "borrowing" of Western knowledge when the tsar traveled to Europe – but rather on Peter's wars and territorial acquisitions, a subject much closer to Putin's heart at that moment.

"Peter the Great waged the Great Northern War for 21 years", said Putin, apparently suggesting that his own "special military operation", though dragging on much longer than expected, was still a reasonable undertaking. He then proceeded to the question of Peter's territorial acquisitions. "On the face of it, he was at war with Sweden, taking something away from it", suggested Putin. But he then proposed a very different interpretation of Peter's conquests: "He was not taking anything away; he was returning." Putin then addressed the issue of the legitimacy of such actions. "When he founded the new capital, none of the European countries recognized this territory as part of Russia", stated Putin. "Everyone recognized it as part of Sweden."

In Putin's mind, the conquest was justified because "from time immemorial, the Slavs had lived there along with the Finno-Ugric peoples, and this territory was under Russia's control." That was a stretch at best when it came to describing the population, and the claims of the medieval Novgorodian republic to that territory belonged to the distant past by the time Peter's forces moved into the area. But Putin continued in the same vein: "He was returning and reinforcing; that is what he was doing." He then added, with a smirk: "Clearly, it fell to our lot to return and reinforce as well." Putin's remarks stood in clear contrast to his "declaration of war" speech of February 24, when he proclaimed that Russia did not "plan to occupy Ukrainian territory".[54]

The Ukrainian response to Putin's remarks was swift. Mykhailo Podoliak, a senior adviser to President Zelensky, saw the Russian president's comments as evidence that imperialism was the true motive behind Russia's aggression against Ukraine. "Putin's confession of land seizures and comparing himself with Peter the Great proved there was no 'conflict,' only the country's bloody seizure under contrived pretexts of people's genocide", tweeted Podoliak. Reports from independent Russian journalists supported Podoliak's interpretation. A few days earlier *Meduza*, a website run by oppositional journalists who had left Russia and found safe haven in Latvia, reported that "the Kremlin was planning to combine all the lands into a new federal district that could be annexed by Russia as soon as this autumn."[55]

"This is a different war to the one Putin began on 24 February 2022", wrote Lawrence Freedman, Emeritus Professor of War Studies at King's College, London, soon after Putin made his remarks about Peter's legacy. "He has now presented himself as a reincarnation of Peter the Great and admitted that this is a war of conquest rather than liberation. It is territory now that he is after, having largely given up on the people of the Donbas, whose supposed vulnerability to a Ukrainian attack provided the pretext for the war. The separatist armies from Donetsk and Luhansk have been used as cannon-fodder, sent into battle unprepared and ill-equipped, to spare regular units."[56]

In September 2022, as military commissions drafted Russian men into the army and sent them to the front lines of Ukraine with no training whatever, Putin's sham referenda were conducted in four partly occupied oblasts of Ukraine. They involved armed soldiers visiting the apartments of Ukrainian citizens and forcing them to vote in favor of Russian annexation of their regions. On September 30, 2022, Putin cited the "will of millions" as he signed decrees formally annexing four oblasts of Ukraine, some of them under Ukrainian control, as was the case with the city of Zaporizhia and its population of some 750,000. Ironically, as Putin delivered his speech, Ukrainian forces were concluding the encirclement of approximately 5,500 Russian troops near the city of Lyman in the newly "annexed" Donetsk oblast of Ukraine. It would fall in the Ukrainians' hands the next day, becoming the first town of the territory formally annexed by Russia to be liberated from its armed forces.[57]

In his "annexation" speech, Putin quoted his favorite Russian émigré philosopher Ivan Ilyin and repeated many themes of his earlier pronouncements. He recalled the imperial history of New Russia – the term he now used to denote the Kherson and Zaporizhia oblasts; decried the destruction of that "great country", the USSR; and spoke about the allegedly free choice of "millions of people who, by their culture, religion, traditions, and language, consider themselves part of Russia." But the overriding subject of the address was Putin's hatred of "the West", which he mentioned thirty-three times.

The West, insisted Putin, was guilty of "the plunder of India and Africa" and "the wars of England and France against China." He blamed the West for the economic hardships of the post-Soviet era, accusing its leaders of neocolonialism – a bizarre claim coming from the leader of a former empire now waging a colonial war against its former subject. Putin claimed that the West "continues looking for another chance to strike a blow at us, to weaken and break up Russia, which they have always dreamed about, to divide our state and set our peoples against each other, and to condemn them to poverty and extinction." Putin's attacks on the West, its colonial policies of the past and alleged neocolonialism of the present, were pathetic at best. The leader waging an imperial war and justifying it through the imperial tropes was trying to emerge as the champion of anti-imperialism.[58]

The formal annexation by Russia in addition to the Crimea of four regions in eastern and southern Ukraine left little doubt that he was on the path of territorial aggrandizement, but they also suggested that the Kremlin had scaled down its war aims. The capture of Kyiv and control of the rest of Ukraine by a puppet government, an apparent goal in February, was unachievable and had to be abandoned. The war initially meant to gain complete control of Ukraine was redesigned to extend Russia's borders. Once again, as in the annexation of the Crimea in 2014, the "Greater Russia" project filled the gap between Russia's aspirations and its capacity to satisfy Putin's imperial ambitions.

There are clear indications that the Ukrainian nation will emerge from this war more united and certain of its identity than at any other point in its modern history. Moreover, Ukraine's successful resistance to Russian aggression is destined to promote Russia's own nation-building project. Russia and its elites now have little choice but to reimagine their country's identity by parting ways not only with the imperialism of the tsarist past but also with the anachronistic model of a Russian nation consisting of Russians, Ukrainians, and Belarusians.

Serhii Plokhy (born 1957) is the Mykhailo Hrushevsky Professor of Ukrainian History and the Director of the Ukrainian Research Institute at Harvard University. He began his academic career at the University of Dnipropetrovsk in Ukraine, where he became a full professor and held a number of administrative positions. He later taught and conducted research at the University of Alberta in Canada, where he served as the Associate Director of the Peter Jacyk Center for Ukrainian Historical Research and founded the Research Program on Religion and Culture at the Canadian Institute of Ukrainian Studies. In 2007, Plokhii became Mykhailo Hrushevsky Professor of Ukrainian history at Harvard. Since 2013, at the Harvard Ukrainian Research Institute, he has led a group of scholars working on The Digital Atlas of Ukraine, an online, GIS-based project.

Plokhy's research interests include the intellectual, cultural, and international history of Eastern Europe, with an emphasis on Ukraine. A leading authority on the region, he has published extensively in English, Ukrainian and Russian. His books deal with history of religion, origins of national identities, history of the Soviet Union and the Soviet-American rivalry in the Cold War, and have won numerous awards, including the Lionel Gelber Prize for the best English-language book on international relations for The Last Empire: The Final Days of the Soviet Union *(2014), Taras Shevchenko National Prize (Ukraine) for* The Gates of Europe: A History of Ukraine *(2015), and Ballie Gifford Prize and Pushkin House Book Prize for* Chernobyl: History of a Tragedy *(2018). His latest book,* The Russo-Ukrainian War: The Return of History *was released by W.W. Norton in the US and Penguin in the UK in May 2023.*

NOTES

1. This essay is based on my book, *The Russo-Ukrainian War: The Return of History* (New York, 2023). It pulls together and presents in a systematic way key historical and historiographic threads and arguments presented in the book.

2. "Putin u menia sprashival, chto o nem napishut v uchebnikakh: glavred 'Ėkha' o lichnom razgovore s prezidentom RF," *Pervyi Russkii*, August 20, 2019, https://tsargrad.tv/news/putin-u-menja-sprashival-chto-o-nem-napishut-v-uchebnikah-glavred-jeha-o-lichnom-razgovore-s-prezidentom-rf_213278.

3. Fiona Hill and Clifford G. Gaddy, *Mr. Putin: Operative in the Kremlin* (Washington, DC, 2015), 64-66.

4. "Putin vozlozhil tsvety k nadgrobiiam Denikina, Il'ina i Shmeleva," *Vesti.ru*, May 24, 2009, https://www.vesti.ru/article/2180162.

5. Plokhy, *Lost Kingdom*, 326.

6. "Putin vozlozhil tsvety k nadgrobiiam Denikina, Il'ina i Shmeleva."

7. Aleksandr Solzhenitsyn, *Kak nam obustroit' Rossiiu?* (Paris, 1990); idem, "Russkii vopros v kontse XX veka" (1994); idem, *Rossiia v obvale* (Moscow, 1998), 79.

8. Simon Franklin and Jonathan Shepard, *The Emergence of Rus, 750-1200* (London, 2014); Mykhailo Hrushevsky, *History of Ukraine-Rus'*, ed. Frank Sysyn et al., vols 1, 2 (Edmonton and Toronto, 1997, 2021).

9. Aleksei Tolochko, *Kievskaia Rus' i Malorossiia v XIX veke* (Kyiv, 2012).

10. Serhii Plokhy, "Empire or Nation?" in idem, *Ukraine and Russia: Representations of the Past* (Toronto, 2008), 19-20.

11. Andreas Kappeler, *The Russian Empire: A Multi-Ethnic History* (London, 2001), 213-46.

12. Alexei Miller, "'Official Nationality'? A Reassessment of Count Sergei Uvarov's Triad in the Context of Nationalism Politics," in idem, *The Romanov Empire and Nationalism: Essays in the Methodology of Historical Research* (Budapest, 2008).

13. Plokhy, *Lost Kingdom*, 81-91.

14. Plokhy, *Lost Kingdom*, 105-36.

15. Alexei Miller, *The Ukrainian Question: Russian Empire and Nationalism in the Nineteenth Century* (Budapest, 2003), 117-210.

16. Terry Martin, *The Affirmative Action Empire: Nations and Nationalism in the Soviet Union, 1923-1939* (Ithaca, NY, 2001), chaps. 1-3; Roman Szporluk, "Lenin, 'Great Russia,' and Ukraine," *Harvard Ukrainian Studies* 28 (1) (2006): 611-26.

17. Plokhy, *Lost Kingdom*, 121-53; Alexei Miller, *The Ukrainian Question: Russian Empire and Nationalism in the 19th Century* (Budapest, 2003), 24-26.

18. Snyder, *The Road to Unfreedom*, 16-35.

19. Aleksandr Solzhenitsyn, "Russkii vopros v kontse XX veka," *Novyi mir*, no. 7 (1994); Vladimir Putin, "Message to the Federal Assembly of the Russian Federation," April 25, 2005, http://kremlin.ru/events/president/transcripts/22931; Serhii Plokhy, *Lost Kingdom: The Quest for Empire and the Making of the Russian Nation from 1470 to the Present* (New York, 2017), 312-15.

20. Ernest Gellner, *Nations and Nationalism* (Ithaca, NY, 1983), 1.

21. Julia Rubin, "Meditations on Russia: Yeltsin Calls for New National 'Idea'", *AP*, August 2, 1996, https://apnews.com/article/122cd732a8cf8b35989afeec4db-69dcd; Vera Tolz, "The Search for a National Identity in the Russia of Yeltsin and Putin," in Yitzhak Brudny, Jonathan Frankel and Stefani Hoffman, eds., *Restructuring Post-Communist Russia* (Cambridge, UK, 2004), 160-78.

22. Timothy Snyder, *The Road to Unfreedom: Russia, Europe, America* (New York, 2019), 88-91; Marlene Laruelle, "Scared of Putin's Shadow: In Sanctioning Dugin, Washington Got the Wrong Man," *Foreign Affairs*, March 25, 2015, https://www.foreignaffairs.com/articles/russian-federation/2015-03-25/scared-putins-shadow; http://newfascismsyllabus.com/contributions/into-the-irrational-core-of-pure-violence-on-the-convergence-of-neo-eurasianism-and-the-kremlins-war-in-ukraine/.

23. Plokhy, *Lost Kingdom*, 331-32; Paul D'Anieri, *Russia and Ukraine: From Civilized Divorce to Uncivil War* (Cambridge, UK, 2019), 193-94.

24. Serhii Plokhy, "The Empire Strikes Back," in idem, *The Frontline: Essays on Ukraine's Past and Present* (Cambridge, MA, 2020), 231; Rajan Menon and Eugene Rumer, *Conflict in Ukraine: The Unwinding of the Post-Cold War Order* (Cambridge, MA and London, 2015), 81-85; Serhy Yekelchyk, *The Conflict in Ukraine: What Everyone Needs to Know* (New York, 2015), 128-31.

25. Vladimir Putin, "Address by President of the Russian Federation," March 18, 2014, http://en.kremlin.ru/events/president/news/20603; Fiona Hill and Clifford G. Gaddy, *Mr. Putin: Operative in the Kremlin* (Washington, DC, 2015), 368-69.

26. Lidia Kelly, "Russian politician proposes new divisions of Ukraine," *Reuters*, March 24, 2014, https://www.reuters.com/article/ukraine-crisis-partition-letter/russian-politician-proposes-new-divisions-of-ukraine-idUSL5N0ML-1LO20140324; "Former Polish FM Says Putin Offered to Divide Ukraine With Poland," *Radio Free Europe/Radio Liberty*, October 21, 2014, https://www.rferl.org/a/26647587.html.

27. Kelly, "Russian politician proposes new divisions of Ukraine"; "President Vladimir Putin met with Polish Prime Minister Donald Tusk," President of Russia, February 8, 2008, http://en.kremlin.ru/events/president/news/43774; Marcel H. Van Herpen, *Putin's Wars: The Rise of Russia's New Imperialism* (Lanham, Boulder, New York, and London, 2015), 4-5.

28. Linda Kinstler, "In eastern Ukraine, protestors are chanting 'New Russia' – an old term that's back in fashion," *New Statesman*, April 8, 2014, https://www.newstatesman.com/politics/2014/04/eastern-ukraine-protestors-are-chanting-new-russia-old-term-s-back-fashion; Veselova, "Plenki Glaz'eva: kto i kak koordiniroval iz Rossii sobytiia 'krymskoi vesny'"; "Direct Line with Vladimir Putin," President of Russia, April 17, 2014, http://kremlin.ru/events/president/news/20796.

29. Marlene Laruelle, *Russian Nationalism: Imaginaries, Doctrines, and Political Battle-fields* (London and New York, 2019), 196.

30. Laruelle, *Russian Nationalism*, 196-206; Marlene Laruelle, "Back from Utopia: How Donbas Fighters Reinvent Themselves in a Post-Novorossiya Russia," *Nationalities Papers* 47, no. 5 (2019): 719-33.

31. Putin, "On the Historical Unity of the Russians and Ukrainians," President of Russia, http://en.kremlin.ru/events/president/news/66181.

32. Serhii Plokhy, *Lost Kingdom: The Quest for Empire and the Making of the Russian Nation from 1470 to the Present* (New York, 2017), 89-91.

33. Putin, "On the Historical Unity of the Russians and Ukrainians."

34. Putin, "On the Historical Unity of the Russians and Ukrainians," 1.

35. Sergei Markov, "Putin ne mozhet uiti ot vlasti, ostaviv Ukrainu okkupirovannoi," Sovet po vneshnei i oboronnoi politike, December 27, 2021, http://svop.ru/main/40348/; "Putin's worsening health set to be a determining factor in Russia's policy over the next four years," Robert Lansing Institute, September 29, 2021, https://lansinginstitute.org/2021/09/29/putins-worsening-health-set-to-be-a-determining-factor-in-russias-policy-over-the-next-four-years/.

36. Edmonds, "Start with the Political: Explaining Russia's Bungled Invasion of Ukraine"; "Otkrytoe pis'mo generala Ivashova – Putinu," https://proza.ru/2022/02/07/189.

37. "Bol'shoe zasedanie Soveta bezopasnosti Rossii. Priamaia transliatsiia," February 21, 2022, https://www.1tv.ru/shows/vystupleniya-prezidenta-rossii/vneocherednoe-zasedanie-soveta-bezopasnosti-rossii/bolshoe-zasedanie-soveta-bezopasnosti-rossii-pryamaya-translyaciya.

38. Aleksandr Iuzovskii, "Khristo Grozev: dazhe Lavrov byl shokirovan nachalom voiny v Ukraine," MINEWSS, May 6, 2022 https://mignews.com/news/politic/hristo-grozev-dazhe-lavrov-byl-shokirovan-nachalom-vojny-v-ukraine.html

39. Address by the President of the Russian Federation. February 21, 2022. 22:35. The Kremlin, Moscow. http://en.kremlin.ru/events/president/news/20603.

40. Serhii Plokhy, "Casus Belli: Did Lenin Create Modern Ukraine?" Harvard Ukrainian Research Institute, February 27, 2022, https://huri.harvard.edu/news/serhii-plokhii-casus-belli-did-lenin-create-modern-ukraine.

41. "Address by the President of the Russian Federation," President of Russia, February 24, 2022, http://en.kremlin.ru/events/president/news/67843.

42. Dan Sabbagh, "Russia is creating lists of Ukrainians 'to be killed or sent to camps,' US claims," *Guardian*, February 21, 2022, https://www.theguardian.com/world/2022/feb/21/us-claims-russia-creating-lists-of-ukrainians-to-be-killed-or-sent-to-camps-report.

43. Jeffrey Edmonds, "Start with the Political: Explaining Russia's Bungled Invasion of Ukraine," *War on the Rocks*, April 28, 2022, https://warontherocks.com/2022/04/start-with-the-political-explaining-russias-bungled-invasion-of-ukraine/.

44. Iurii Bratiuk, "U Pereiaslavi demontuvaly pam'iatnyk 'vozz'iednanniu' z Rosiieiu," *Zaxid.net*, July 7, 2022, https://zaxid.net/u_pereyaslavi_demontuvali_pamyatnik_vozzyednannya_z_rosiyeyu_n1545835; Serhii Plokhy, "Vladimir Putin's war is banishing for good the outdated myth that Ukrainians and Russians are the same," *Telegraph*, March 3, 2022, https://www.telegraph.co.uk/authors/s/sa-se/serhii-plokhy/.

45. Margaret Besheer, "Ukraine's Cultural Heritage Under Attack, Official Says," *Voice of America*, July 15, 2022, https://www.voanews.com/a/ukraine-s-cultural-heritage-under-attack-official-says/6661269.html; Andrei Krasniashchikh, "Kak gorit pod bombami russkaia kul'tura," *Ukraïns'ka pravda*, May 3, 2022, https://www.pravda.com.ua/rus/columns/2022/05/3/7343653/.

46. Krasniashchikh, "Kak gorit pod bombami russkaia kul'tura,".

47. "Udar Rosiï po muzeiu Skovorody ie splanovanoiu aktsiieiu – Tkachenko," *Ukrinform*, May 7, 2022, https://www.ukrinform.ua/rubric-culture/3477358-udar-rosii-po-muzeu-skovorodi-e-splanovanou-akcieu-tkacenko.html.

48. Olenka Pevny, "Recreating a Monumental Past: Self-Identity and Ukraine's Medieval Monuments," J. B. Rudnyckyj Memorial Lecture, University of Manitoba, https://www.researchgate.net/publication/337623350_Olenka_Pevny_RECREATING_A_MONUMENTAL_PAST_SELF-IDENTITY_AND_UKRAINE'S_MEDIEVAL_MONUMENTS; "Ukrainian cultural heritage is also under Russian bombing – Olenka Z Pevny," *Breaking Latest News*, March 19, 2022; "Building of Chernihiv Collegium Cossack Baroque Architectural Style Historical Heritage of Ukraine," YouTube, November 17, 2016, https://www.youtube.com/watch?v=kewDM45N8t4.

49. David Axe, "Ukraine's Best Tank Brigade Has Won the Battle For Chernihiv," *Forbes*, March 31, 2022, https://www.forbes.com/sites/davidaxe/2022/03/31/ukraines-best-tank-brigade-has-won-the-battle-for-chernihiv/?sh=554db-4c7db9a.

50. Plokhy, "Vladimir Putin's war is banishing for good the outdated myth that Ukrainians and Russians are the same."

51. Lena Rudenko, "Mitropolit UPTs MP 'poblagodaril' patriarkha Kirilla za prolituiu v Ukraine krov': vy otvetite pered Bogom," *Apostrof*, June 6, 2022, https://apostrophe.ua/news/society/2022-06-06/mitropolit-upts-mp-poblagodaril-patriarha-kirilla-za-prolituyu-v-ukraine-krov-vyi-otvetite-pered-bogom/271059

52. "Postanova Soboru Ukraïns'koï Pravoslavnoï Tserkvy vid 27 travnia 2022 roku," Ukraïns'ka Pravoslavna Tserkva, https://news.church.ua/2022/05/27/postanova-soboru-ukrajinskoji-pravoslavnoji-cerkvi-vid-27-travnya-2022-roku/; "Eparkhiia UPTs MP v okupirovannykh Roven'kakh reshila ne upominat' Onufriia kak predstoiatelia tserkvi," *Gordonua.com*, May 31, 2022, https://gordonua.com/news/society/eparhiya-upc-mp-v-okkupirovannyh-rovenkah-reshila-ne-upominat-onufriya-kak-predstoyatelya-cerkvi-1611113.html.

53. Dmitrii Akimov, "Rossiia otmechaet 350 let so dnia rozhdeniia Petra Velikogo," *Smotrim*, June 9, 2022, https://smotrim.ru/article/2789489; "Putin posetil vystavku o Petre I na VDNKh," *Vesti.ru*, June 9, 2022, https://www.vesti.ru/article/2790684.

54. "Meeting with young entrepreneurs, engineers and scientists," President of Russia, June 9, 2022, http://en.kremlin.ru/events/president/news/68606; "Putin compares himself to Peter the Great in Russian territorial push," YouTube, June 9, 2022, https://www.youtube.com/watch?v=N2sfJjl7_Zk; "Address by the President of the Russian Federation," President of Russia, February 24, 2022, http://en.kremlin.ru/events/president/news/67843.

55. Andrew Roth, "Putin compares himself to Peter the Great in quest to take back Russian lands," *Guardian*, June 10, 2022, https://www.theguardian.com/world/2022/jun/10/putin-compares-himself-to-peter-the-great-in-quest-to-take-back-russian-lands.

56. Lawrence Freedman, "Spirits of the Past. The Role of History in the Russo-Ukraine War," *Comment is Freed*, June 12, 2022, https://samf.substack.com/p/spirits-of-the-past?s=w&utm_medium=web.

57. Andrew E. Kramer, "Russia-Ukraine War: Armed Russian Soldiers Oversee Referendum Voting," *New York Times*, September 24, 2022, https://www.nytimes.com/live/2022/09/24/world/russia-ukraine-putin-news; Anthony Blinken, Secretary of State, "Russia's Sham Referenda in Ukraine," Press Statement, U.S. Department of State, September 29, 2022, https://www.state.gov/russias-sham-referenda-in-ukraine/; Joshua Berlinger, Anna Chernova and Tim Lister, "Putin announces annexation of Ukrainian regions in defiance of international law," *CNN*, September 30, 2022 https://www.cnn.com/2022/09/30/europe/putin-russia-ukraine-annexation-intl; Thomas Gibbons-Neff, "Russia's withdrawal from Lyman comes a day after Putin said he was annexing the region." *The New York Times*, October 1, 2022, https://www.nytimes.com/live/2022/10/01/world/russia-ukraine-war-news#ukraine-moves-to-encircle-lyman-a-strategic-eastern-rail-hub

58. "Signing of treaties on accession of Donetsk and Lugansk people's republics and Zaporozhye and Kherson regions to Russia," President of Russia, September 30, 2022, http://en.kremlin.ru/events/president/news/69465.

IVAN BAHRIANYI: A TRAGIC OPTIMIST

—

Olha Poliukhovych

This new creation.

Ivan Bahrianyi (1906-1963) was a Ukrainian writer, poet, journalist, politician, and consistent critic of the Soviet system. Born Ivan Lozoviaha in Okhtyrka, now Sumy oblast, in north-eastern Ukraine, he started writing poetry and prose under the pseudonym "Ivan Bahrianyi" ("bahrianyi"is Ukrainian for "crimson"). After years of repression and multiple imprisonments by the Soviet authorities and his own political and armed resistance, in 1945 he ended up in Germany, where he continued to write novels and agitate for Ukrainian independence until his death.

—

The censorship and repressions that Ukrainian cultural figures faced in the USSR were so overwhelming, that Ivan Bahrianyi insisted that Ukrainian literature had to be upheld by Ukrainian writers displaced abroad. Within the bounds of their responsibility lay not only presentation, he believed, but the creation of a new national literature which may "swallow whole, then master" the European example.

Bahrianyi himself was a personal example of this new creation: in 1950 he wrote *The Garden of Gethsemane*, which was later translated into French and German and upon release was compared to other works dealing with the struggle against a totalitarian system, such as Arthur Koestler's *Darkness at Noon* and Boris Pasternak's *Doctor Zhivago*. However, in contrast to the heroes of those works, Bahrianyi portrayed a person who "resists until the end and finally triumphs against the inhuman force that wishes to desecrate him." Despite the tragedies Bahrianyi experienced and portrayed in his works, in his life and creations he displayed optimism to the end.

Bahrianyi Uncensored

Bahrianyi's personal resistance started in his school days with challenges to educational doctrine in the Russian Empire. "I wrote my first poem at ten years old, in my first class of the 'Educational Institute'. I wrote in Ukrainian out of protest against the teacher who would hit me over the head with a ruler because I could not speak Russian. Later on I already could, but by then I did not want to speak it", the writer recalled of his literary debut.

In 1925 the nineteen-year-old published his first book, *Black Silhouettes: Five Novellas*, under the pseudonym of Ivan Poliarnyi. By that time the young writer had already learnt the trade of a locksmith before studying at art and ceramics school, had worked in his trade, and even managed to travel. He later moved to Kyiv and entered art school there. Although he never completed his studies, he acquired many friends and colleagues in the art world. Magazines, literary critics, discussions and readings were all available to and enjoyed by him. Bahrianyi was acquainted with vanguard literary figures such as the "Martians", members of *MARS* (acronym for *Maisternia literaturnoho slova*, or "Workshop of the Literary Word"). Its members included the writers Borys Antonenko-Davydovych, Hryhorii Kosynka, Valerian Pidmohylnyi, and Yevhen Pluzhnyk.

During this time Bahrianyi actively wrote poetry and experimented with drama. His works were published in the prestigious Ukrainian journals of the time: *Globus, Life and Revolution*, and *The Red Path*. He relished the attention and praise of critics: "It is something fresh and new, authentic and sincere", as the critic Hryhorii Kostiuk put it, sharing his impressions on seeing Bahrianyi's poetry for the first time in print. Bahrianyi's verse engaged creatively and critically with post-revolutionary reality. Some of his texts did not get past the censors, however, and others were subjected to their additions and interventions: "barbaric acts" that caused the writer to feel "repressed and enraged", in his own words.

Although the situation appeared to be a lost cause, Bahrianyi firmly stood up for his creative freedom. He later left Kyiv and went back to his native Okhtyrka. While he was there, in 1929 the arrival of his long poem *Ave Maria* on the shelves of bookshops in Kyiv and beyond created quite the stir. It was released by the publisher *SAM* ("Oneself"), that at the time was completely unknown; as it later turned out, Bahrianyi had arranged the printing with an acquaintance at a press in Okhtyrka and distributed it himself to booksellers. *Ave Maria* was banned and confiscated, but several hundred copies were still sold, as interest in this particular forbidden fruit went off the scale.

A response to the poet's brazenness was quick to arrive. On 22 January 1930, at the *Molodniak* All-Ukrainian Congress of Comsomol Writers, his works were denounced as "pulp" and "trash fiction". Bahrianyi was publicly accused of "pushing forward in his artistic work ideas hostile to our era".

Bahrianyi's Many Arrests

At the beginning of the 1930s, Bahrianyi settled into the legendary Slovo House in Kharkiv, where the most prominent Ukrainian writers of the time lived. He stayed in poet Vasyl Vrazhlyvyi's "rotating apartment" where many poets of the era would settle temporarily when they arrived in Kharkiv. One early evening Ivan left the building, and suddenly two "subjects" from a local criminal investigation interdicted him.

In an attempt to scrape together evidence against him, the NKVD officers concocted interpretations of his poetic and literary fantasy as if a representation of his real-life beliefs. "They were very persistent in their questioning, [asking] to which friend I devoted my preface to *Ave Maria*. I laughed at them. In the same way they stubbornly demanded to know who I meant, when I dedicated its themes to 'rebels and Protestants'. I laughed at this too, just as I laughed at the imaginary friend. This angered them", as Bahrianyi described his first arrest to Kostiuk.

After several months of futile confession "extractions", the "troika" courts exiled him for three years to the north of the USSR's Far East. "The Sea of Okhotsk. Taiga. Tundra. Huntsmen. There was a settlement of our people from Ukraine who had moved there long ago. If I must be sincere, all this was rather interesting to me, even. But later I was overcome by a terrible longing for Ukraine. An unconquerable one. So I got on a train and travelled west", Bahrianyi later recalled.

He was intercepted in Tomsk and was sentenced to three further years of imprisonment, in Baikal Amur Corrective Labour Camp. Afterwards he returned to Okhtyrka. Less than half a year later, in 1938, he was arrested again. "Once again", recounted Bahrianyi, "the investigations unit in the Kharkiv Kholodnohirsk prison. Once again, boundless bureaucratic rigma-role, frayed nerves, demands to 'confess' to certain connections and terrorist intentions." Despite the Stalininst terror, the psychological pressure and physical abuse, he did not sign the verdict against him and after six months was released.

During the Second World War he was called up to fight, but during transportation of his party of recruits, the formation was bombed, and Bahrianyi deserted the Red Army. Bahrianyi described this personal experience of fleeing both Soviets and Nazis in his novel, *A Man Runs Over the Abyss* (1965). Later he recalled to Kostiuk: "For all this horror that we experienced, it was still good that it happened. We came to know the world of our reality very deeply, even if not comprehensively."

Later Bahrianyi joined the Organisation of Ukrainian Nationalists, or OUN. In that period he wrote his most famous novel, *The Tiger Trappers* (also translated as *The Hunters and the Hunted*), whilst hiding from the Gestapo in the Carpathian Mountains. In it he told the story of a Ukrainian man, Hryhorii Mnohohrishnoho (which can be translated as "Gregory Mostsinsul), who fled from ogreish Bolshevik manhunters in the USSR's Far East. In 1944 this novel won first prize at the Krakow-Lviv literary festival for Ukrainian publishing. A shortened version of the book was published in the monthly magazine *Evening Hour* (Krakow), with the title *The Beast Catchers*. However, in the chaos of war, the manuscript was lost; and while in an Allied displaced persons' camp, Bahrianyi rewrote and restored the lost text from memory, and the full book, *The Tiger Trappers*, was printed in Germany by Prometheus Press.

An Advocate for an Optimistic Young Nation

Immediately following the war, Bahrianyi became an active member of the Artistic Ukrainian Movement (*Mystetskyi ukrainskyi rukh*, or MUR), an organisation formed of Ukrainian writers in exile. The aim of its initiator, academic Yurii Sherekh-Shevelyov (known by western academia as George Shevelov), was to create a robust Ukrainian literature of wide breadth. By virtue of his talent and his ability, Bahrianyi was among the most important postwar writers from Ukraine.

For the Ukrainian émigré readership, Bahrianyi was the star and symbol of human indomitability. Described as "still young in years, and what is more – in will and soul", he did not lose his drive and enchanted his audiences with expressive readings of "harsh and fascinating poems" from his collection *The Golden Boomerang*. George Shevelov argued that Bahrianyi's temperament matched that of poet and "father of the nation" Taras Shevchenko, in terms of the power of his poetic utterance. "Bahrianyi begins where he gives free rein to his poetic temperament. And this happens in places where he creates magnified pictures of ruin and defeat, or solemn hymns to heroism and victory. The poet does not search here for purely national images, but in a queer way they echo back to those rage- and pathos-filled parts of Shevchenko, as in *Hosea: Chapter XIV* or sublime moments in *From Jeremiah*", continued Shevelov, raising him to the rank of the Neo-Shevchenkovites.

Bahrianyi did not stand aside during fierce debates of MUR members on the question of what Ukrainian postwar literature should look like. He reimagined it according to the legacy of an idol of his youth, Mykola Khvylovyi, who had had the idea of a "psychological Europe" – even as the significance of which had changed for Ukrainian literature in the new postwar world. "As for Europe, we no longer need her as a reference point. We need her for something else; not as something to imitate, not for us to foster trivial epigones of Goethe and Petrarch – but for us to swallow whole (figuratively speaking), master, and thereon move forward", he wrote in an article, "Thoughts on Literature".

Because Ukrainian literature in Soviet Ukraine had become the object of repression and censorship, it was upon exiled Ukrainian authors whom Bahrianyi placed the mantle of "a deep sense of responsibility". He included himself in this formulation, explaining his own work as follows: "I am an advocate for healthy optimism, an advocate of creative optimism, heroic optimism – whichever one may like, only it is the optimism of a healthy, young, and not yet exhausted nation. I am an advocate of exuberant, self-affirming, breakthrough literature." This approach was applied not only to his creative output, but to his political views and real-life actions.

Contesting Stalinist Propaganda

According to the agreements made between the USSR and the Allies following victory in the Second World War, people who had been citizens of the Soviet Republics in 1939 had to return home after hostilities ended. As such, Soviet repatriation commissions hunted down Ukrainians in displaced persons camps in order to forcibly return them "home". Bahrianyi too was not allowed peace after the victory. In 1946 he published a high-profile pamphlet that resonated with many, *Why I Don't Want to Return to the USSR*, in which he described his personal experience of the Bolshevik terror. The text was translated into several languages and was actively distributed in the Allied nations.

In Germany, Bahrianyi still had enough energy to create his own party branch of the Ukrainian Revolutionary Democratic Party. "Only triumphant, foolhardy daredevils in these gloomy, hopeless times can plan something effective, creative, and large-scale", commented Kostiuk in regards to this initiative.

The party had its own newspaper, *Ukrainski visti* (Ukrainian News), which was edited by Bahrianyi, and its own publishing house, Prometheus. In addition to great Ukrainian émigré classics, it published a Ukrainian translation of Orwell's Stalinist satire *Animal Farm*, with a new preface by the author. The publisher had further plans for translations of work into Ukrainian that "consistently revealed the falsehood behind the Soviet myth and shone a light on the true nature of the Stalinist slave society system." But due to the living conditions in camps, as well as the fact that ideas of Western intellectuals were not as well-received in the Ukrainian diaspora, these plans did not come to fruition.

The political atmosphere in the displaced persons camps was tense. Bahrianyi and his party opposed the OUN's B faction (The "B" faction of the Organisation of Ukrainian Nationalists was headed by the more radical Stepan Bandera, in contrast to the OUN-M, headed by more moderate Andrii Melnyk). Some of their more aggressive rivals prevented the distribution of *Ukrainski visti* and spread rumours that it was "Communist propaganda". On the night before Easter in April 1947, a group attacked his dwelling in Neu Ulm, smashing his windows with stones and attempting to break down the doors, while shouting crude insults and chanting: "Beat the Muscovites, Communists, Soviets!" The board of MUR staunchly condemned such "physical and spiritual Bolshevism" as practised by some of these so-called "Bandera-ites", noting that the persecution of Bahrianyi was being carried out on political grounds, not criminal, or on any other basis.

The Empire Strikes Back

The Soviet secret services also persecuted Bahrianyi for his political convictions. On 12 June 1956, his son, Borys Zosymov, was forced to address his father on the radio. The announcer first condemned emigration from Ukraine in highly abusive terms; the next direct target were "independents and nationalists", with Bahrianyi as their "ringleader". Then, unexpectedly, Bahrianyi's son took the microphone. He said that he had intended to publicly disown his "no-good father", even though his "filial sentiments" had prevailed, and so he called on his father to "repent" and to stop the "shameful slandering of his fatherland

and the deception of his fellow countrymen also suffering in a foreign land." The story was related by Bahrianyi's friend, the literary scholar and memoirist, Dmytro Nytchenko-Chub.

Bahrianyi offered a brief answer to his son, referring to the tale *Taras Bulba* by Mykola Hohol (better known as Nikolai Gogol), where the Cossack Taras addresses his sons Ostap and Andrii, one loyal, the other a traitor: "If you are Ostap – then you and I may find a common language, but if you are Andrii, then we have nothing to speak about." Notwithstanding the outward calmness of his response to such Soviet provocation, Bahrianyi afterwards suffered a serious nervous breakdown, severely worsening his health, already weakened by Stalinist Gulags and exile.

That year Bahrianyi published another, no less scathing, pamphlet: *The Fireworks of "Collective" Demagoguery (A Word Following Khrushchev's Report)*. In it Bahrianyi debunked Nikita Khrushchev's cynical assertions during his "secret speech" about the supposed changes occurring in the USSR, calling them false and pretty tricks of distraction. Khrushchev's speech, Bahrianyi argued, included nothing on taking responsibility for the crimes committed and, worse, was intended to bury this responsibility alongside yesteryear's "great leader and teacher", Stalin.

A Writer Without a Country, But Standing Up for His Country

Very few people knew about Bahrianyi's novels in postwar Soviet Ukraine, although they were well-received by contemporaries and critics abroad. Perhaps his success was due to the fact that Bahrianyi spoke about the experience of Stalinist terror from the perspective of a survivor.

His novel, *The Garden of Gethsemane* (Neu Ulm, 1950), was the first text in Ukrainian literature to describe in detail the "saddening and tragic era of terror inflicted on the Ukrainian people by the bloodthirsty Stalinist viceroy Yezhov", Kostiuk wrote. He would also compare Bahrianyi's work to novels such as Arthur Koestler's *Darkness at Noon* and Victor Serge's *The Case of Comrade Tulayev*.

Poet and critic Jósef Łobodowski noticed too the novel's similarity to Koestler's own: "Bahrianyi has portrayed an existence so terrifying, of which Koestler never could have dreamt. Yet while *Darkness at Noon* remains a gloomy and oppressive book, *The Garden of Gethsemane* on the other hand has a sense – and let us not be afraid of this banal expression – of spiritual empowerment. The more terrible the acts in the book, the greater the faith inspired in the reader."

Bahrianyi's novels have been much-translated into other languages. In this way, Ukrainian literary culture was made known to the world. Grigory Aleksinsky, who translated *The Garden of Gethsemane* into French, appreciated this novel on the same level as other international texts that represented the hero's struggle against a totalitarian system, as in the aforementioned *Darkness at Noon* and *Doctor Zhivago*. However, despite such company, noted Aleksinsky, Bahrianyi's protagonist is significantly different: "Their [Koestler and Pasternak's] protagonists are crushed by the totalitarian Moloch, whereas Bahrianyi's protagonist, the worker's son, is a human personality who resists until the end and finally triumphs against the inhuman force that wishes to desecrate him."

In 1963 the process for nominating Bahrianyi for the Nobel Prize for Literature was commenced, but was stopped when the writer died that same year.

Unlike most other Ukrainian émigré writers, Bahrianyi never left Germany for America, Canada or Australia, because of his poor long-term health, suffering as he did from tuberculosis. He never returned to Ukraine and was buried in Neu Ulm. The inscription on his tombstone in German reads tersely: *Iwan Bahrianyj – Ukrainischer Schriftsteller (Ivan Bahrianyi – Ukrainian Writer)*.

Does such an inscription say too little, or conversely a great deal, at a time when Ukraine did not exist on the world map – and yet unequivocally did so for Bahrianyi and other such "eternal rebels", who believed in and struggled for their country against all the odds?

Translated, from the Ukrainian, by Daisy Gibbons.

See biographical note for Daisy Gibbons on p 135.

Olha Poliukhovych holds a PhD in the Philosophy of Literature from the National University of Kyiv-Mohyla Academy. She is an Associate professor at The Volodymyr Morenets Department of Literature at Kyiv-Mohyla Academy. In 2017-2018, she was a Fulbright Fellow at the Harvard Ukrainian Research Institute of Harvard University. In 2020 she became a co-founder of the New Ukrainian Academic Community NGO (Kyiv). Since the full-scale war began, she has been featured on LitHub podcasts and has published essays in AGNI, Consequence Forum, *and* Prospect Magazine. *Her research interests include modernist literature, identity politics, power relations, memory studies, gender studies, displacement and émigré literature.*

TWO STORIES

—

Yuri Andrukhovych

WOODSMAN
Without unnecessary exposure.

For a period of several years, brief but densely packed with hard-to-clarify events, Granny Iza from time to time received visitors. They came from some previous lives of hers where she, exhausted by her husband's endless absence, would travel through the mountains on a donkey or take up teaching at distant settlements. To me, some of those visitors seemed odd. I would involuntarily take a closer look at them. Or to be more precise, my memory stocked up its notes for the future, and I was its eyes and ears.

Dani showed up only after dark.

He called Granny Iza "auntie", which suggested that Dani could be someone from our family, its branches numerous and – no way to hide the truth – quite twisted. Because of this to this date I have been unable to put together even an approximate genealogy of this contradictory and argument-fractured familial unit. And if I did not succeed in doing this by now, I would never be able to do it. So Dani too will stay in eternal uncertainty – who, where from, and why.

He would visit us without any advance notice, always saturated with a sharp scent of forest wildness, most often in badly neglected clothes soaked in swampy mists and also strongly smelling of smoke. This mixture of moisture and soot probably attracted me the strongest. No bonfire could fully dry out all the layers of his clothes which, covered with ever-new grayish-green stains, became an increasingly adventurous type of camouflage.

Dani almost never came empty-handed. The most frequent of his offerings was mushrooms: birch boletes, the flirts, and at times even slippery jacks or porcini. Dani would string them on a thick thread and would wrap himself with them, like a suicide bomber with grenades, under his raincoat. But you should have seen that raincoat! Made in ancient prewar days out of British naval tarp and all thoroughly stained through countless life-threatening adventures, it rather resembled an itinerant preacher's cloak that had witnessed a great deal. In its pocket one could perceive an outline of either a Luger pistol or leaden knuckle-dusters.

Berries were another popular gift from Dani. From the pocket of his impressive military breeches, he would produce entire fistfuls of either ling-onberries or bilberries.

Memory also notes his Yugoslav garrison cap – the kind Marshal Tito was fond of posing in. It was a good fit for Dani's face – of which not that much was left, mostly cheekbones and eye sockets.

One of Dani's pragmatic goals was changing the sweater. The fact is, Dani had a pair of them – rough and thick like a wild boar's hide. One of them Dani always left with us for washing, after which it had to wait for Dani's next visit, to replace its dirty work buddy on Dani's body. Since Dani's visits could not happen regularly, the dirty sweater quite often had to wait for its next washing long past all the established sanitary and hygiene norms, sometimes for many months.

I do not recall Dani ever washing, but it is possible that memory wiped out those pictures of a bony, unnaturally long torso without any hint of muscle bent over the washbasin. Or perhaps, foolhardily pouring all over himself scoopfuls of water full of tiny prickly shards of ice. Or of Dani, with enthusiastic crackling sounds, squashing parasites on his body or digging up from somewhere behind his ear and then shaking off onto the floor various little beetles and ticks.

Dinner was the other goal. Dani ate hastily, pouring into his mouth stuffed with hot boiled potatoes glassfuls of kefir, thin like Dani himself. During this, his excessively protruding Adam's apple would go energetically up and down, reminiscent of a piston. Not having patience to mash potatoes with a spoon or break them into smaller pieces, Dani swallowed them whole. I was afraid that one day he would choke and suddenly die in front of me, a potato stuck in his throat. However, this never happened, Dani was lucky. Sometimes I right away sighed with relief: Granny Iza announced that *this time* she made for him porridge with milk. I remember that once (but only once!) she served him real chicken broth, which by then one was officially recommended to call bouillon. Dani loudly ate up an entire large bowl of it in less than five minutes. With noodles and all, you should know.

To conclude the banquet, Dani would down one after another two, or sometimes even three mugs of hot rosehips infusion. Personally, I hated this swill, but grandma forced me to drink it instead of the much more expensive tea, justifying this by its high vitamin C levels. So rosehips were omnipresent in our home. Dani also complimented it and asked for more, not without some passion and pathos. A few times Dani even said that thanks to this rosehips abomination his bald patch was growing back hair.

The hot vitamin infusion was finally accompanied by conversation. I tried to listen closely, but mostly just observed. By then I had already learned the expression about the *corner of one's eye*: my observation point was a distant corner close to the windowsill, where I studiously pretended to be doing school homework. I should add right away that later I could not fall asleep for a long time, in the neighboring smaller room. Dani brought with him a spirit of anxiety. Because of it, with him it felt both scary and interesting. Besides, Mom in those years was often away. She would go to the capital for some advanced training courses and would be away from home for weeks. The only positive for me consequence of those work trips consisted in the new toys mom occasionally brought me in her generosity, proving not with words, but with actions how much she missed me.

Well, let's not get distracted by trifles. How can I convey the essence of those conversations between Dani and grandma?

By education, Dani was an engineer or something, he knew about electricity and steam boilers (in a future book the copyeditor, in a rush to make dinner for her husband, would in her haste change them to "steamed meatballs"). No, Dani wasn't a specialist in steamed meatballs. But in diesel engines – definitely. Still, he and Granny Iza spoke about other things. Although once Dani did fix Mom's umbrella, which confirmed the old rumor that before the Great Previous War he went to a vocational school.

In general Dani's arrival caused certain typical changes. Thus, for some reason only when he was present Granny Iza would retrieve from a secret drawer yet another pillowcase she had not finished embroidering and would resume her red-and-black cross-stitch, listening to Dani and occasionally reacting with a brief remark to all his reports, which gradually transitioned into the half-asleep and increasingly less controlled mumbling.

Dani shared news from various aspects of life.

The film director Tarkovsky is still struggling to get his *Andrei Rublyov* released in theaters, even though it had already been mercilessly cut by the Committee. Grand Master Blumenthal has been advised to ask for asylum in Canada. The British band the Monkey Men has set out on a Great Danubian tour with a new program titled Sticky Fingers; several concerts at stadiums have just been announced. The Americans are readying the astronauts for walking on the Moon. Sakharov did reach China, and Mao has ordered to start carrying out the plan.

Dani saw in all this the unambiguous signs of a nearing fall of the regime. An unfamiliar mystical glow would appear in Dani's eyes. "Auntie, you must understand", he got excited, "this is the coming of a new world order!"

After those words he would still go on shouting for a while, waving his hands, but soon he would get exhausted and again switch to the more familiar underground half-whisper.

Grandma would only give surprised sobs from time to time – and not so much because of the shocking contents but because of the yet another confirmation of the fact that Dani, even in his distant woods, somehow managed to catch the frequency of Radio Free Argentina, much loved by us all.

The last thing Dani would manage to mumble half-asleep would not even be borderline fantastic – it truly was fantastic, in the clearest, most unbelievable way: apparently at the Vatican they had ultimately decided that the current Polish cardinal would serve as the next Pope.

Dani would fall asleep without finishing his phrase, with his mouth open, his back pressing against the tiled surface of the stove warmed up specially for him, pushing the faded Yugoslav cap over his eyes and from time to time trying to shout something alarming from the Mariana trenches of his sleep.

In this state everything got suspended for four or five, or at times even six hours. On such nights Grandma did not go to sleep, continuing her embroidery exercises and simultaneously, it seemed, watching over the brief restless sleep of her secret visitor.

Dani had to leave us before dawn, to slip out of the house without the participation of extra pairs of eyes, or, to use the parlance they were already beginning to use, without unnecessary exposure. His main task was not to stumble into his old confidant Mr. Acid or, even worse, into Fenya the Heartfelt, an extraordinarily slovenly lady who was believed to be an orderly at the state hospital for the veterans of the Great Previous War and who had an unpleasant habit of eavesdropping after the lives in the neighboring apartments, strolling, as it were, for no particular reason down the shared hallway and using the occasion for a public showing of her utterly not fresh nightgowns, stained here and there with various shades of yellow. No, it would not be a good idea to be spotted by the eyes of that untidy neighbor!

Keeping trouble away, Dani slipped out carefully and noiselessly, and for the sake of ideal silence solemnly carrying in his hands, the way one carries military decorations at a hero's funeral, his well-worn and by now somewhat hole-ridden boots dating to the late Czecho-Slovak years.

While everything around him was beginning to get grayer and lighter, Dani managed to cross most of the park – at least the part where a human might be encountered more often than a squirrel or a raccoon.

Then, after a few hours of determined walking, the energetic waving of the tarp folds manifesting in all directions the strength of his spirit, Dani crossed the boundary between the park and that which was no longer considered the park. Using familiar paths to avoid two or three rocket bases, he entered the thickest parts of the forest and disappeared in it – dissolved, led a guerrilla life, lay in wait, watched, vegetated, naturalized, blended with nature, with its body and background, became a part of nature, an element of the environment, an ecosystem, a landscape elevation, a hillock, a tree stump, finally an anthill.

And once, he also stayed one.

For some time I could not avoid asking about him. "Where is Dani? Why did he stop coming by?" I would not leave the adults in peace.

Iza would answer, "There is no Dani. This is all in your imagination."

Mother added, "And don't you ever mention him at school. Do you hear me? Never!"

SACRIFICE

Amidst the wild Carpathian grasses.

At the very tail end of summer, Mom resolved that the permit from the office of the camp's supreme commandant was not coming in time. Her petition was registered on the first of June – and she began feeling hopeful already the next day. Permits of this type were delivered not by the neighborhood mail carriers, but by a special courier known to the entire city, a morose gangling skewed-eyed guy dressed in a now-faded ceremonial uniform jacket. You had to certify the receipt of the permit-containing encrypted telegram with your signature, and then treat the courier to a glass of rum or port.

For the entire summer we did not travel anywhere, not even for a day: we were afraid of missing the courier. Especially since the permit could be not only urgently dated – for today or tomorrow – but also valid only for single use. Who is not at home misses the boat. The courier does not knock twice, good-bye.

That summer I lived with the increasingly sharper sense of wasting it. The vacation flowed away like sand between your fingers, like water into sand. I aimlessly played ball in the courtyard, kicking up simoom-like clouds of dust; I played cards with the dumb Yulio – endless rounds of War – counted identical days from yesterday's competition of fates to the next one and killed time the best I could, wandering around the Park with Petard and other, younger pals.

The Park was not much of a salvation, but still prevented us from totally sinking into boredom. Its offerings weren't pleasingly sophisticated, but their constancy was satisfying.

They contained, for example, nighttime screenings at a movable cinema – weekly, or even more frequent. Although all those movies, which we had seen a million times already, had long become super annoying in the heroic feats they plied, their inevitable victories of the Good over the slightly worse good, and the dialogues that sounded artificial even to us kids. On top of it, the film reels were often mercilessly damaged, completely torn here and there.

There were outings with Grandma, carrying empty jars neatly stacked in a cart to a park drinking fountain, the furthest and correspondingly the hardest to reach by the thirsty consumptives. In and of themselves those walking trips did not promise anything interesting, but on the way, one could spy a little at the rail-thin jailed deserters who toiled hard on the bed of a canal between two artificial lakes. On the way back Grandma generously yielded to my nagging, and we paused at the Officer Café where I could get a small mug of kvass, which by then would be close to spoiling but in general still drinkable.

There were also digs – not quite archeological, but of that general style. Petard proffered tall tales about crawling into a brigands' cave where a treasure of 4728 coins was hidden. And to get to it, we needed to clear an entrance covered up with stones and then saw through its grates. We did not get very far.

There were, finally, bats in the summer twilight, there was us watching them. It was as if each time they crossed out in the air some erroneous text invisible to us, decisively ridding themselves of it. But it must have reappeared again and again, because they again incessantly rushed to cross it out with their whole bodies.

———

Ah yes! Something else happened that summer: for a while, hobos settled down in the Park. At first a small group of them, but then it grew. However, despite their often-strange manners, there was no entertainment to be had from them. Once I saw one of them, a Bearded Weirdo in a Hat, stumbling through the alley, suddenly freeze above a crumpled newspaper thrown on the ground. He straightened it out for a while with the tip of his crutch, and when I passed by him, I heard him proclaim, "AMERICANS ON THE MOON!" – perhaps specially for me, although I already knew that without him: this was the paper from the day before yesterday. It seems, it was then that he uttered in my wake one of his famous phrases, "If this world is only a construct of my imagination, I am pleasantly surprised by its power!"

Though no. It was not that summer, but the following one. Besides, I could have made up that phrase myself many years later. Or I might have only thought I heard it.

On August 23, Mom put an end to the futile expectations. The vacation's final week was starting, and if by some miracle the permit was issued now, we still would not be able to make it to a visitation at the southern camps and be back by September 1. Pulling the plug on all of this, Mom let me go to the mountains to visit Grandpa. For about a year, he was working as a foreman at the construction site for a resort with a frivolous name, the Bijou. "It's a name fit for a filly", Mom said.

Grandpa, Mom's father, had a name that was not so frivolous: Emi. When I was very little, I enjoyed choosing between the versions of Pop-pop Empop and Gramps Emps. For many long decades he worked his butt off at various construction trusts, finally rising to a senior hydraulics foreman. Here, of course, one must subtract two or three jail terms, but mostly for laughably light offenses, like a bottle of cognac pinched from a country store, where no one would have ever bought it anyway given the exorbitant price. Unfortunately, there was also a more serious one: participation in undercover trade in poisonous substances. But I would prefer not to dwell on that one.

Staying with Grandpa in the mountains was the best thing ever.

I had at my disposal an entire separate room in the unfinished wing of the building, and at night no one would lean over me to check whether my hands were above the blanket.

I had great sleep on the floor, where they set for me a mattress that rested on eight bricks.

Actually, I had great lack of sleep on the floor: for half the night, I would listen to banned music from the jammed stations, hugging with my free hand my radio girlfriend with the unforgettable name Selga.

In the stream, I had great time pretending to wash up.

Late in the evening, I had great time eating thick porridge from a giant pot, shared with a dozen or so hardworking guys – invariably accompanied by chitchat about the recent or tomorrow's win of our Fortuna.

During the day, I had great time exploring the rocks and the woods – even in all sorts of weather, for Grandpa let me use a pair of comfortably trodden rubber boots and a homemade oilcloth cape. I scaled those tenebrous desolate spaces and searched for the continuation of the refrain, "And the summer was so ra-a-a-iny . . ." – but the right words evaded me, until I finally thought that the only good rhyme was "miscellany". But a word like "miscellany" does not fit a song, and so I reckoned the problem was irresolvable. Why didn't "zany" ever come to my mind then, I haven't figured out to this day.

In addition to that, going with the guys to the club beyond the mountain pass to watch Yugoslav westerns about Winnetou. Returning at night, once under the stars thickly scattered all over the sky. You can rarely see things like that in our mountains; apparently, this only happens in late August.

Every now and then smoking "Extrafine" cigarettes pinched from Grandpa's desk drawer. Just one or two, not more than that.

Sitting with everyone else around the fire, getting saturated with warmth and smoke, like a wild mushroom drying on a string.

Disappearing without a trace in one of the favorite directions:

to the old, looted spa at the mineral springs, with an option of bathing in moss-covered stone pools

the tactical military road to the defenses of the first line, where with luck one could find a hole-ridden old helmet, and if it had a spike, it was from the Kaiser's army

another, lower road, along the Mlynivka – to the ruins of a mill and the old Czechoslovak customs house

or at least to the train track that smelled thickly of ozokerite, and twice a day the stupid lumber mill draisine would crawl by.

All this stuff was old, abandoned, destroyed, cracked, half-erased. But I loved to loiter there.

———

Grandpa Emi let me be. He did not obsess over me, did not warn me, did not pry, did not educate, did not force me to do anything. Instead, he brought me along to outings for mushrooms, for wild blueberries, or even visiting locals:

to see how they make cheese, slaughter lambs, or castrate young bulls. All sorts of skills might come handy later in one's life.

In my thoughts I started calling him Deedo-Freedo. Ah, to abandon forever the nasty middle school and wander with him through all those construction sites, near and far, mountainous, and not really. I would be his best helper, would hand him wrenches, tighten the nuts, and would run to refill the soda siphon: Grandpa could not live without sparkling water.

I think he loved me more than his children. At that time, I was his only grandson. I am not sure Mom approved of his pouring me a small glass of his home brew before dinner, *for good appetite*. Perhaps she was jealous.

———

One early evening, from the slope above which the construction hummed along, I saw down below on the highway a convoy of cars, dirty-green military in color, consisting of five or six trucks and cargo vans. The convoy carefully crawled in the direction of the mountain pass. There was also a jeep, I think, but I cannot recall if it went first, or for some reason last. Or maybe somewhere in the middle? I don't remember. In general, I was not expected to remember much at all: all sort of transport could suddenly appear on the road in those militarized times. There wasn't anything unusual in that, and I would not have remembered anything, were it not for one of the vans stopping. And then the entire convoy stopped.

Suddenly there was fuss and commotion, various drivers and mechanics dashed around the cars, took turns rummaging in the stalled engine, fiercely turned the cranks, the commanders barked something unintelligible, but all the attempts to start it and get going again looked increasingly disgraceful. The convoy got stuck. Meanwhile, I relocated to my habitual hideout in the burdock jungle and savored my second extra fine cig. When I returned to the observation post, a roadside council was in session – and judging by the voices and phrases, an extremely nervous one. Thereupon the van was pushed off the road, closer to the forest, and left there. The rest moved forward.

Dusk was falling over the mountains, and figuring out that nothing else interesting was going to happen, I wandered over to the construction site trailer, where they were dealing the cards for that evening's first round of Schnapsen.

———

In the morning, we all saw that the left behind van was still there. Every now and then a carbine-armed soldier would get out of the cabin. Making two or three circles and then shifting on his feet, he would again hide in the cabin.

In the afternoon Grandpa Emi, muttering something unintelligible, packed a basket with food, coffee, and various other sundries. With a whistle that usually called me to joint outings, Grandpa let me know that he needed me.

"Take this to the soldier, he's hungry", said Grandpa.

"This is not our soldier", I protested.

"A soldier is a soldier; he wants to eat."

"I will approach him, and he'll shoot at me", I suggested to Grandpa an entirely plausible scenario.

Grandpa thought about it, and not saying anything else, picked up the basket himself. I caught up with him on the slope as he descended to the highway.

"Can I go with you?"

"Let it be", said Grandpa, his habitual phrase.

(Whenever his wife and my grandma Chloe gave birth to yet another daughter, he always repeated "let it be". But as we can see, he could also say this on other occasions.)

Closer to the van we discovered that the soldier, having opened wide the back door, was loudly rearranging the van's contents, moving here and there various boxes of canned food, tins large and small, paper sacks which appeared to contain various grains, and other kinds of rear goodies. Above it all rose a doubtfully edible gray dust from the macaroni spilled on the floor here and there.

"You watch over food, but are hungry yourself", said Grandpa and pushed the basket towards the soldier.

He decisively, jerkily, like a dog, sniffed Grandpa's gifts and, briefly forgetting about the carbine pushed to the side, dashed head-on, like down a precipice, chowing down on the first things his hands fell upon: pieces of lamb, crunchy pigeon wings baked in dough, tomatoes, butter, a bun, cheese slices . . .

"Munch, munch", encouraged Grandpa Emi, "when will they feed you again."

The soldier almost didn't get our local language, but just in case, agreed with everything and forced a smile, nodding often and not for a moment stopping to chew on whatever he saw. Finally, he seemed to have satisfied his primeval hunger and wanted a smoke. Grandpa gave him one of his extra fines and poured some barley coffee from a thermos. The soldier puffed a cloud of smoke, sipped loudly, grinned, and patted with satisfaction his stuffed belly. His tiny Trans-Ural eyes were now covered with a veil of thoughtless tranquillity.

"To the Czechs?" asked Grandpa.

The soldier pointed in the direction of the mountain pass.

"Prague. Down there."

"To the Czechs", confirmed Grandpa, and for some reason winked at me.

Soon the soldier started yawning – impossible to contain, with his entire wide mouth with a few natural teeth and numerous metal crowns. He gestured that he was going to sleep and without waiting for our departure, climbed back into the cabin.

——

When Mom came for me by a tightly packed and mercilessly bumpy commuter bus, it was the penultimate day of summer. With regret, I returned home, and the van with the soldier still stood where it was before. It stood there a week later, and a month later, and later still. From time to time, Grandpa brought food to it, but each time he had to leave it next to the cabin. The soldier no longer climbed out and did not reveal himself in any other way.

He slept, and his service term went on.

The food was taken care of by the ravens and the foxes.

Eventually Grandpa stopped bringing anything there. Operation Danube happily concluded, and the army, using its victor's prerogative, stayed on to keep the peace and mutual understanding beyond the pass, in the lands of the Czechs. The commanders evidently forgot about the cargo van, even if it was fully packed with various grains. Was it the only one lost without a trace in that lightning-like brilliant peacemaking operation?

The locals gradually got used to the shack-like thing by the forest, its immovable proximity. However, they were afraid to come close to it: rumors flowed through the villages that some guerrillas mined the approaches to it. What for, no one knew.

Shortly before New Year, the Bijou Resort Hotel was opened – as always, solemnly and noisily, with Mr. Supreme Commissar himself present. Naturally, they did not invite Grandpa to the ceremony: he had already migrated, together with his team of the world's best hydraulics workers, to another site, somewhere in the flatlands, and therefore, probably boring.

Right before departure, Grandpa with careful soft steps came close to the van and from the sidestep peeked into the tightly sealed cabin. The soldier slept like the dead, pressing to his chest the carbine clutched with both hands. He slept, and his service went on. One did not feel like waking him up.

That winter, the van got covered above its roof with snow. Back then it used to snow in our mountains.

When spring came, the van, all peeling and rusty, gradually got covered with growth and greenery – no longer the army camouflage paint but now the wild Carpathian grasses. Nature took it back, together with the skeleton and the grains.

Grandpa Emi, on the rare occasions someone recalled that episode, would only barely raise his eyebrows and smile faintly – like a truly modest and responsible person for whom it was impossible not to fulfil one's duty.

Translated, from the Ukrainian, by Vitaly Chernetsky

Yuri Andrukhovych was born in 1960 in Ivano-Frankivsk, Ukraine. In 1985, he founded the literary performance group Bu-Ba-Bu (Burlesk-Balahan-Bufonada / Burlesque-Bluster-Buffoonery). He has published five poetry books, seven novels and four books of essays. Andrukhovych's novels Recreations *(1992),* The Moscoviad *(1993),* Perverzion *(1996),* Twelve Circles *(2003),* Mystery *(2007),* Darlings of Justice *(1918) and* Radio Night *(2021) have had considerable impact on readers in Ukraine and abroad. His books have been translated into 22 languages. He has received a number of prestigious international literary awards: The Herder Preis (Hamburg, 2001), The Erich-Maria Remarque Friedenspreis (Osnabrück, 2005), The Leipziger Buchpreis zur Europäischen Verständigung (2006), The Central-European Literary Award "Angelus" (Wrocław, 2006), The Hannah-Arendt-Preis für politisches Denken (Bremen, 2014), The Vilenica Award (2017) and The Heinrich-Heine-Preis (2022).*

Vitaly Chernetsky is a Professor of Slavic Languages and Literatures at the University of Kansas. A native of Odesa, Ukraine, he received his PhD from the University of Pennsylvania and has been translating poetry and prose into English since the mid-1990s. His translations into English include Yuri Andrukhovych's novels The Moscoviad *(2008) and* Twelve Circles *(2015) and a volume of his selected poems,* Songs for a Dead Rooster *(2018, with Ostap Kin); a book by the Ukrainian artist Alevtina Kakhidze,* Zhdanovka *(2006); two children's books by Romana Romanyshyn and Andriy Lesiv,* Sound *(2020) and* Sight *(2021); and* Winter King, *a poetry collection by Ostap Slyvynsky (2023, with Iryna Shuvalova). A translation of Sophia Andrukhovych's novel* Felix Austria *is forthcoming from Harvard University Press.*

UKRAINE: A LOVE STORY

Patrick Breslin

Focused on the future.

We met over *pad Thai* in a Washington DC restaurant. "A blind date", I called it later. "A business lunch", she insisted. A friend had arranged it because I was trying to write about what I'd seen in Moscow in 1991 as the USSR was collapsing. "There's a beautiful Ukrainian lawyer in town you should meet", the friend said. "She knew some of the dissidents." The adjective flickered like a tiny neon sign in my mind the week before we met.

Three months later, we were living together, Moscow impressions fading, and I was learning about a new country. It's hard to remember, now, how little was known, west of that curtain from the Baltic to the Adriatic, about the nations east of it. Once, a fellow Washington bus rider asked her where in Africa Ukraine was. I wasn't that clueless, but close. In my entire life, the only connections I could recall for her were the Ukrainian Jewish shopkeepers on Westchester Avenue in the South Bronx. With our nickels and dimes, my friends and I would fuel up for stickball games with huge sour pickles speared like fish from a wooden vat, and knishes, Yiddish or Ukrainian for hot, mashed potato pastries. She found that memory appealing.

I'd never even heard the name of her hometown, Kharkiv, Ukraine's second city. Some Americans had. "You were near the top of our target list", a US Air Force colonel told her at a party. He was talking about nuclear weapons, but I think he meant it as a compliment. Kharkiv, I learned, with a population close to two million, was one of the major research and defense manufacturing cities in the entire Soviet Union. The law institute, where she was a tenured professor, was its largest law school.

She'd been among the first 17 Soviet lawyers chosen for brief internships in the US four years before, and was now in Washington for a postdoctoral program. After finishing, she chose to make a life with me, giving up her professorship. The break was painful but she soon found opportunities to pursue her passion for environmental law, first writing a citizen's guide for Russian environmental activists on how to use the law, then advising US organizations on support for democratic approaches to environmental protection in the former USSR.

In 1995, she helped organize a conference in the Carpathian mountains in western Ukraine, the first chance to show me her country. We flew into Kyiv late one summer morning with a scant three hours to catch the only overnight train that would get us to the conference in time. But Delta Airlines had misplaced her checked baggage – several boxes of crucial conference documents. They were coming on a Lufthansa flight, too late for our train. Lufthansa had a solution – a taxi driver would await the boxes, drive 620 kilometers through the night, and meet us in Ivano-Frankivsk.

"Should we take a chance?" she asked.

I'd noticed the driver when he entered the office, a stocky, dark-haired man who looked to be in his mid-40s. Something about him had reminded me of her mother's take-charge approach to the world.

"Try it."

The next morning, he was standing by his car at the Ivano-Frankivsk station as our train shuddered to a stop. A sample of one, admittedly, but ever since I assume Ukrainians come through and 30 years in and out of the country has only reinforced that.

The conference was at a large mountain lodge south of Ivano-Frankivsk, one of those places where agriculture fits into the landscape instead of obliterating it, where farms interlace with forest and both are beautiful. On the slopes, bare-chested men harvested hay with scythes that flashed in the sun. The haystacks were ghostly in morning fog, golden in late afternoon. Most were tall, like shawled madonnas, propped up by sapling lengths or slats. Some had little slanted wooden roofs to shunt away rain. Sometimes a tall gaunt stack looking like Don Quixote leaned next to a plump Sancho Panza. There were apple and pear trees, wild berries abundant in the meadows, fields marked off by split rail fences where tall sunflowers patrolled the rows of corn or nodded beside tin-roofed wooden houses that had intricate wood carvings on the walls, lace curtains and flower boxes in the windows, and pyramids of fruit or two-liter bottles of homemade wine for sale on tables by the road. In the villages, the churches had bright aluminum roofs and kerchiefed women led goats on long ropes home along the streets at dusk.

Surrounding the farms were hardwood and pine forests, interspersed with alpine pastures where belled cows chimed as they lowered their heads to the grass. Trains followed the riverbanks or crossed high trestles on their way through the mountains. From the tallest ridges you could see into Romania,

Hungary, Slovakia or Poland, sometimes all four at once. This is Europe's geographic center, so said the Austro-Hungarian Empire on an 1887 stone marker it erected beside a highway. It's also a cultural fault line. Local road signs used both Roman and Cyrillic alphabets.

Behind the beauty of the landscape that entranced me was a struggle for power and wealth in a nation taking shape. Our train had taken us through fiefdoms where a local strongman's word was law. She wanted to bar our sleeping compartment's door, not trusting the attendant. I extended the legs of my heavy tripod and wedged it between the handle and the frame. In the morning, we learned that another conference participant was kicked out of his bed at 2:00 a.m. when he made the mistake of opening his door to the insistent knocking of a strongman who had just boarded.

More violent struggles were taking place farther east, for bigger prizes than a sleeping compartment or farmland. In the Donbas, along Ukraine's border with Russia, enormous factories or coal and iron mines were up for grabs. Rumor had it that the repetitive cement or tarmac repairs on local highways hid the bodies of losers in those struggles.

After the conference, we stopped briefly in Kyiv and an old friend of hers gave us a nighttime tour of the city center. I remember broad avenues, darkened streets, garish lights from casinos or expensive restaurants, thick-necked bodyguards in black jackets over black t-shirts standing by black SUVs –trappings of a new and wealthy class, its style sense seemingly borrowed from the villains in James Bond movies. A US embassy official told us about his visit to one oligarch's office where a shark cruised in an enormous glass tank.

Kharkiv seemed more normal. I liked the streets speckled with university students from all over the world, wide plazas and green gardens, factories and tall Khrushchev-era concrete slab apartments on the outskirts, old, architec-turally interesting buildings with high ceilings in the center of town. She had grown up in one, near the opera house, six floors of apartments and private clinics built by a group of doctors before the revolution, split into communal apartments after. Seven families shared the kitchen and bath in hers.

My introduction to her extended family apparently went well. We married the following year, just before another business trip to Ukraine. We stopped in Italy for a Tuscan honeymoon, then went on to Kyiv, where she had meetings and I would entertain myself. It was the anniversary of the October 1917 revolution. At the end of Khreshchatyk, the wide, stately boulevard in the city's center, I photographed aging communists marching with red banners under the Marlboro cowboy's chiseled features, his narrowed gaze from a huge billboard taking in the few hundred true believers left behind by history. It was the last demonstration I witnessed in Ukraine about the past. The ones to come would be about the future.

(The Marlboro billboard wasn't just photographer's luck. At that time, it would have been hard to march anywhere in a Ukrainian city not dominated by western cigarette advertisements. The highway from Boryspil International Airport was a gauntlet – a billboard every few hundred meters of the 30 kilometers into Kyiv, every last one pushing smoking. The cancer connection they'd long suppressed was finally catching up with tobacco companies in the West. Behind the fallen Iron Curtain were millions of new customers/victims.)

In the next few years, I tagged along on other business trips. One took us to Crimea where she convened scientists and local conservationists to create a biodiversity plan for the entire peninsula. Published in Russian, English, Ukrainian and Crimean Tatar, it was still Crimea's basic working document for conservation a decade later. While she worked, I fell under the spell of another aspect of Ukraine's beauty, riding long-distance trolleys down to Yalta and along the light-drenched coast, drinking in the Mediterranean-like landscape of cliffs and coves, vineyards and elegant cypresses, pillars of two thousand-year-old Greek temples framing the setting sun. Inland, I toured monuments of a Tatar Muslim civilization in Crimea that went back to the thirteenth century. The Russian Empire had repressed the Tatars and Stalin had deported the entire population in freight trains. Now the survivors and descendants were trickling back.

On another trip around Ukraine we met local environmentalists – forest rangers, researchers, activists – fighting to preserve natural treasures from the incursions of privatizing politicians and oligarchs. Her project funded many of them and I saw similarities to grassroots leaders and activists I knew from my own work in Latin America. Their organizations were locally-based, democratically run. She thought democracy natural to Ukrainians, Russia's traditions more authoritarian. Over the next couple of decades, that difference would play out in a series of intensifying crises, stepping stones to the current war.

But back then, I was just trying to understand her country. I wasn't the only one curious. A nation bigger than France, its population close to 50 million, had suddenly appeared in Europe. People needed a way to see it.

During the first decades of Ukraine's independence, most saw it through a sort of bifocal lens that seemed to reveal two Ukraines – a western half, much of it once part of the Austro-Hungarian empire, Ukrainian the main language; an eastern half, once part of the Russian empire, later the Soviet,

Russian widely spoken. The Dnieper River, running through the capital, Kyiv, a neat dividing line. The language division supposedly explained everything: culture, religion, political orientation, loyalties, economy. The west was agricultural and leaned towards Europe, the east industrial and oriented to Russia.

But up close, the division wasn't so neat. Starting with her. She came from the east, a scant 30 kilometers from the Russian border. Her home language was Russian. Kharkiv was a major cultural center but as a student and young professor, she would also ride the overnight train to concerts and art exhibitions in Moscow, not Kyiv. Yet she proudly spoke fluent Ukrainian. Back then, economic and personal networks spanned the porous border between eastern Ukraine and Russia. She knew many people in Moscow, but after 1991 the assumption, even among liberal Russians, that Ukrainian independence was an amusing and transitory myth, began to grate. Eventually, she stopped going to Moscow.

Other realities didn't divide neatly either. In addition to its mines and factories, the east was also agricultural, dense ranks of sunflowers and rippling grain blanketing vast steppes rolling to the horizon. In its villages, people spoke Ukrainian. And despite the assumed affinity for Russia, it, along with every part of the country, had voted decisively for independence in 1991. Most people considered themselves Ukrainian, no matter their language or where they lived.

The other lens through which the west saw Ukraine after independence focused on widespread corruption. But corruption doesn't quite capture what happened in Ukraine. Looting is the better word. After the USSR's collapse, there were room-where-it-happened meetings when former party functionaries and managers, some of them Russians, divided up Ukraine's factories and mines and infrastructure and media. As a well-known lawyer in Kharkiv she was invited more than once to those rooms. She declined. Those who attended became fabulously wealthy. A new class appeared – the oligarchs.

Westerners, especially the Americans, have been tut-tutting about Ukrainian corruption ever since. But it was the predictable outcome of the rush by American policy makers to privatize economic infrastructure and resources, to drive a stake through the heart of communism, worrying little about the lack of public accountability and transparency in government actions, about the concentration of great wealth and therefore power in few hands, and thus the inevitable impoverishment of much of the population. And so the country was looted, and not only by Ukrainians. In December 2013, for example, a subsidiary of Archer Daniels Midland Company (ADM) pled guilty to paying, along with a second ADM subsidary, $22 million in bribes to obtain over $100 million in VAT refunds.

Ukrainians like political jokes. It's part of the way they absorb the politics they've been dealt. You could tell the history of independent Ukraine in a series of such jokes. I remember one that captured the brazen scale of looting and, significantly, included an American actor:

An ambitious Ukrainian oligarch goes to New York and is invited to a wealthy American's penthouse apartment for drinks.

"How did you make your money?" the Ukrainian asks.

The American draws him to the window overlooking the Hudson River.

"You see that?" he says, pointing to the span of the George Washington bridge. "Fifty percent for the bridge, fifty percent for me."

A few years later, the American visits Kyiv and is invited to the Ukrainian's much larger penthouse apartment.

"You've done very well since I saw you. How did you do it?"

His host draws him to the window and points to a stretch of the Dnieper River.

"I took your advice and got a contract to build a bridge."

"But there's no bridge out there", the American says.

"Exactly", says the Ukrainian oligarch, with a smile.

One of the most infamous insider deals came in 2004. With presidential elections approaching, the government sold Ukraine's largest steel mill to a couple of oligarchs, one of them the son-in-law of retiring President Leonid Kuchma, for $850 million. The opposition, led by a former prime minister, Viktor Yushchenko, and Yulia Tymoshenko, a fiery orator and perhaps the cleverest politician in Ukraine, complained loudly that the price was a fraction of the mill's worth.

In the elections, Kuchma's chosen successor was Viktor Yanukovych, who despite starting his career with prison sentences for assault and robbery eventually rose to become prime minister. Russian President Vladimir Putin visited Kyiv the week before the election to underline his support for Yanukovych. During the campaign, Yushchenko fell dangerously ill from dioxin poisoning. He recovered after emergency treatment in a Vienna clinic and returned to the campaign, his distorted face a reminder that politics could be a dangerous game in the region. (News reports on Putin's opponents often contain some variant of the words "suspected poison" or "fall from an upper-story window". More recently, "presumed dead in plane crash" has made the list.)

Charges of voter suppression and blatant cheating marred the first round of voting, and escalated in the November 21 runoff between Yushchenko and Yanukovych. When the opposition protested the official count, which flatly contradicted reputable exit polls, thousands of Ukrainians massed on the wintry Maidan, the vast square in the center of Kyiv, and along wide Khreshchatyk, and vowed to stay until a new and transparent election was called.

In Washington, we devoured every report about the protest and about Kyiv's citizens rushing to bring the demonstrators food and warm clothing. She said she had to be there. After an overnight flight we went to the apartment of a friend, a prominent lawyer. Normally reserved, now he was giddy with excitement. He led us down to Khreshchatyk, where tents of all shapes and sizes, from camouflage military surplus that could sleep a dozen to bright single backpackers' domes, filled the wide avenue. Orange, the color of Yushchenko's campaign, was everywhere: in the flickering flames in the oil drums full of wood scraps around which people gathered and guitarists warmed their fingers; in the armbands worn by volunteers policing the occupied area, the scarfs and sweaters and hats most of the demonstrators wore. One smiling guy stuck an orange ball on his nose, the way circus clowns do. There was a teenager, his Cossack-style braid tied with an orange band, showing off his breakdance moves. Women and girls wore orange bands or scrunchies in their hair. Dogs out for a walk sported orange sweaters. The grey, glowering sculptures of long dead philosophers or politicians held paper orange flowers in their rigid hands.

Russia charged the entire protest was American-funded, and that the demonstrators were drugged. Demonstrators in one tent mocked the accusation, stenciling USA on a traditional Ukrainian felt boot worn against the cold and displaying it on a barrier beside a weather-withered orange pierced by hypodermic needles.

But behind the impressive fortitude of the protestors, the Orange Revolution was less a revolution than a mobilization of the political parties cheated in the elections. The crowds gave Yushchenko and his allies leverage as they demanded a rerun. We were in the enormous crowd filling the Maidan to celebrate when Ukraine's Supreme Court ordered just that. There were speeches and songs, orange banners and Ukrainian flags. In the light from the fireworks her face was radiant with pride. Three weeks later, the runoff was rerun and votes counted before international observers. Yushchenko won by almost eight points. Yulia Tymoshenko became prime minister and Yanukovych remained head of the opposition bloc in the Parliament.

That steel mill? The new government renationalized it, then put it up for bids on the open market, where it brought $4.8 billion – six times the price in the sweetheart deal.

There was a political lesson in the Orange Revolution that, even though it blocked him from the presidency, Yanukovych forgot: Ukrainians would put up with a lot from their politicians. But cross a line, they would come out. There were also lessons for Putin. He understood the first – Ukraine's democratic example could threaten his own authoritarian system. A Russian TV reporter had spelled it out in the kicker to his reporting from the Maidan: "if Ukrainians can do it, why can't we?" Putin couldn't accept a second lesson – Ukrainians didn't like the idea that outsiders might poison their candidates or tamper with their votes. They wanted to run their own country.

Despite the elation of the Orange Revolution, and the new government's promising beginning, the following years were filled with internal political struggles. Yushchenko's government seemed increasingly ineffective. The three main political figures began to play at shifting alliances and musical chairs. At one point Tymoshenko, heroine of the Orange Revolution, was sidelined and Yanukovych, whom the protests had foiled, became prime minister.

An ingenious joke from those years captured the political leaders in one short scene:

The three, along with Yushchenko's wife, are at high tea in Buckingham Palace, across the table from the Queen of England.

Yushchenko's wife wants a souvenir and whispers that he should put one of the silver teaspoons in his pocket.

"I'm the president of Ukraine. I can't steal a teaspoon from the Queen of England."

"Your friend Viktor's an accomplished thief. Ask him to do it."

Yanukovych whispers that he'd like to help, but he's already pocketed one spoon.

Yushchenko turns to Julia and explains the problem. She thinks for a moment, then brightly addresses the Queen.

"Your Majesty, you welcomed us with lovely compliments about our country and our talented people. But perhaps you weren't told of our talent as magicians. Let me demonstrate."

She lifts a teaspoon from the table.

"Watch closely as I place this lovely spoon in our president's pocket."

"And now," she says with a malicious smile at her rival, "watch while I withdraw the same teaspoon from the pocket of our prime minister."

In 2007, we moved to Kyiv. She'd been hired to lead a two-year European Union-funded effort to improve an environmental treaty for the Black Sea. We settled into an apartment overlooking Khreshchatyk, a few blocks down the hill from the gargoyle-encrusted presidential office building on Bankova Street, a short walk from the Maidan, the cockpit of Ukrainian democracy.

Much of the talk those years was about metastasizing corruption. With so much of the country's major resources already swallowed by oligarchs, extortion reached into every institution, and down to street level.

Her project put her in contact with working level officials in various ministries, where she learned of the envelopes with required salary kickbacks that flowed upwards each monthly payday, as routinely as water through the pipes, to a minister's office.

In cars, drivers kept banknotes folded above their visors, an instant get-out-of-jail pass handed to a policeman who'd waved them over for some traffic offense, or none.

Almost routinely, in downtown restaurants, something other than what you'd ordered would show up on the bill, at a higher price. Her secretary explained:

"Most people who go to those restaurants didn't earn their money. They stole it. Why shouldn't they share some of it with the restaurant?"

On Khreshchatyk, near the Bessarabia Market, fast-talking guys ran scams on pedestrians. Pickpockets circled the train station like attentive crows. In winter, luxury cars or black SUVs parked, with in-your-face arrogance, diagonally on the sidewalks, forcing walkers into the icy or slushy streets to get around them. A couple of times, I talked her out of raking her keys along their doors, fearing some iron-pumping bodyguard might be inside, behind the tinted windows.

It wasn't only Kyiv. When my brother-in-law opened a car wash in his Kharkiv neighborhood, a pair of city officials promptly appeared to explain how $10,000 would make the problems they could devise for him go away.

Meanwhile, economic conditions were worsening for ordinary Ukrainians. The national currency, the hryvna, steadily lost ground to inflation, which didn't hurt us since our income was in euros or dollars, but ravaged people in the local economy. One evening in a Silpo supermarket in Kharkiv, our cart already quite full, she was looking for something in the cereal aisle. Next to her was a retirement age couple, dressed simply, the man holding a basket with a small package of processed cheese. After studying the prices they turned away, resignedly. "It looks like we can't allow ourselves oatmeal anymore", the woman said to the man. Translating the women's words for me, she had tears in her eyes.

The disillusionment was so general that in 2010 Ukrainians voted Yanukovych into the office the Orange Revolution had stopped him from stealing in 2004. His image had been touched up in the meantime, thanks in part to American political consultant Paul Manafort. A smiling Yanukovych beamed from a huge campaign billboard on my mother-in-law's street, the skin on his face so Botox-tight I thought the billboard might go all black hole at any moment. Manafort later moved like a Monopoly board game token, to Fifth Avenue, where he briefly managed Donald Trump's presidential campaign, and then to jail for bank and tax fraud related to his international consulting. Trump pardoned him before leaving office.

We'd intended to return to Washington when her project ended, but shortly before that her mother suffered a paralyzing stroke. For the next several years, we split our time between Kharkiv and Washington. I came to like Kharkiv more and more, which pleased her. There was always something new — a museum opening, an opera, a concert from one of the city's three classical orchestras, sophisticated jazz, seasonal flowerbeds in the city's parks, hip restaurants where young Ukrainian chefs offered local food and excellent service, and the bills mirrored the meals you'd eaten.

Meanwhile, Yanukovych was taking looting to a new dimension, while balancing popular pressure for closer ties with Europe against Putin's insistence on welding Ukraine and Russia together. For a couple of years, he kept both balls in the air, dealing with Putin but permitting the meticulous negotiations towards a trade and cooperation agreement with the EU to continue. On one of her consultancies she helped produce the environmental chapter for that agreement. When the overall agreement was ready to be signed in Vilnius, Lithuania in November 2013, Yanukovych abruptly reversed himself and announced that he would accept Putin's embrace instead. Weirdly, he also announced that he'd still be going — Banquo's ghost in a business suit — to the Vilnius meeting, where he no longer had a role to play. He'd been keeping two balls in the air for so long he didn't seem to know how to stop, even after kicking one away.

Yanukovych's U-turn was a particular shock to young Ukrainians who already identified as European. They'd traveled west, found work, made friends, learned skills, like some of the young chefs who'd returned to open those chic restaurants in Kharkiv. Yanukovych's announcement threatened that freedom. It also dashed hopes that the financial transparency required by the

EU agreement would finally limit the corruption that crippled their country. Young protesters gathered on the Maidan, put up signs and tents, talked with passers-by, played guitars, and danced in circles at night.

The day after the Vilnius meeting, Yanukovych sent helmeted riot police out at 4:00 a.m. to clear the Maidan. Cameras and cell phones captured appalling scenes of the police headhunting with their nightsticks, dragging girls along the pavement, stomping youths who were pleading for mercy. Television screens, which earlier in the evening had shown young people dancing and laughing and singing now showed garbage trucks hauling away their tents and protest signs, and city workers hosing their blood off the pavement.

Public reaction was swift and massive. By the next afternoon, an angry and enormous crowd –estimates ran as high as 350,000 – swept into the square, pushed the barricades aside as the police melted away, occupied city hall and set up a command center where ad hoc leaders promised to continue the occupation, which would be dubbed Euromaidan, until the government resigned.

Several days later, when the riot police, restrained by public outcry from using their clubs, tried to shove people away from the area with their heavy plastic shields, hundreds of Kyiv residents raced to reinforce the protestors and the police were pushed back. The same frigid night, water sprayed from fire hoses on the upper floors froze a police operation against the occupied city hall. After that, barriers of snow and ice blocked the streets leading into the square and supporters poured in from around the country.

In Kharkiv, we watched television coverage or attended rallies on Sumskaya Street where every night, young people with backpacks received rousing sendoffs as they boarded buses to join the uprising in Kyiv. We followed soon after, for a few days of reporting on the Maidan before a scheduled trip to Washington, where we would be speaking on events in Ukraine.

What we saw was an alternative, self-governing nation housed in over 200 tents, enough steaming soup cauldrons and sandwich prep tables to serve tens of thousands of meals a day, 24-hour medical services and psychological counseling, five thousand volunteers to defend the four-meter high barricades of ice, snow, wooden beams and rubber tires and guard the narrow checkpoints to bar provocateurs and drunks. Housing coordinators placed out-of-town protestors in rooms donated by Kyiv residents. One tent distributed donated clothing – warm sweaters, scarves, socks, hats and gloves. Volunteers with jeeps or hatchbacks came at night to haul trash away. Entertainment, by popular singers and poets, was as continuous as in a Las Vegas casino, except when priests led prayers from the stage. On a smaller stage, university professors offered open-air classes and their students stood on mats someone had thoughtfully laid down to insulate feet from the frozen concrete. Drifting smoke from scores of bonfires in blackened steel drums clung to clothing and hair. Like a stamp in a passport, the whiff of woodsmoke marked you as a resident of, or at least a visitor to, this republic of protest.

As soon as we walked onto Maidan, press credentials hanging from our necks, everyone wanted to talk. The most common response as to why they were there was corruption. Everyone had a story. One 53-year-old former businessman told us that in the previous decade businesses in his native Donetsk had to turn over half their profits to Yanukovych's circle. Now, he said, medium and large businesses were taken over entirely, through physical threats or decisions by corrupt courts. He said he was forced out of his own small business five years before.

"I've been sitting on my couch since, watching television", he said. "But with Maidan, I got up from the couch. It was my duty to come here." By mid-December, he was working as a volunteer guard on the barricades.

Surveys confirmed our impression that, unlike the Orange Revolution, which had scant support in the east, Yanukovych's base, the Euromaidan protestors came in roughly equal thirds from Ukraine's east, centre and west. Another survey found that 92 percent of the people on the Euromaidan claimed no political party affiliation. So what was happening there?

"It's like quantum mechanics", the son of one of her childhood classmates who was deeply engaged in the uprising told us. "When you try to analyze it, you change it." But he was sure about what was not happening. "Political leaders are not driving the process", he said. "They are following what happens here. There was not a single moment when those political leaders came to the empty square first, and then the crowd came. Always, it was first the crowd, and then the politicians."

We saw a moment one night that confirmed his point. Negotiations with the government were generally handled by three politicians – one from the party of Tymoshenko, who had been jailed by Yanukovych ("Lock her up" was not invented by Trump supporters), one leader of Right Sector, the right wing political party strongest in western Ukraine, and Vitali Klitschko, who'd entered Ukrainian politics after dominating world heavyweight boxing for years. On this night we watched the three climb to the Maidan stage to report on the talks and be booed because they were proposing to give away too much, to settle for not enough. As a boxer, Klitschko had left a long line of opponents crumpled on the canvas, but at the Euromaidan he stood with his head bowed, like the others, as the crowd sent them back to do better.

Again and again, the people we talked to said they've been transformed by the experience. We left convinced that much of the international press coverage, focused on the power struggle, was missing the real story: a grass-roots process that was fundamentally transforming how Ukrainians thought about themselves, their country and their politics.

We were back in Washington in January and February when events reached their bloody climax. Almost 100 protestors died, many from police sniper fire. Thirteen police officers were also killed. The protesters' perimeter shrank to a corner of the square, but they built a ring of fire to defend themselves, and then counter-attacked. Police lines broke. Up on Bankova Street, political negotiations were ongoing as the police disappeared from the streets. Yanukovych raced to his opulent residence, gathered up the valuables he could carry, and fled, eventually winding up under Putin's protection in Russia.

He left behind a country close to default. During his three years in power, the interim prime minister reported, the Central Bank's foreign reserves, including gold, had dropped from $37 billion to $15 billion, as much as $70 billion had been sent out of the country. Forbes Ukraine reported that Yanukovych's son, a dentist, had increased his wealth to an estimated $510 million during his father's truncated term.

In snap presidential elections with 21 candidates, Petro Poroshenko, a chocolate business millionaire – Ukrainians love chocolate – who'd played a visible role in the protests, won 54.7 percent of the vote. Russian charges that Euromaidan brought fascists and the far right to power in Ukraine looked ridiculous when the two right-wing candidates, one of them the highly visible political leader on the Maidan, got less than two percent of the vote, combined.

Three months before the election, Putin had dropped his political attempts to bring Ukraine to heel and started his war on the country. He sent troops without insignia to annex Crimea before a shocked, and leader-less, Ukraine could react. Next, he fomented rebellion in Ukraine's eastern Donbas oblasts and his troops intervened to back the separatists whenever Ukrainian forces threatened them.

The war seemed low intensity to much of the world, but Ukrainian soldiers were dying in savage battles and over 1.5 million refugees fled the region. In Kharkiv, the sometimes daily rattle of helicopters meant wounded soldiers arriving and she and her friends would drop what they were doing to rush medical supplies, linens and clothing to hospitals. Ukrainians used cellphones to create support networks overnight. One afternoon we interviewed a young woman who was coordinating the collection and delivery of supplies to soldiers fighting in the Donbas. Her phone rang with a call from the front lines with a list of needs — socks, rain gear, sweaters, batteries. Within minutes, she and her group were busy rounding up the items, to be packed in cars and driven to the front that same day.

Many of the refugees came to Kharkiv. Others, mainly elderly people, couldn't or wouldn't leave their homes. That summer, along what was called the line of contact, I photographed some of them by the light coming through holes in their rocketed roofs for an international refugee agency, and then documented the volunteer relief effort that sprang up across the country.

Up till then, I hadn't really been on my own in Ukraine, save occasional wanderings with my camera while she was working. Now, I was the guide, trying to explain Ukraine to the refugee agency officials. Ukraine puzzled them. There were no blue tents. They had years of experience in refugee crises around the world and they were used to seeing the neat rows of blue United Nations tents go up in empty fields. Ukraine absorbed its refugees into its towns and cities. Many fled to the homes of family or friends. In our Kharkiv neighborhood, cars with Donbas license plates filled the streets.

I started to feel a sort of home-town pride, calling the refugee officials' attention to Ukrainians' spontaneous mobilizations to support their fellow citizens, describing the civic culture behind them. We talked with volunteers at an information desk in Kharkiv's train station who directed arriving refugees to lodging, meals, nursery schools, job centers, all set up and run by other volunteers. In Kyiv, I photographed the support center a young businessman created in an empty building in the Podil neighborhood. He got donated playground equipment and placed it on foam pads so kids could be safe on the swings and slides and seesaws. Next to the pop-up playground were pop-up plywood rooms displaying clothing. A constant procession of local citizens donated bags of freshly laundered clothing that was sorted by gender and size on long tables, then placed on hangars or shelves in the display rooms. In the room with women's clothing, a gorgeous volunteer in a fashion t-shirt helped refugees select the items that most flattered them, creating all by herself the atmosphere of an elegant store in London or Paris.

The war in Donbas dragged on, threatening to become the kind of "frozen conflict" that Russia has created in former Soviet countries like Moldova and Georgia, crippling their sovereignty and insuring that Russia keeps outsized influence over their policies. With Ukraine's 2019 presidential election on the horizon, a TV series, *Servant of the People*, about a teacher who becomes president after a high school student captures and posts his angry tirade over corruption, made its leading actor, Volodymyr Zelenskiy, the real life leading candidate. In a runoff with Poroshenko, he won over 73 percent of the vote. Once again, Ukrainians had voted for abrupt change.

Zelenskiy had promised to end the conflict with Russia, but Putin rebuffed him. It was a propitious moment for Putin, with Crimea firmly in his grip, the ongoing conflict in the east sapping Ukraine, and a politically untested television comedian as president in Kyiv.

And then came Covid. The macho Russian leader was notoriously afraid of the disease. For months, the very few visitors permitted in the same spacious room with him sat at the other end of a very long table, enough room between for a ping pong match. Despite running a country spanning nine time zones, he found time in his bubble to, personally, the Kremlin said, research and write a tract insisting that Ukraine was never a country, always an historical part of Russia. Professional historians around the world ridiculed his arguments, but Putin had convinced himself, and in February 2022 he launched his armies to gather Ukraine in.

She knew it was coming. When Putin first came to power, intriguing most of the world's media, she'd told me he was a KGB thug, exactly like the agents who interrogated her after her internship in the US. George W. Bush's discovery of Putin's soul failed to convince her. In the days leading up to the invasion, friends and family in Ukraine assured her the Russian troops massing on the border were only a show of force. And then the bombs fell on Kyiv and Kharkiv and tank columns rolled down Ukrainian highways. Russian troops reached the center of Kharkiv before being pushed back. Mariupol was besieged and reports of war crimes came from Bucha and Irpin, and, sick with worry, she called her mother every day and agonized about how to help her besieged country.

Alerted by a journalist friend to Kharkiv's overwhelmed firefighters, she drew on her experience with grassroots groups, knowing to ask – not decide from afar – what they needed. The firefighters were already receiving shipments of well-intentioned but superfluous equipment. She also knew to be flexible when needs changed, as they will, during a war. All this involved dozens of phone calls with her contact in Kharkiv. "Should I be concerned that this fireman keeps calling you at 3:00 a.m.?" I asked.

The most pressing needs were for delivery trucks to move their people more efficiently in response to dozens of daily calls for help digging survivors out of the rubble of collapsed buildings and distributing emergency and relief supplies.

To counter her despair about the war, she plunged into a fundraising campaign. Together with two friends and an association of women firefighters in San Francisco, and appeals to friends around the US and in Europe, we raised about €56,000 to buy two used delivery trucks and to cover 57 percent of the cost of an 18-wheel truck and trailer so they could pick up equipment on the Polish border. When the trucks arrived in Kharkiv, the firemen sent photos. But any sense of success during a war is fleeting. While we were raising funds to support them, five Kharkiv firemen died from Russian rockets or mines.

Three months after the war started, we finally convinced her mother to leave. With the elevator in her building not working, firemen carried her down from her fifth-floor apartment. Friends and family helped her travel eight hundred kilometers to a border crossing near Lublin where we waited. She rolled across the border in her wheelchair, cursing Putin for forcing her from her home. Later that night, she admitted she'd lived in fear of the daily attacks.

"But you told us you were fine, and didn't want to leave."

"I lied. I didn't want you to worry."

By the time she escaped, Ukraine's actor-president had become a courageous and inspiring leader and the Russian invasion a shambles. Putin sent a powerful army so sure of capturing Kyiv in a few days that officers packed dress uniforms for the victory parade on Khreshchatyk. Zelenskiy refused to flee. In a month of fighting, fierce Ukrainian resistance blunted the attack north of Kyiv. Destroyed Russian equipment lined the roads for miles.

Another joke, this one a cartoon, captured Ukrainian insouciance in the face of Putin's invasion and recalled those long lines of destroyed Russian tanks:

A woman seen through a kitchen window tends steaming pots on the stove. In the next room, a boy, maybe 10, grips a Javelin missile launcher as he peers out another window.

"Ok, Pasha", the woman calls. "Just one more tank and then you have to come for your borscht."

Later in the war's first year, Russia suffered more defeats, including the rapid loss of land it had initially captured around Kharkiv. Its forces have largely hunkered in defensive positions, indicating Putin's strategy is to hold territory, continue to inflict maximum damage on civilians and infrastructure, and hope that Ukraine's supporters grow weary, or that Trump returns to the American presidency next year. His bombs and rockets continue to target Kyiv and Kharkiv and scores of other cities. Death and destruction are general over Ukraine and we wonder what will be left of her country when the war finally ends.

But two things are already clear. Putin's obsession with rebuilding the Russian empire is weakening the Russian nation. And Ukraine's resistance is a convincing argument for the superiority of democratic government over authoritarianism, a question widely debated around the world today.

One bright winter day years ago, when we were living in Kyiv, her brother visited with his wife and daughter. We walked down Khreshchatyk to the park above the Dnieper and took photos near the eight-metre tall sculpture of two workers with linked arms beneath a soaring titanium arch, built in 1982 to symbolize friendship between Russians and Ukrainians. Now her brother lives alone, looking after their home and business in Kharkiv. His wife, daughter and young son are refugees in Lithuania. After Putin's 2014 invasion, someone drew a symbolic jagged crack across the arch with black paint. After Putin launched his full-scale war, a symbolic crack wasn't enough. Two months and two days into it, a crane rolled up, neatly decapitated the Russian figure, lifted the rest of the sculpture from its plinth and dropped it like rusted plumbing from a house demolition.

In the years before that sculpture became intolerable, Russia had a country on its western border with links of language, culture, family. Putin's determination to control rather than live with it, his decision to go to war with it, and what his army did, in Bucha, in Mariupol, in Irpin, in Izium, what his rockets continue to do in Kyiv and Kharkiv and across the country, have destroyed those links and will color how Ukrainians think about Russia for generations.

Putin talks of restoring the Russian empire, but history suggests that when empires shatter, the shards don't reassemble. In the aftermath of the Second World War, imperial powers in Western Europe soon lost most of their colonies. Faced with the impossibility of regaining them, historian Timothy Snyder points out, they came up with the European Union. Russia has not found a similar alternative. Like those aging communist marchers I saw in Kyiv in 1996, it looks only to the past.

Meanwhile, in just over three decades of independence, through the Orange Revolution, the Maidan uprising and the war with Russia, Ukrainians have forged a democratic nation focused on the future. Putin intervened aggressively at each of those junctures, and the result each time has been stronger Ukrainian unity, and growing hostility, now openly professed hatred, towards Russia. Ultimately, the war is about choosing the future, which Ukraine rushes to embrace, or the past, a false version of which Putin seeks to drape like a funeral shroud over his own country and its neighbors.

The war also reconfirms a World War II lesson that seems to be fading. Even within nations that believe themselves exemplars of democratic government, many question whether democracy is too ineffective to deal with today's problems? Would a strong, authoritarian hand be better? Evidence from the war so far confirms the lesson that democracies can defend themselves, and that leaving everything to an authoritarian leader eventually means a debacle.

But for now, the war rages on as we watch from Western Europe. She continues to find ways to help in Ukraine. Her paralyzed mother, officially a refugee, continues to insist she will return to Kharkiv. We watch and we wait for the Russian lines to break north of the Azov Sea, or for another rough beast to slouch toward Moscow. And in a few weeks, thirty years on, we'll look for a Thai restaurant.

See Patrick Breslin's biographical note in "Portfolio".

TWO POEMS

—

Moya Cannon

On the road.

DÚCHAS

The Rock, Sixmilecross, Loughmacrory,
she spoke the names affectionately,
all the consonants softened,
all the vowels lengthened –
Pomeroy, Donaghmore, Beragh, Omagh –
hamlets, villages, towns
that surrounded her childhood,
"Sweet Tyrone among the bushes"
intimations of a kindlier, sunnier country –

To us children,
summer-holiday names
almost as exotic as Samarkand
but we sometimes wondered
which rock among so many?
Six miles from where?
Who was MacRory
and how did he get his own lake?
And, later, what king and why an apple?

Later still, those names shrilled –
night raids, armed soldiers shouting
in the kitchen of our small, favourite aunt,
bewildered young cousins interned,
armoured cars and murderous
night-time road-blocks
and then, a bombing, heinous, catastrophic.

What's in a place-name — an earth-crumpling,
a rise, a hollow, in the earth's crust;
a hill where a glacier paused, exhausted;
a stony river crossing?

Is it power, dramatic incident,
or primal poetry
that allows specific syllables
first meld to field,
forest, house or hill?
— before life and time
play on them
to ring joybells
or knells of dread
inside our heads.

And can place-names
once, maybe, tenderly spoken —
Wounded Knee, Xwéda, Babi Yar, Hiroshima,
Kosovo, Kabul, Bakhmut, Omagh —
ever be cleansed of their pain?

And what's in any name?
What does *omphalos* mean?
Or *dúchas*?
What does *dúchas* mean
and why has such violence
been wreaked in its gentle name?

Dúchas (from the Irish): one's heritage, what is native, natural to one.

SINGER

i.m. Ruby DeBúrca Connolly, 2003-2022

I knew you only as a little, brown-haired girl
and now, a young woman, you are gone
leaving a crater, a caldera, an inland sea
of grief where you used to be.
You are gone as if you had been on loan
to the green planet which you so loved.

Yesterday, in the house of that good friend,
just hours after doctors removed tubes
which supported the last sparks of your life,
we met your stunned young mother
your heart-stricken young father,
your dear grandmother,
all in a daze of sorrow,
a maze, a labyrinth of sorrow.

And, today, in a deep valley
where, even in May sunshine, beech buds
were small, furled, brown umbrellas,
and bluebells bowed their blue heads
and a river ran brightly over granite rocks
I thought all day of you, little singer,
gone out of the world and of how, yesterday,

as we left and closed the gate
of that good friend's house
and stepped off the path,

there, on the road, was the body
of a young thrush, the tree-top singer,
brown wing-feathers fanned wide

and the singing heart stopped.

Moya Cannon was born in 1956 in Dunfanaghy, Co Donegal and now lives in Dublin. She holds degrees in History and Politics and in International Relations from, respectively, University College, Dublin and Corpus Christi College, Cambridge. She is the author of six collections of poetry, most recently Keats Lives *(2015) and* Donegal Tarantella *(2019), both from Carcanet. She is a member of Aosdána.*

THE AWAKENING

(an extract from *The Longest Journey*, a novel)

—

Oksana Zabuzhko

Where identity begins.

That was to be my first trip since 2020 to do a book presentation in another country.

The first – after two years of lockdowns, covids (I managed to get both the Delta and the Omicron variants!), canceled book fairs, countless exhausting conversations with pixels on the screen in place of actual people, and a newly developed – and highly unusual in the country that has lived through three Maidan revolutions in the thirty years of its independence – fear of any human gathering. It seemed incredible that all of this has ended, that the book market was returning to normal life. I had been prepared to make my peace with things being changed forever.

I should have felt happy. And yet, somehow, I couldn't. As I packed my suitcase on February 23 (a small one, I was only going for three days, and not far at all, it's an hour's flight from Kyiv to Warsaw, like going across the street: two public appearances – so two dresses, two changes of underwear, and my make-up bag), pouring out my gels and tonics into travel-sized bottles and breaking off a few vitamins and contact lenses from the large packs that wouldn't fit into my purse, I mentally palpated the state of my soul like a doctor palpates an aching organ – and had to admit I felt no anticipation or excitement whatsoever. More: that, however strange it seemed, I would have been relieved if at the last moment this trip had to be canceled. (I would have felt bad about my publisher: they spent so much time and effort on this book, and for them this was also going to be the first visit of a foreign author after a two-year hiatus, and the book was complicated, a collection of essays that wasn't going to advertise itself ... Alright, enough of this fruitless procrastination, better figure out what shoes to take!)

—

That was how I tried to deal with my oddly sedate state of mind: by rationalizing, by telling myself to snap out of it. I actually have an extraordinarily rich array of stress states – traumatic, post-traumatic and pre-traumatic (it's when you're go nuts like a dog before an earthquake, and only later realize why!), shock-induced, anxiety-induced, or panicked – every possible kind, an entire psychology textbook of personal experience, where I generously draw blood and flesh for my books' characters, but this particular state was unlike any I could recognize. Today, I would define it as a state of soldierly fatalism, *an awareness of being a tool* when you sense you are given a role in a drama written by someone else and you just have to play it the best you can, not asking about its meaning or purpose. (I am only able to be so perceptive today because I have lived in this state for the last three months. Back on February 23, it was still new and unfamiliar, and I was still trying to fit it into the confines of common sense like everything I needed for three days into a carry-on bag.)

There were a few other moments that for some reason stuck in my mind. Such as a sudden flare-up of hesitation when I was almost ready to go and glanced at the laptop on my desk: should I go ahead and bring it? (Nah, the common sense told me, don't be silly, you've got fourteen interviews and two public appearances in three days, not to mention all your friends in Warsaw you at least have to say hello to – when do you think you'll have the time to open that laptop, in your hotel room before bed? To post something on Facebook? You can do that on your phone, don't overpack, you'll survive until Saturday …)

And – a prick of an oddly cold, distanced disbelief as I was walking down the stairs and putting my apartment keys into my purse: here I am, I'm going, the trip is not being cancelled …

And – my last phone call with Rostyk before I boarded the flight at Boryspil, the view of the runways through the window, and my own voice that sounded like someone else's, saying "That's alright, I'll be back on Saturday …"

… That night (long after midnight, after the buzz of the first interviews-meetings-conversations I plunged into as soon as I landed at the Chopin airport in Warsaw had settled), nestled in my hotel bed and having set my alarm for eight (my interview marathon started at 9:30 a.m. the next morning, I could sleep in!), before I put my phone away and despite being already quite sleepy, I wrote on Facebook so I wouldn't forget:

I've never seen so many Russian-speaking people with "different", meaning not Ukrainian Accents – Belarusians, Armenians and others I could not identify – crowded together in one place as I did today at Boryspil.

Such frightened people.

These people are visibly nervous. They fuss, they push and shove, they look for ways to get ahead of the line, as if they can't believe that the flight won't leave without them. The sound of Ukrainian language makes them freeze: it's obvious they don't understand it and it scares them.

"Mom, are we going to come back when the war is over?" a boy behind me in line asks.

"What are you talking about!" a terrified woman's voice snaps at him, with an audible note of anger ("you better watch yourself now!")

Looks like these are Putin's "peacekeepers", the potential cannon-fodder from those Russian satellite countries one of which Ukraine had refused to become, fleeing through Kyiv, the long way round, any possible way, with families and their worldly goods.

I could not think of another explanation for this "russkiy mir" incursion.

I posted this at 1:53 a.m. on February 24. And fell into the rock-like sleep of a proletarian after a hard day of honest work.

And at six (at six!!!) my phone rang as if possessed. Rostyk was calling.

"Idiot!" I groaned mentally, forcing myself to open my eyes. "What is he doing waking me up so early, doesn't he know what a demanding day I'm about to have? What a demanding trip this is?"

But I picked up – it didn't matter, I was awake.

And heard, instead of a "good morning":

"It's started, baby. They're bombing us."

———

I don't remember what my first thought was. It was just like eight years earlier when they called very early in the morning from the hospital to report my Mom's death, and Rostyk picked up, sat up in bed, grunted a few times, asked a question, and then exhaled somewhere into the space beside me, *"Mom is gone, baby. She's left"* – there's a gaping seconds-long blackout after this in my memory, as if a breaker popped, and then I'm in the bathroom, looking at myself in the mirror as if learning to recognize myself anew.

This was the same – it wasn't that we didn't expect this to happen, but that with our entire beings, to the very depths of our consciousness, down to childlike magic, in the name of all that is holy *we willed it not to happen* – and the next moment I'm aware of how I am looking at myself in the hotel bathroom's mirror and thinking, now you are in trouble, how are you going to make it home?

That irrational, irresistible, instinctive animal urge in the hour of danger – home! To your den, your cave, your shelter, to your kin – burrow into their bodies, become one with the warmth of your pack, dig deep, cover your head with your paws ...

Even when your den is being bombed.

This is where any identity begins: for an individual, it's always the safety belt, even when it offers no safety in the current conditions. Even when someone's declared a war on it.

Even when it's a war of extermination.

———

Much later, I realized I had taken one of the last regularly scheduled flights out of Kyiv. And that those crowds of skittish "foreigners of the Russian zone" that confused me so much at Boryspil must have been, in fact, Russians, citizens of the Russian Federation. And that they were, in fact, fleeing, I hadn't imagined it – because they knew something that we in Ukraine didn't know yet.

At 14:30 Kyiv time, when my flight LO752 took off, the first units of the Russian army were already moving across the Ukrainian border.

Translated, from the Ukrainian, by Nina Murray.

Oksana Zabuzhko (born 1960) is one of Ukraine's major contemporary writers and public intellectuals, the author of more than twenty books of poetry, fiction and non-fiction. She made her poetry debut at the age of 12; but since her parents had been blacklisted during the Soviet purges of the 1970s, it was not until perestroika that her first book saw the light of day. She graduated from the Department of Philosophy of Kyiv Shevchenko University; took her PhD in philosophy of arts; and subsequently worked as a research associate for the Institute of Philosophy of the Ukrainian Academy of Sciences. In the early 1990s she was a Fulbright Fellow and a Writer-in-Residence at Penn State University, Harvard University, and University of Pittsburgh. Following the publication of her novel Field Work in Ukrainian Sex *(1996) – named in 2006 as "the most influential Ukrainian book over 15 years of independence" – she has been working as a free-lance author.*

Zabuzhko's books have been translated into Bulgarian, Croatian, Czech, Dutch, English, Estonian, French, Georgian, German, Hebrew, Hungarian, Italian, Latvian, Lithuanian, Norwegian, Persian, Polish, Romanian, Russian, Serbian, Slovenian and Swedish. Among her awards are a

MacArthur Grant (2002), the Antonovych Prize (2009), the Ukrainian National Award (the Order of Princess Olha, 2010), Shevchenko National Prize of Ukraine (2019), the French National Order of the Legion of Honor (2023), and several other national and international awards. Her opus magnum, The Museum of Abandoned Secrets (2010), won the Angelus Central European Literary Prize for the best novel of Eastern and Central Europe (2013), and her recent work, The Longest Journey (2022), a book-long essay on the cultural and historical background of the current Russo-Ukrainian war, won in Ukraine The Book of the Year, and has been translated into nine languages. Since 2013 she along with her partner, the artist Rostyslav Luzhetsky, have operated a small publishing house promoting quality non-commercial literature.

Nina Murray is a Ukrainian-American poet and translator. She is the author of the poetry collections Glapthorn Circular (LiveCanon Poetry, 2023) and Alcestis in the Underworld (Circling Rivers Press, 2019) as well as several chapbooks. Her award-winning translations include Oksana Zabuzhko's Museum of Abandoned Secrets (AmazonCrossing, 2012), and Oksana Lutsyshyna's Ivan and Phoebe (Deep Vellum, 2023). Her translation of Lesia Ukrainka's Cassandra was performed at the Omnibus Theatre in London in 2022, and toured to Cambridge and Oxford in 2023. Nina grew up in Lviv and lives, for the moment, in Cambridgeshire.

AT THE FRONT

———

Sándor Jászberényi

YOU'VE GOT YOUR FAMILY WAITING FOR YOU

Pics.

1

When the missiles hit too close, I always woke up.

Didn't matter whether we'd had a warm cup of something before turning in or I'd taken a sleeping pill or anything. When I heard the roars, my eyes opened.

I would wait, ready to jump out of bed in my bulletproof vest, grab my helmet and boots, and run barefoot out of the building.

Not that it would have made any difference.

If the place took a direct hit, I'd be dead before I could run anywhere, and if it didn't, it would be pretty pointless to run out into the night. Still, I was always ready to jump. The blood screamed in my head, and I struggled to hold back my animal instincts.

"It's ok", Petyus said from the bed next to mine.

He was a miner from Kharkiv. A hundred and twenty kilos of fat and muscle, with dog eyes and a raspy baritone voice. He was awake, because when he slept, the wooden building shook from his snoring. It was like sharing a room with a bear.

"It's ok", he repeated. He sounded as if he were talking to his son. Not that I knew how he sounded when he talked to his son, but there was something in his tone that made it seem like the whole Russian invasion was just a bad dream, with missiles thundering down.

Of course, the instincts howling inside me would not let me go back to sleep. Petyus knew this, so he got up, pulled his backpack out from under the bed, and took out a jar.

"Come on, yeah", he said. His English was terrible, but I hardly noticed anymore.

I got up and walked over to the window that yawned into the night. Petyus screwed the lid off the jar and took out his knife. I took my knife out of my vest pocket, dipped it in the jar, and ran my tongue down the blade.

There was thick, black honey in the jar. Not the sickeningly sweet stuff you get in the store.

"I was dreaming about my wife", he said.

"I wasn't dreaming about anything."

"We were in little house in Ilovaisk, the one I tell you about. Her father's house."

"And?"

"The kids were in bed and she was in kitchen cleaning up."

"Do I have to listen to one of your sex stories? It'll give me nightmares."

"Did not get to sex. I was smelling her hair when the Russians woke me up and fucked up my dream."

"Too bad."

"They fucked up your dream too."

"I wasn't dreaming anything."

"You will if you stay here long enough."

"You know perfectly well this is my last day at the front."

"What time is it?"

"Sun will rise in two hours."

"We'll eat the honey in meantime, and I make coffee."

There were some crimson hints of dawn on the horizon, but we were still standing by the window. We sipped our instant coffees, smoked, and watched the glints of light shimmering in the shards of glass on the ground below from the windowpanes that had been shattered by the shifts in air pressure from the explosions.

2

They had found a bunk for me in a ghost village with the 72nd Ukrainian Motorized Rifle Division two weeks earlier.

The place was on a hillside next to a coal-fired power station lake. A narrow concrete bridge cut across the lake, the only way into the town on the far side. Wild ducks nested in the mud under its pillars.

Gray block houses stared at us from the opposite hillside. The Ukrainians had put the artillery units between the buildings, but there were still plenty of people living in the town. In the evenings, I watched the lights in the apartments go out.

The village was in total darkness. No one wanted to give the Russian artillery any clues as to which building the soldiers were sleeping in. The anti-aircraft guns still shot down a Russian missile or two every day, and it was not safe to spend more than one night in the same house.

The cannons rumbled during the day, but the real show started after the sun went down. The Russians seemed to have given up on occupying anything apart from ruins.

On the front, you learn pretty quickly to distinguish between the sound of your own artillery and that of the enemy. After two days, I had gotten it down. Most of the shells hit kilometers away from us, but when one struck closer, I would throw myself to the ground out of reflex. Always gave the soldiers a good laugh.

3

A young boy took me from Kiev to Dnipropetrovsk in a camouflage all-terrain vehicle with no license plate. The closer we got to the front in the east, the more checkpoints there were.

The boy would pull up in front of the roadblocks, roll down the window, and shout out the latest password, which was sent to the soldiers every day by the Ministry of War. We set out at dawn, and by afternoon we had reached the town. At a gas station, I had to switch cars. They put me in a car driven by two snipers from the 72nd Brigade. I shared the back seat with AKM machine guns and a hand grenade launcher all the way to Donetsk province. No one had to tell us we had reached the front. The continuous roar of the artillery made that clear enough.

For two or three hours, no one bothered with me. I took pictures of soldiers trying to fix shot-up SUVs in the yards of the houses they had requisitioned. The sun had already set by the time a soldier in his twenties who wouldn't stop grinning came up to me and told me that the commander of the unit wanted to see me.

He took me to a two-story wooden house. The ground floor was full of soldiers eating eggs and chicken with potatoes roasted in their peels. They were sitting on crates of NLAW anti-tank rockets that had been pushed up against the wall. An older man gave me a plate and gestured for me to eat. His name was Nazar. He was the unit commander. I had a few bites to eat. There was an uncomfortable silence in the room, and everyone was looking at me.

"So you are Hungarian?" Nazar asked.

"Yes."

"I know a Hungarian."

My stomach was in knots. I sincerely hoped that I wasn't going to have to explain Hungarian foreign policy to a bunch of armed men fighting in the middle of the night.

"Yes?"

"The best Hungarian, I think. The most talented. Do you know her name?"

"No."

"Michelle Wild."

The men in the room who were over forty laughed. The men in their twenties had no idea what he was talking about.

"She had a big influence on me too", I said.

"Are you talking about a politician?" a twenty-year-old kid named Vitya said in English.

"No", Nazar replied, "talented actress."

"How come I never hear of her?"

"Because by time you were born, she already retired."

"I could still know her."

"You don't know her because you're homo and you don't watch porn."

"Yes I watch porn!"

"But you don't watch classic porn. Because you're homo."

"I'm not a homo!"

"Yes, you are," Nazar said, bringing the debate to an end, "So what you come here for, Hungarian?"

"To film."

"Porn?" Vitya asked.

"Yes."

"Welcome to Ukraine!" Nazar said.

Someone found a bottle of American whiskey, and by the time we had finished it, they had assigned me to Vitya, who would take me to the front. The war had been going on for eight months, and we all knew that eight months was more than enough time for people in the West to forget that the Russians had invaded a European country. Ukrainian resistance depended on getting military support. The presence of foreign journalists was a necessary evil to secure arms supplies.

4

The day I arrived, I met Petyus. I was put on the first floor of a wooden house, and he was my roommate. When I first stepped into the room with my back-pack slung across my back, he was standing in front of me in his underwear and a poison green T-shirt. He was a huge man, with a shaved head, you could feel the floor shift under his weight. He looked me up and down.

"I warn you that I snore like chainsaw."

"It won't bother me. Actually makes me feel at home."

"That's what my wife says."

"Does she snore?"

"I don't know. I never heard her snore."

"I snore."

"No problem."

I unpacked my stuff next to my bed, undressed, and went to bed. I listened to the night noises, the rumble of the cannons in the distance. The branches of the trees were heavy with fruit, and you could hear the wasps and bees buzzing around the rotting apples and pears in the leaves on the ground.

"Do you have a family?" Petyus asked.

"A wife and a son from my first marriage. How about you? Do you have any children?"

"Two. Two boys. Eight and twelve years old. Do you want to see picture?"

"Yes."

Petyus stood up. The boards creaked underneath him as he stepped over to my bed. He held up a battered smartphone. A pic of two little boys eating ice cream. Blond kids wearing striped T-shirts.

"They are very handsome", I said. Then I shuddered because a shell had struck maybe a kilometer or two away.

"Do you have picture of your son?"

I took out my phone and brought up a pic of my son.

"He looks just like you."

"Yeah. Lots of people say I had myself cloned."

"My children look nothing like me, fortunately. They look like their mother."

"Lucky for them", I said with a grin.

"You're not most handsome man in world either, Sasha."

5

During the day, I toured the Ukrainian positions with Vitya and conducted interviews. Nazar had given orders that I was not to be taken to the active front until he was sure I could take it. I did interviews about ten kilometers from the front with the guys coming back in tanks or I hunted pheasants at the edges of the fields of wheat. The birds were confused by the thunder of the mortar shells, so they would run out to the side of the road, and you could just shoot them. There was always something freshly killed for dinner. During the two weeks I spent at the front, the soldiers shot pheasant for the most part. I managed to bag some wild rabbits once. Everyone was overjoyed that day.

I usually chatted with Petyus in the evenings. He was stationed at the Browning machine guns. The Russians would shell the hell out of the Ukrainian positions dug in the ground between the stunted trees and then try to overrun them with infantry. There were more and more unburied bodies in the wheat fields under the October sky.

On the third night, Petyus asked if I had a picture of my wife.

"Yes."

"Show me."

I showed him one of the pics on my phone. He looked at it for a long time.

"Too Jewish for me."

"Jewish cunts are warmer, you know."

"My wife's cunt is hotter. Want to see picture?"

"Of your wife's cunt?"

"No, idiot. Of wife."

"Sure."

Petyus stepped over to my bed and put his phone in my hand. On the screen was a pic of a natural blond, a stunningly beautiful woman.

"She's my Tyina", he said.

"Poor thing, she must be blind."

"Why you say she is blind?"

"She married you."

"What do you know about true love?"

"Everything. What the hell does she see in you?"

"I don't know. We met at a presentation. She was so beautiful I could not breathe."

"What did you do to trick her into talking to you?"

"Nothing. I knew her father from factory. He introduced me. It was love at first sight. I courted her for one month before she let me hold her hand. No one had ever kissed me like that in my life."

"Gimme a tissue so I can wipe away my tears."

"Her kiss was sweet like honey."

"You were born to be a poet, Petyus, not a soldier."

"After one year, I married her. The wedding was in Ilovaisk. And then came Petyuska and then little Volodya."

"You think about them a lot."

"I do not think about anything else."

"When was the last time you saw them?"

"Seven months ago."

"That's a lot. Do you talk to them often?"

"Yes. Every day."

6

The days passed by. In the evenings, Petyus talked about his family. He told me what his children's favorite food was, how his wife made it, how they kept bees at his father-in-law's place, twelve hives in all. I'd been among the soldiers for a week when Petyus came to dinner one night with a bandage on his hand.

"What happened?"

"It's nothing."

He ate, drank some whisky, and went to bed. I played cards with the others.

"The Russians tried to break through today."

"They did?"

"Fifty rounds left in the Browning. Can you imagine?"

"What happened to Petyus?"

"He's the only one left alive. A bullet went through his hand. We had to shout at him to get him to leave the post. He grabbed the gun, just in case."

Petyus was already snoring when I got back to the room. I went to bed. I woke up to him moaning and swearing.

"What happened?"

"I rolled on hand. Stitches are torn, I think."

The bandage was dripping with blood.

"We should go to the hospital."

The hospital was about twenty kilometers away. I wasn't allowed to take any pictures there. Anywhere but there. The Ukrainians wouldn't let us report their losses.

"Fuck it", he said. "Just bandage it up again."

"I'm not a doctor."

"Just bandage the fucking thing. I will go to hospital in the morning."

"Okay."

"First aid kit is on the vest."

I unzipped the pouch marked with the white cross and took out the tourniquets. The gauze and iodine were at the bottom. I used the small scissors to cut the bandage on Petyus' hand. The stitches had torn badly. A mix of red and black blood.

"Clean it out."

I wiped the wound with iodine and even poured a little in it. Petyus cursed like a sailor. When it looked clean enough, I started to bandage it up.

"There you go", I said. "But you should take better care of yourself. You've got your family waiting for you back home."

"They will have to wait a little longer."

"There's no telling how long this war will last."

"It lasts while it lasts. We will be together in the end anyway."

"I sincerely hope so."

"You don't have to hope. We will be together for sure. But not now. I still have some Russians to kill."

"I hope you get home soon."

"You are a good man, Sasha."

7

At Kharkiv, the Ukrainians counterattacked and broke through the Russian lines. I was only informed of this at the last minute, of course.

While playing cards, Nazar said, "tomorrow you can take the Hungarian out after the attack has started." When I asked what attack he was talking about, no one said a word, not surprisingly.

It later turned out that, contrary to expectations, the Ukrainian forces had launched a successful counterattack at Kharkiv. Nazar had hoped that this would distract the Russians enough to keep the artillery fire on the positions down a little while I was out.

...continues after Portfolio

PORTFOLIO

———

Patrick Breslin

Ukraine: A Love Story

Born in 1940, Patrick Breslin is an Irish-American photographer and writer who grew up in the immigrant communities of New York City's South Bronx. After graduating from Manhattan College, he worked as a newspaper reporter and then as a Peace Corps volunteer in Colombia, where he gained a lifelong interest in the problems of poverty.

Breslin earned his Master's and PhD degrees in political science from New York University and the University of California, respectively. Concurrently, he worked as a Peace Corps trainer, a journalist, and a research director at the Carnegie Endowment for International Peace. He studied photography at the Corcoran Gallery and the Smithsonian in Washington, DC.

His solo exhibition "Georgian Reflections" – 43 photographs juxtaposing sculpture and people in public spaces in Tbilisi, Georgia – was presented at the Kharkiv Municipal Art Gallery in April-May, 2011.

Other photographs have appeared in group exhibitions in Washington, DC, Belo Horizonte (Brazil), New York, El Paso, Texas, and Hawaii. His photographic work has appeared in *The Audubon, Garden, Grassroots Development, National Conference of Catholic Bishops, World Wildlife Fund* and *Urban Age Magazine.*

Breslin has also published two books, *Interventions* (Doubleday, 1980), a novel set in the turbulent period of the 1973 military coup against President Salvador Allende in Chile, and *Development and Dignity (1987)*, on the Inter-American Foundation, a semi-independent US government agency. That year, Breslin joined the Inter-American Foundation staff, where he directed research, wrote numerous articles, handled country portfolios in Honduras and Colombia, and was principal staff photographer for the IAF journal. From 2000 to 2007, he was the Vice President for External Affairs, overseeing publications and representing the Foundation before Congress. He wrote the Preface to Cathal Ó Searcaigh's *Errigal: Sacred Mountain*, published by The Irish Pages Press/Cló An Mhíl Bhuí in 2023.

His essay, "Ukraine: A Love Story", appears on page 78 of this issue.

i

Carpathians
Western Ukraine, 1997

Carpathians
Western Ukraine, 1997

Carpathians
Western Ukraine, 1997

The Sviatohirsk Cave Monastery
Ukraine, 2011

Crimea, 1998

Crimea, 1998

Crimea, 1998

Orange Revolution
Kyiv, 2005

Orange Revolution
Kyiv, 2005

Orange Revolution
Kyiv, 2005

Orange Revolution
Kyiv, 2005

Maidan Uprising
Kyiv, 2013

Maidan Uprising
Kyiv, 2013

Maidan Uprising
Kyiv, 2013

Maidan Uprising
Kyiv, 2013

Maidan Uprising
Kyiv, 2013

Maidan Uprising
Kyiv, 2013

Maidan Uprising
Kyiv, 2013

Refugees
Ukraine, 2015

Refugees
Ukraine, 2015

Refugees
Ukraine, 2015

Babi Yar Trees
Ukraine, 2007

October Revolution Memorial
Kyiv, 1996

Kharkiv, 2019

Crimea, 1998

Odesa, 1998

Kharkiv, 2010

We were cutting across fields of wheat, with the sun shining resplendently in the sky above us, when the Russians started shelling the position we were headed for. Two shells hit right next to our car, and it felt as if someone had pushed my head under water.

Vitya drove the car into the woods, and we jumped out. The soldiers knelt to the ground and listened and then ran to take cover in the trees.

Dusty earth and mud. The trenches were like something out of a World War I movie. Petyus was grinning as he came up from underground.

"Want some coffee?" he asked.

We did. I looked at the field where the barrels of the Browning machine guns were pointed. The Russians were less than a kilometer away on the far side. You couldn't see the dead bodies because of the tall grass, but I knew there were a lot of them lying unburied in the field, because when the wind shifted, it brought with it the sweet smell of decay.

I had a cup of coffee in my hand when I heard the shriek of the mortar shell. I lurched to one side and splattered the whole cup on Vitya.

"That was more than ten meters away", he said after it struck, and he pulled me up off the ground. I was ashamed that my nerves had given out.

The biggest problem with modern-day artillery is that you can't see it at all. The legend that 82mm mortar shells were deliberately designed to whistle before impact is widely held. It's nonsense, of course. No engineer would design a weapon so that the targets would know before it hit that it was about to strike.

Mortar shells whistle because they cut through the air and leave a vacuum behind them.

But you only hear the whistle of the shells that God intended for someone else.

The Ukrainians knew when the Russians were firing missiles. I guess the front was close and they could hear them launching. Though I'm not really sure. I only know that on the way back to the car, Vitya suddenly grabbed me and pulled me down into a hole.

I didn't have any time to think. The ground shook. I heard a big crash, then nothing.

When Vitya pulled me to my feet, I had no idea which way to go. He led me to the car. I thought my eardrums had burst, but neither of my ears was bleeding. I couldn't hear anything until we got back to the ghost village. Once my hearing had returned, with every shell that hit, I felt as if an electric current were tearing through my body. It took concerted effort not to throw myself to the ground each time, but I did okay, as long as the hits weren't too close.

8

Nazar told me that there was a car leaving for Kiev at eight o'clock, and I would leave the front in it.

The brigade was hard at work. All the equipment had to be moved to a new location because the Russian missiles were getting closer and closer. Old flatbed trucks were rolling down the dirt roads, loaded up with fuel, rocket launchers, and ammunition. They drafted me to lend a hand, so I was lugging boxes too, muttering something all the while about how nice it'd be if the Russians could please not fire any fucking rockets for just a little while.

The new headquarters was in a granary. It was a concrete building from the Cold War era, with bullet holes and boarded-up windows. We were still hard at work when a green all-terrain vehicle pulled up in front of the entrance.

"What about you?" I asked Petyus.

"I am coming with you."

"See, I told you you'd make it home", I said, giving him a slap on the back. "I'm good luck for you."

There were five of us in the all-terrain, and the trip back was a good twelve hours. Wasn't exactly first-class. I was longing to get a shower and finally take a shit in a toilet, but most of all just to stretch my legs once we reached Kiev.

But that was out of the question. Nazar and the others insisted that we get a round of drinks.

In the city center, we went to a pub called Gorky's. It was in a cellar, with heavy wooden tables and a bar. We could barely get a seat. I was shocked by the bustle. It felt as if we had arrived in a different country, a country that wasn't being ripped apart by war.

The guys ordered Ukrainian vodka and beer. The waiter brought dried salted fish and five shot glasses.

Nazar filled everyone's glass, and when he was done, he raised his own.

"A toast to those who gave their lives."

He lifted his glass on high, then poured the vodka on the ground and threw the glass on the floor with all his might. The others did exactly the same thing. The place fell dead silent, and everyone looked at us.

"Is there a problem?" Nazar asked the bartender.

"Glory to Ukraine!" the bartender replied.

"Glory to the heroes!" the soldiers said, and everyone in the pub echoed their shout.

New glasses were brought to the table. Nazar filled them.

"And now a toast to the living", he said, and he knocked it back in one gulp.

We drank quickly, and a lot.

"And now", Nazar said after the second vodka, "we go to see the patriotic whores."

I had heard that since the offensive had started, the whorehouses in the city center had been offering a twenty percent discount to anyone who had been fighting on the front lines. As there was an eleven o'clock curfew, my guess was that the desire to keep the places running had also been a factor in the decision to offer a discount, as well as the desire to make a show of devotion to the national cause, of course. But the adjective "patriotic" had stuck.

I was dizzy from alcohol and fatigue. I didn't want to go, but I couldn't get out of it. The whorehouse was in a four-story building. We went on foot. Nazar rang the bell, and the door swung open.

The women were on the fourth floor. Two old, moderately spacious apartments that had been turned into one. There was a big Ukrainian flag on the wall in the hallway. A woman who must have been about fifty and whose cheeks were caked with rouge walked over to us and sat us down on the sofa.

She and Nazar started haggling in Ukrainian. It took me a while to realize that they were arguing about me. I was not a soldier, she was saying, and so I did not get any discount. I cast a glance at Petyus, hoping he could get me out of the whole thing, but he was just staring at the wall. Eventually, Nazar must have reached some kind of agreement with the woman, because she walked over to the counter, picked up a bell, and gave it a shake.

The three doors off the hallway swung open, and soon six women were standing in front of us with business smiles on their faces. They were dressed in bras and panties.

"Take your pick", the woman said, and even I understood.

I also understood the silence that fell over us. When it comes to committing a sinful act, no one wants to go first. Several seconds of silence passed, several unbearably awkward seconds.

And then Petyus stood up. He had a bleary look in his eyes. He walked over to one of the brunettes, a girl who must have been in her twenties.

"Let's go, sweetheart", he said. She took his hand and led him into the room. The other two soldiers immediately followed suit. I stared in shock.

"What?" Nazar asked, lighting a cigarette. "You look like you have seen a ghost."

"No", I replied, "I'm just a little surprised. Petyus was always talking about his wife. I never would have thought he'd sleep with another woman."

Nazar took a drag on his cigarette, grimaced a little, stubbed it out in the ashtray, and stood up.

"Petya's apartment in Kharkiv was hit by a rocket the day after the invasion started", he said. "His family was killed."

He then walked over to one of the girls, took her hand, and withdrew with her into one of the rooms.

DAYS IN THE WILD

The sky above, blackout below.

The jeep cut across the field. The wheat was tall. It crunched under the wheels of the car. Scents of hay blew in through the rolled-down windows, washing the smell of burning houses and fuel from our noses. I stared at the seemingly endless yellow field. The sun was setting. Twilight would be upon us in an hour, and then darkness. Somewhere in the distance, mortars thundered with a deep rumble. The Russians had started shelling the village.

The sergeant must have taken it as a sign to break the silence.

"We did what we had to do. You know that, right?"

"Yeah."

"Those animals shot the men dead and raped all the women in the village."

"I know. I saw the mass grave."

"They're not people. They're animals."

"Yeah. I would have done the same thing."

And I meant what I said. I had not a drop of sympathy for the Russians who had been shot, and it didn't bother me in the slightest that I didn't care.

What the Russians had done to the Ukrainians since the launch of the offensive had drastically chipped away at my enthusiasm for the Geneva Convention. I began by taking pictures of the mass graves, as I had done in all the towns and villages that had been liberated. Didn't take much digging. The soil that had been thrown on the piles of bodies was more a marker than anything else.

The bodies of the men were clothed, with their hands tied behind their backs and their faces to the ground. The female corpses were naked, little girls, old women, and everything in between. The sergeant had not been speaking figuratively. It was what the Russians did, everywhere.

The twelve soldiers who had survived the Ukrainian attack had gotten off light. Certainly nothing even resembling torture.

They had killed almost all of them with the first shot. Only one had had to be shot in the back of his head, lying on the ground.

The Ukrainians were remarkably disciplined. They didn't desecrate the bodies, didn't spit on them, didn't strip them naked. They just carried them into one of the houses that was still standing in the village after the shelling.

Except for one blond kid in his twenties, who had written "Buryats for sale" in chalk on the wooden door of the house.

Russia, as always over the course of its history, was sending its minorities to war. Starving wretches from the edges of the empire, Buryats, Chechens, Dagestanis. The men who had been taken prisoner had been Buryats.

The kid's joke had met with general amusement among the soldiers until the commander had seen it. He was in his fifties, graying, and had lips as thin as blades. He smacked the private so hard that his nose bled. I watched him make the kid erase the whimsical little sign.

When the private had finished, the commander came up to me and began to explain in terrible English, as if he owed me an explanation.

He was talking to my blue Kevlar helmet, i.e. the international press.

Without help from the West, the Ukrainians would have lost the war, but thanks to the influx of arms, they had not only stopped the Russian invasion, they had even managed to launch a successful counterattack.

So successful that the enemy had left everything behind and fled the eastern front. The Western shoulder-launched surface-to-surface and surface-to-air missiles became so popular that people were naming their kids after them, and sometimes you could see them in the hands of the saints on icons.

As a Western journalist, I was treated like an uncle from abroad whose family lived off the money he sent. And it mattered what I thought about the resistance the Ukrainians had put up.

I didn't understand much of what the commander said. All I could manage to decipher was that he had ordered the execution of the prisoners of war because the Russians were expected to counterattack in a matter of minutes, and he simply didn't have enough men to secure the village and guard the prisoners. This was also perfectly clear from the fact that he gave orders to the sergeant in Ukrainian, who then turned to me and said, "we must go".

The outlines of acacia trees shimmered in the distance. We were close to the Ukrainian base. They were moving house to house every other day because of Russian missile attacks. I knew nothing about where I was going to sleep, but I was hardly counting on anything luxurious. I'd been sleeping on various bunks next to NLAW missiles for a week, using latrines built out of empty ammunition crates, like everyone else in the detachment.

And the sergeant clearly felt he had to explain himself. He spoke with tears in his eyes.

"We're defending our country, you know. We are not animals. Everyone in the detachment's a teacher or an engineer or a doctor or a farmer."

"I know, Petya", I said. He was bald, hefty, with a 1970s porn moustache. Came from somewhere near Ternopil. He had been assigned to me when I arrived in Donbass because he spoke English.

"These beasts are just in it for the kill. We do it so we can go home at last and get on with our lives."

"What did you do before the war?"

"I had a little stand where I sold fried fish."

"You going back to it when the war's over?"

"I don't know. I guess so, if I ever get back home."

"The Russians are fleeing."

"Yeah. But the war's not over yet. As long as the invaders still have one scrap of our land in their hands."

We fell silent. We were both thinking the same thing, but neither of us said it. That officially, Russia was not yet at war with Ukraine. The collapse of the front did not mean that peace was any closer. The Ukrainians had only won a month or two while the Russians conscripted another quarter million soldiers. Everyone knew they were coming. The war had been going on for eight years now.

We got out of the fields and drove down a white dirt road in the evening light. There were acacia trees on either side of the road with Ukrainian T-64 tanks behind them. Their crews were sitting on the turrets, smoking, waiting for orders over the radio, and waving as we passed by.

"So you're not angry that you couldn't take pictures?"

"No. I know why you took the camera, and besides, you gave it back."

"I was following orders."

"Petya, stop explaining. The Russians got what they deserved. Why did they come here in the first place?"

"You're a good man. I'm glad you understand."

As I watched the shadows of the trees dancing on the dirt road, I thought of the psychologist from Budapest. She was a slender, short-haired woman, a blonde I had met before I had left for the front. We had had a little fling which had ruled out a doctor-patient relationship, but we had become very fond of each other. We got together for a drink fairly often when I happened to be home.

She was the only person I would put up with that gibberish from, the psychoanalysis talk that I guess you run into with every shrink. What would she say, I wondered, if I were to tell her that I had felt nothing when the Russians had been executed in front of me. I imagined her eyes widening and the pace of her breathing shifting nervously as she tried to appear calm. I remembered the expression she had had on her face two weeks earlier, holding a glass of wine in one hand and earnestly explaining.

"What exactly are you trying to prove?" she had asked.

"Nothing."

"How long do you think you'll survive with your skin intact?"

"I've always managed to pull through so far."

"I meant how long do you think you'll stay the same man?"

"I've been doing this for eleven years."

"That's quite a big ego you've got."

"Yeah, not just my ego."

She smiled for a moment but then her face grew stern again.

"If you dance with the devil people will mistake you for the devil."

"That's a cliché."

"Doesn't mean it's not true. No one comes home from a war. The people who come home aren't the people who went."

"That's clever. What film did you get that from?"

"I don't know. But you didn't answer the question. Why are you leaving again."

"For the money."

I had no intention of lecturing Marti about how I'd rather be in the middle of a patriotic war surrounded by heavy shelling than feeling sorry for myself on the terrace of some bar with craft beers, sipping a sparkling rosé with hints of almond and wondering whether I was a boy or a girl.

I'd rather be where history was being made than yammering on about stirring depictions of violence from behind a lectern at some smalltown college while life ticked away beside me.

In Ukraine, a new nation was being born, with new myths. The Ukrainians were standing up to an empire, and the empire had begun to crack.

They were all fucking heroes, heroes from the novels of yesteryear. My place was there, with them. Especially since I'd been writing about their struggle for freedom since the revolution had broken out in 2014.

There was a checkpoint at the end of the dirt road. Concrete blocks narrowed the road leading to the village. Nearby, pits charred black indicated that the Russians were constantly shelling the Ukrainian checkpoints. At the side of the road, you could see the entrance to the trench where the soldiers lived. One of the soldiers came out at the sound of the car, but Petya didn't slow down. He just shouted out the password that was sent twice a day by the Ukrainian Ministry of Defense. The soldier gave a wave, telling us to move on.

We drove through a ghost village. The doorways of the mud-brick and wooden houses yawned in the darkness. Everywhere the sweet smell of fruit rotting in the grass. Everywhere silence, stern and grave. Nothing but the buzzing of hungry wasps and the screech of the wheels of the jeep.

The Ukrainian forces had set up headquarters in a primary school. It was a two-story building, white, modern, with a large playground surrounded by a fence. The only signs that there had been fighting around the building were the bullet holes in the walls and a few boarded-up windows here and there. In the middle of the playground there were troop transports with caterpillar-treads, the little jungle gyms and monkey bars crushed and contorted underneath them.

The whole base was bustling with life.

Behind the school, four men were frying meat by the outhouses, and some soldiers were sitting on benches under the trees and smoking. Fifteen Russian soldiers were kneeling in the middle of the square, their hands clasped behind their heads. Three Ukrainians with rifles were standing over them.

Petya parked the car, and we grabbed my backpacks and headed inside. I stopped in my tracks when I got to the prisoners. Four women were kneeling next to the fifteen Russian soldiers. Two were dressed in camouflage and were in their mid-twenties. The other two were in their fifties. They were wearing skirts and cloth jackets.

"Who are they?" I asked.

Mercenaries and collaborators", Petya replied. "Go get something to eat. I'll find out where they're putting you up."

I put my bags on a bench and went into the school. I followed the soldiers with plastic bowls in their hands. There was no gas in the school kitchen, but that was where they served the meals. Potatoes and chicken today. And three slices of bread. It was always the same, potatoes with chicken or potatoes with eggs.

I went back to my bags, sat down on the bench, and started eating. I saw the female prisoners being lined up and led into one of the two-story outbuildings, which I suppose must have been the groundskeeper's house. They marched right past me. One of the female soldiers had shoulder-length hair. A natural redhead.

By the time I had finished eating, Petya had come back. They had found a spot for me on the second floor in the school, a large room with ten soldiers. I took out my sleeping bag, unrolled it, uploaded my pictures to the cloud, and fell asleep.

I slept for two hours. I looked at the clock when I woke up. Not yet midnight. The room was thick with the smell of men. I put on my boots, taking care not to wake anyone, and went out into the yard.

I sat down on a bench and lit a cigarette, when suddenly I heard screaming. I set off in the direction of the sound. It was coming from the groundskeeper's house. Soldiers were laughing and smoking cigarettes outside. The lights were on upstairs. The men were coming in and out of the door. The screaming was getting louder and louder, but it didn't bother anyone.

When they saw me coming, they started shouting, and Petya came out from behind the little building and started walking towards me. He was drunk. He was trying hard to cover it up, but he was oozing with the stench of hard liquor.

"What's going on here?"

"They are interrogating the prisoners. It's top secret. Please return to your quarters. We are leaving at four in the morning."

"But..."

"Go."

I turned around and started back. I could feel Petya's stare on my back. I stopped in front of the school, sat down on a bench, and lit a cigarette. I waited for the screaming to stop, but it didn't. It was getting cold. I'd have to buy a decent coat. I looked up. Stars glittering in the sky above, blackout below. It occurred to me that I was 1,700 kilometers from Budapest, and the journey home wasn't going to be an easy one.

Translated, from the Hungarian, by Thomas Cooper.

Sandor Jászberényi is a Hungarian journalist and writer. He is the author of The Devil Is a Black Dog: Stories from the Middle East and Beyond *(New Europe Books, 2014) and* The Most Beautiful Night of the Soul: More Stories from the Middle East. *In 2017 he received Hungary's Libri Literary Prize. As a correspondent for Hungarian news sites, he has covered the conflict with Islamic State, the war in Ukraine, the revolutions in Egypt and Libya, and the Gaza War. His writing has appeared in the* Wall Street Journal, The New York Times Magazine, AGNI, *and* The Brooklyn Rail. *He divides his time between Budapest and Cairo.*

POEM

——

Ostap Slyvynsky

LOVE

1

A prickling feeling,
like when you touch a warm cup
with a very cold hand,

or when a body, stiff from sleep,
crosses the room,
                    still a little wobbly
yet smiling.

A kind of prickling,
like when your father,
whom, for some reason, they had not shaved for a few days,
lay,
        as
a salty overheated stone lies,
and hugged us one by one.

A kind of prickling,
like when you carry a Christmas tree
through the air tightened with frost,
knowing that
               among all the people
lulled to sleep by the Most Sacred of Messages
one is awake and waiting.

2

Love
does not promise, does not acquit,
does not convince, does not serve as evidence,
does not prevent war.
Let it go.
Let it go to civilians,
let it go to old people and children.
Let it go to animals.
Or it might burst into tears in a bomb shelter.
Or it might betray our passport names.
We will call it back once we've set up
our mic.
Once our radio station starts running again.
Until then,
we need seasoned professionals,
men and women.
That's all.

Translated, from the Ukrainian, by Iryna Shuvalova.

Ostap Slyvynsky (born 1978) is a poet, translator, and literary scholar from Lviv, where he teaches Polish Literature and Literary Theory at the Ivan Franko University. He has published six volumes of poetry, as well as over a dozen translations from Polish, English, Bulgarian, and Russian, including work by Czesław Miłosz, Olga Tokarczuk, Derek Walcott, William Carlos Williams, James Tate and Georgi Gospodinov. He has been awarded, among other prizes, the LitAccent Award, the Anonych Literary Prize, the Hubert Burda Prize for Young Poets from Eastern Europe, the Medal for Merit to Polish Culture, and the Kovaliv Fund Prize. He coordinated the International Literary Festival at the Publishers Forum in Lviv in 2006-2007; and in 2016, he helped organize a series of readings entitled "Literature Against Aggression" during the Forum. In 2019, he was awarded the EU Prize for Literature (Ukraine), an annual initiative recognizing the best emerging fiction writers in Europe.

TWO POEMS

—

Yuliya Musakovska

YOUR ENEMY'S DAUGHTER

And there, you meet your enemy face to face,
in the olive garden,
   on the sand whiter than the bones of your dead.
What will you say to him?
   A walnut tree with a crack grows by the gate,
spurring new branches like bayonets that will grind him.
Your enemy's daughter is dancing under the vine's tender arch.
The birds have returned to rebuild their ravaged nests.
The neighbor, the machine gunner, is back, unhurt,
although he flinches from thunder
   and screams at night like a seagull.
When you catch a glimpse of your enemy in the crowd,
without any doubt,
   you wish you could hit the target
but words or bullets cannot take one by surprise.
Crawling on the blue railings are the smells
   of elderberry and fried eggs,
among them another sharp scent: hate.
The red heat is spreading its tenacious crab claws,
groping the golden crosses, the rust on them is centuries-old.
Your enemy's daughter is throwing her foot to the side,
   childlike, awkward.
She is dancing, with her eyes like berries
from which wine is squeezed during harvest time.

THE LILY OF DARKNESS

In place of a mouth the executioner has a lily,
white, suffocating, and endless.

He turns around and I see the darkness
of his throat.

A rollercoaster ride on which
I choke on vomit.

I held this lily by the stem,
the executioner by the throat.
I dug the earth up with my bare hands,
to pull up all the roots,
the snake's lair.

But it slithered out between my fingers.
It always
slithers away at the last second,
the darkest
before dawn,

so that tomorrow it can
uncurl again
beneath the cradle.

Translated, from the Ukrainian, by Olena Jennings and the author.

Yuliya Musakovska is an award-winning Ukrainian poet and translator. She was born in 1982 in Lviv, where she lives and works. She has published five poetry collections in Ukrainian, among them Hunting for Silence *(2014) and* Men, Women, and Children *(2015). The most recent,* The God of Freedom *(2021), is forthcoming in English translation in 2024 with Arrowsmith Press. Yuliya's work has been translated into over thirty languages and widely published around the globe. Her poems have appeared in* The Southern Review, AGNI, Tupelo Quarterly, NELLE, The Common, *amongst other journals and anthologies.*

Olena Jennings is the author of the poetry collection The Age of Secrets *(Lost Horse Press, 2022) and the chapbook* Memory Project. *Her novel* Temporary Shelter *was published in 2021 by Cervena Barva Press. She is the translator (together with Oksana Lutsyshyna) of Kateryna Kalytko's* Nobody Knows Us Here And We Don't Know Anyone *(Lost Horse Press, 2022), as well as of Vasyl Makhno's* Paper Bridge *(Plamen Press, 2022). She was shortlisted for the Ukrainian Literature in Translation Prize 2023 for her translations of Yuliya Musakovska's poetry. She lives in Queens, NYC, and is the founder and curator of the* Poets of Queens *reading series and press.*

CRIME WITHOUT PUNISHMENT, PUNISHMENT WITHOUT CRIME

———

Tetyana Ogarkova & Volodymyr Yermolenko

Because they can.

"It's not a war crime if you had fun while doing it."

This message was inscribed by Russian soldiers on a wall in one of many ruined villages in Kharkiv region, eastern Ukraine. Our friends posted a photograph of it online, after a trip made to the liberated region. The village in question is Velyka Komyshuvakha, not far from the town of Barvinkove. Komyshuvakha was mercilessly bombed by the Russians during their offensive campaign of spring 2022. After that, the village was occupied for half a year before being liberated in September 2022.

Next to the above message was another inscription:

"If someone asks about Ukraine, there are two answers —

1. This never happened

2. They deserved it."

And the last one, which drew our especial attention:

"I'm gonna set fire to other people's villages with a smile on my face."

There are many things one could say about why in twenty-first-century Russia, the largest country on the planet by landmass with vast natural resources and limitless unpopulated territories, chose an armed takeover of the lands of its neighbouring country. Russia chose war over peace, degeneration over development, mass destruction over the mutually beneficial cooperation enjoyed by countries of the West.

At the same time, these cynical messages left by an unnamed Russian occupying soldier in the village of Velyka Komyshuvakha, population of circa 800, bear witness to something very important and extending to great depth within Russian aggression against Ukraine. They hint that this is not a war for territory, or even a war for resources: the deeper motives behind this war contradict Russian propaganda, which justifies its attack on Ukraine as revenge for the non-existent "genocide" committed by Ukraine in Donbas, or as a war on "nazis", or waged out of concern for NATO's eastward expansion.

Those who talk of the primacy of their own pleasure over adherence to law – "it's not a war crime if you had fun" – or who blur the bounds of reality – "this never happened, but they deserved it anyway" – wish to say something quite apart from the above claims.

"Am I a trembling creature, or do I have the right?"

In Russian culture there are two literary works that succinctly represent the broken link between crime and punishment, which is the deeper motive behind this insane war.

In the first, Dostoevsky in his world-famous novel *Crime and Punishment* presents us with "crime without punishment". Let us remind you why the protagonist Raskolnikov murders the elderly pawnbroker and her sister Liz-aveta. The pragmatic motive has merely a fraction to do with it: Raskolnikov's enjoyment of transgression and the right to decide outweighed the egotistical motive of improving his financial condition and the chance to rid the rest of the world of this old pawnbroker, who, according to the protagonist, was an amoral being.

People, as Dostoevsky's character theorised, are divided into two cate-gories: firstly, those who are no good for anything; and the elect, those who have the right to everything, even to crime. This right is without set limits. Their right does not end where the rights of others begin – but no matter, for the latter *deserve as such*.

Raskolnikov attempted to test his capabilities of belonging to the second category, the elect who have the right to take voluntaristic decisions such as about who should live and who should die. Having committed his crime, Raskolnikov becomes convinced that he, in fact, does not belong to the elect after all. Fear, emotional disturbance, and emptiness ensue. Eventually, it is not conscience or remorse that leads him to confess to his crime, but his own weakness. His journey as he gradually approaches his decision to confess to the murder resembles the flight of a moth, fluttering around a candle before finally throwing itself into the flame. The French thinker Gaston Bachelard called this fascination with fire as a "magnifying reverie" that can propel the "reverer" into change (or death), the "Empedocles complex", named after the Ancient Greek philosopher who committed suicide by jumping into a volcano. Raskolnikov imagined himself as Napoleon, but he was merely a moth flitting around the candle in reverie, when he decided to burn himself and confess – not the Ubermensch he professed to be.

The punishment imposed by the court is miraculously lenient: eight years of hard labour for the murder of two people. Yet while undertaking hard labour in exile Raskolnikov was still bereft of internal acknowledgment and processing of his crime – as well as his punishment. He reproaches himself for a "near miss", for "erring", not for committing a crime. It is only in the final lines of the novel's epilogue, as Sonya Marmeladova sits next to Raskolnikov with a Bible in her hands, where Dostoevsky hints that before his protagonist lies the path of renewal, rebirth, transition from one world to another, and so on. However, we are not told this story.

Even if this is precisely the story that we would like to hear.

Therefore, a philosophical question of the nineteenth century – whether the law and institutions could enable the reformation of a criminal – received a negative answer from Dostoevsky. He makes it clear that it is Christian faith that can give Raskolnikov hope and rebirth: religion, not rights. Mysticism, not state institutions. Metaphysics, but not respect for the law.

Nonetheless, Russian nihilism still undermines the religious foundations for morals. "If there is no God, everything is permitted", says another one of Dostoevsky's characters, Ivan Karamazov.

The nameless Russian occupier who wrote "It's not considered a war crime if you had fun doing it" on the wall in Komyshuvakha was guided by this logic of denial of rights and by the belief in the bankruptcy of social norms, i.e. their inability to regulate life within a society.

Putin, who does not recognise Ukraine's existence and calls it an "artificial state" (a statement he made on the 32nd anniversary of Ukraine's independence), sends tanks, destroys Ukrainian towns and villages for the sake of ghostly "possession" of them, and has entered four Ukrainian oblasts – Luhansk, Donetsk, Zaporizhzhia, and Kherson – that are partly Russian-occupied, as well as all of Crimea, into the Russian Federation's Constitution as "Russian". His fight is not with Ukraine. He sows doubt in international law and rights. He asserts the right of Russia to have a centre and to have no borders.

In this, Putin seems to forget that the Russian Federation itself recognised Ukraine's independence more than thirty years ago and did so within its internationally recognised borders.

Russians fail to recognise the law and international rights not because they poorly understand them. They do this because they cultivate superiority above others. It is also because they consider law to be for the weak – as demonstrated by Russian political nihilism in the literature of the nineteenth century.

Yuliia Payevska, a legendary Ukrainian paramedic who is better known by her callsign "Taira", was taken prisoner by Russian troops in Mariupol in March 2022. In lieu of this she became a witness to torture, abuse, and inhumane treatment of Ukrainian POWs, and after being freed in autumn 2022 she had much to tell. One of her most powerful testimonies is the following. One time a Russian soldier asked her: "Do you know why we are doing this to you?".

"Because you can", Taira merely replied. The pragmatic reasoning for the "why" was not relevant.

Perhaps there is no more fitting answer than this to the endless whys that arise when we observe the mindless violence committed by Russia. They do it just because they can; because they know they will not meet a level response. The concept of impunity is key to understanding the Russian Federation's aggression against Ukraine.

The cognisance of such impunity, i.e. the acknowledgment of the absence of punishment, is what pushed Putin towards a full-scale war: Russia has a population four times the number of Ukraine's, has a significantly stronger military potential with weapons manufactured after the Soviet era, and a nuclear arsenal. Valerii Zaluzhnyi, the commander-in-chief of the Armed Forces of Ukraine until February 2024, justly stated in one of his articles that the key to understanding Russia's actions is precisely this asymmetry between its and Ukraine's capabilities, and consequently its conscious acknowledgment of its own impunity. To illustrate: in 2022 Russia launched missiles from a range of over two thousand kilometres, hitting targets close to Ukraine's western border. Conversely, the Ukrainian army spent months demanding its foreign partner nations for platforms with capabilities to strike enemy targets at ranges of one hundred kilometres.

By 2024 Ukrainian drones are flying deep into the Russian interior, but the bulk of Ukraine's partners are still handing out military assistance in doses, fearing the reaction of the Russian Federation as a nuclear state. Russia has concluded that if its opponent is weaker, and other parties still fear its trump card – nuclear weapons – then it can keep endlessly committing crimes without punishment.

Thus a nuclear state with an ever-growing totalitarian regime is strengthening its alliances with similar states to itself – Iran, North Korea, in part, China – and is continuing to attack. Because it can.

This aggression devastates human lives, wipes cities and villages off the face of the earth, and lays waste to an economy. The lands that Russia has managed to grab – making up almost twenty percent of Ukraine's territories – are no longer resources. They are ruins.

Moreover, this aggression hurts Russia itself. It has already lost hundreds of thousands of soldiers in this war, disposed of the majority of its armament reserve inherited from the USSR, and weakened its own economy due to Western sanctions. Such aggression is self-destructive. The reasons behind this aggression do not occur within the realms of rationality. Yet Russia stubbornly continues to fight. What is it trying to prove? And to whom?

Together with this "crime without punishment" is found the idea of "punishment without the crime". The second work that represents the broken link between the above is a twentieth-century counterpart to Dostoevsky's *Crime and Punishment*: the novella *The Old Woman* by Daniil Kharms. Kharms, whose real surname was Yuvachev, lived between 1905 and 1942 and belonged to the generation of avant-gardists who were mercilessly squeezed out by the Soviet totalitarian system of the 1930s. An author of avant-garde poetry and *Zaum* "transrational" verse, Kharms was accused of "anti-revolutionary activity" in the 1930s, was exiled to Kursk, and banned from publishing his work. He would later die in 1942 from starvation in a psychiatric hospital. According to later accounts, he was in fact shot. His body of work became famous first in *samizdat* abroad, and only after perestroika would it return to the Soviet Union.

In his novella *The Old Woman*, Kharms' narrator finds himself in a "Raskolnikov situation", with the difference that he does not murder anyone. The old woman enters his flat of her own volition, then suddenly dies. The narrator's fate is subsequently involved with the attempt to rid himself of the body. He behaves like a guilty man and attempts to hide the body as if he really had murdered the woman. He eventually stuffs the body into a suitcase and takes it on the train out of the city. The suitcase disappears from the train under mysterious circumstances. The protagonist exits the train, then enters a forest and prays.

The story of the protagonist's adventures in *The Old Woman* is a succinct metaphor for one's state under totalitarianism, which causes one to experience "punishment for no crime". In a totalitarian society, everyone behaves as though they are guilty or could become so at any moment; as though they have a corpse lying at home and your mission is to hide the crime they did not commit. Everything and everyone would testify against them, for there is no hope in trusting in the rule of law and fairness.

Kharms' work subtly documented the condition of Soviet totalitarian society of the 1930s. A person in such a society was a subhuman, a cog in the system, who forever owed something to someone. In a liberal society, everyone has a skeleton in the closet – but in a totalitarian society, everyone has a corpse at home.

Excessive punishment in Russia was historically known. Mykhailo Drahomanov, the leading Ukrainian political thinker, mentioned in his text titled "An Introduction to the Hromada" ("hromada" being a specific type of Ukrainian civil community at the time) the following note: "What in Galicia is punishable by three months in prison, in Russia was punished by 6-12 years of hard labour." Evidently, the current sentences given in the Russian Federation for peaceful protests have a long history behind them.

In Russian culture, one can either hope to be a superhuman and commit crimes without punishment, or be a subhuman and accept restriction and punishment for no fault whatsoever. Such learned helplessness is therein consolidated in conscious acknowledgment of the self as "the small man", and in the responses, "But what can we do?", and, "We are beyond politics". In such a context, the most difficult thing to do is to stay human; that is, to understand one's boundaries, respect the boundaries of others, to continue to act, and not to refuse to take part in the struggle.

Russian totalitarianism is the other side of the coin to Russian nihilism. In Putin's Empire, they become inseparable. This is an empire that can continue to exist only on account of export of violence outwards, and the mirrored increase of violence inwards, onto its own citizens.

Soviet totalitarianism killed tens of millions of people on one-sixth of the Earth's landmass, but it was never tried for its crimes nor did it receive any punishment whatsoever. The absence of a public process for condemning the Communist regime has led to the fact that no-one has taken full account of what happened; no one has apologised, and nothing has been corrected. This is highlighted by the fact that since the early 2010s in Russia, sympathies with Stalin have sharply grown. Now, in 2024 there is a trend for men's suits that are similar to those once worn by the Soviet leader.

The defeat of the Soviet Union in the Cold War and the chaos of the 1990s did not pose for Russia a chance to choose another future. Instead during these times Moscow mirrored Raskolnikov in exile in the hard labour camps, mentally reprimanding itself for its "errors", but without Sonya Marmeladova with her Bible to provide hope of new life.

Those who consider their crime an "error", or just a mistake, are doomed to return sooner or later to the idea of payback for their punishment. Russia's current war against Ukraine and the West is a reprisal for its defeat in the Cold War.

Russia furthermore systematically blurs the boundaries between victim and executioner. It parasitises on the boundaries of the ethical. As such, the terrorist attack on Moscow's Crocus City, as a result of which around 150 Russian citizens were killed, and for which the Islamic State claimed responsibility – became a pretext for Russia's attempt to extricate itself from international isolation and reassume the role of victim. It claimed that Russians were just as much victims of international terrorism as Americans and French people, and that countries should cooperate to fight together against a common threat.

When Russia as the aggressive party was cornered, it did not accept defeat and draw new conclusions, but overturned the chessboard and proposed a new game to play, in which its role as aggressor unexpectedly turns into the role of victim: the victim of imaginary threat from the expansion of NATO, American hegemony, capitalism, Ukrainian "Nazism", "oppression of Russian speakers" – you name it. The aggressor's defeat transforms it into a victim that does not address a need to understand the causes of transgression, punish the guilty, pay reparations for losses, restore justice, or renew world balance. Russia perceives any punishment, even if fair, as a humiliation, and thereafter demands retribution. Its vengeance is usually not long in coming.

The disconnect between crime and punishment that leads to the conditions of unpunished crime and punishment in return for no crime, undermines our belief in the foundations of our world order. Cynicism, nihilism, voluntarism, pseudo-realpolitik – for as long as we allow immersion into extremes, unpunished evil can expand its boundaries. It is naïve to believe that this evil can stop itself, by itself.

Recently a journalist on a children's television channel in Canada decided to make a programme about Russia's war in Ukraine. She gathered questions from children aged 8 to 12 years old, selected the most interesting ones, and put them back to the children for answers. One of the questions was the following:

"Why did Russia, which is the largest country in the world by size and natural resources, invade and take over the territories of its neighbouring country?"

It is doubtful that Canadian schoolchildren have an in-depth knowledge of the works of Dostoevsky and Kharms. Yet their answer ran along similar lines – if sounding more simple, childlike:

"Because it can."

Translated, from the Ukrainian, by Daisy Gibbons.

Tetyana Ogarkova (born 1979) is a Ukrainian literary scholar, journalist and essayist. She runs the International Department of the Ukraine Crisis Media Center; is co-founder of Kult: Podcast *(in Ukrainian); and is anchor at* L'Ukraine, face à la guerre *(podcast in French). She is also Senior Lecturer in the Department of Literature at the Kyiv-Mohyla Academy, a member of PEN Ukraine, and Docteur ès lettres (University of Paris-XII Val-de-Marne). Amongst others, her essays include ones on the history of French literature, the history of avant-garde, and the theory of literature.*

Born in Kiev in 1980 into a family of philosophers, Volodymyr Yermolenko is a philosopher, essayist, journalist, editor and writer, as well as President of PEN Ukraine. He took PhDs in both Political Studies (France) and Philosophy (Ukraine), and is now Associate Professor at Kyiv-Mohyla Academy. He is also Analytics Director at Internews Ukraine *(one of the biggest and oldest Ukrainian media NGOs), as well as Editor-in-Chief of* Ukraine World. org *(a multimedia project in English about Ukraine). He is the author of four books, most recently* Fluid Ideologies, *winner of the Yurii Sheveliov Prize (2018), the Ukrainian Book of the Year Prize (2018) and the Petro Mohyla Prize (2021). He is also the Chair of the Board of International Renaissance Foundation; and co-founder and author of podcasts for* Kult:Podcast *(in Ukrainian) and* Explaining Ukraine *(in English). He has written numerous articles for Ukrainian and major international media, and been interviewed by the BBC, CNN, Al Jazeera, France 24, amongst other channels. His texts and interviews have been published in Ukrainian, English, French, German, Polish, Italian, Russian, Dutch, Norwegian, Czech, Greek and Chinese.*

Daisy Gibbons is a prize-winning literary translator from Ukrainian into English. A graduate of Cambridge University's Slavonic Department, she lived in Ukraine for several periods after 2016, when she took up translation and interpreting. Her book translations have been (or are to be) published with Simon & Schuster, Seven Stories Press, Deep Vellum, and ibidem-Verlag; her translation extracts or short pieces have been published by The Guardian, Harper's Magazine, Vanity Fair, *amongst others. She spends much of her time in the UK but is frequently spotted in Ukraine.*

THREE POEMS

Michael Longley

Stumble-stones.

THE FOLLOWING DAY

I met him in The Crown
By chance the following day,
The cameraman whose film
Had shown around the world
Our blood-drenched tarmacadam,
And when I asked him how
In nightmare's aftermath
He could compose himself,
"I take out my light-meter
And I focus the lens",
He said the following day.

BEQUESTS

I
I have on my desk my dad's
Blackthorn swagger-stick and
Nineteen-seventeen compass,
So that when I write a poem
I draw panoramas
As Edward Thomas did,
A map-reading instructor
Before the bloody battle,
Squinting through a prism
To read rainbow numbers
For a sense of direction —
And I keep within reach

My dad's brass-capped, oxter-
Polished authority-wand.

II
Were they meant for you, clever wife,
Your mathematical father's
Rosary and Polyphase slide-rule
Put to use when he and Schrödinger,
Jewish refugee from the Nazis,
Genius, Nobel laureate,
Wrote *Boolean Algebra and
Probability Theory*
Published in nineteen-forty
In Dublin (Price One Shilling) –
Calculus at his fingertips,
Logarithms, exponentials
As well as the shiny rosary's
Simple arithmetic?

EVICTIONS

I
Brass squares among the cobblestones record
Who were evicted from their homes and shops
And where they were taken away to die.
I bow before the dead to read their names
And I stumble over these "stumble-stones".
It will take me a lifetime to walk home.

II
At dawn a German couple is waiting
In the shadowy hallway while you pack
A few belongings for the rest of your lives,
Your bed still warm for them where you made love.

III
Outside the block of flats in Plavecka
In Prague a new stumble-stone remembers
HELENA HERRMANNOVA / NÉE KATZ
BORN 1916 / DEPORTED 1942 TO TEREZÍN
1944 TO AUSCHWITZ / LIBERATED
There's a second stone for her husband Pavel
MURDERED 1945 / ON A DEATH MARCH
And a third stone for her mother Elsa
DEPORTED TO LUBLIN 1942 / MURDERED
Helena Herrmannova married Harry
An old flame and lived the rest of her life
Just around the corner in south Belfast
As Helen Lewis, choreographer,
Teacher of dancing who had danced in Hell.

Michael Longley was born in Belfast in 1939 and educated at the Royal Belfast Academical Institution and Trinity College, Dublin, where he read Classics. He has published twelve collections of poetry, most recently Angel Hill *(2017),* The Candlelight Master *(2020), and* The Slain Birds *(2022), all from Cape. In 2001 he received the Queen's Gold Medal for Poetry, and in 2010 was awarded a CBE. In 2022, he was the recipient of the Feltrinelli International Prize for Poetry for "the extraordinary relevance of his themes and their cultural implications", one of the major European honours for poetry, awarded every five years by the Italian Accademia dei Lincei. He was Ireland Professor of Poetry from 2007-2010, and continues to live in Belfast.*

INTERVIEW WITH JURKO PROCHASKO

A CONVERSATION ABOUT EVIL

———

Jurko Prochasko and Marci Shore

On the algebra of true evil.

Marci: I'm teaching a seminar now on this war and the problem of evil. It seems to me that we need to return to an idea of evil without scare quotes.

Jurko: Yes, absolutely. And when I say "absolutely", I mean, too, that there is such a thing as that which is absolutely evil. This is not just a question of our doing bad things, because we can do bad things unintentionally. Something I regard as good can always be bad for someone else. Moreover, every human act contains a dialectic of good and evil. And so I want to detach the concept of evil from the concept of violence. There is violence that is unavoidable. For example, in order to turn earth into a field, we have to plow it, right? And in plowing a field, we're killing an improbable number of life forms, forms whose existence we don't even suspect. This, too, is violence. In literally every aspect of our existence, we cannot act without causing violence. When we ride in a car, we're releasing carbon dioxide, poisoning the atmosphere, and constricting someone's life. And yet isn't driving a car an expression of human vitality? Vitality is Eros, creativity, vigor. And every expression of vitality contains violence as its other side. This cannot be wholly avoided – and this unavoidable violence is not evil. For me, true evil – what in German is called *das Böse* – is bound up with deriving pleasure from carrying out evil.

Marci: So sadism ...

Jurko: Yes – intentionally enacting violence and deriving pleasure from it.

Marci: What is the source of the pleasure?

Jurko: Freud believes that it's the *Verflechtung*, the intertwining of Eros and Thanatos. He believes that sadism is a derivative of what he calls the *Bemächtigungstrieb*, the drive – *Trieb* – to rule over something or someone. For Freud every sexual act that brings pleasure, every instance of *Lust*, inherently contains elements of *Bemächtigung*. In psychoanalysis the question of sadism is very complicated, all the more so as Freud's own view underwent a large evolution. In his later reflections, he perceived in sadism *Triebentflechtung*, a decoupling of drives, when sadism disentangles itself from Eros and becomes self-activating.

Another way of looking at sadism is through the theory of narcissism. Among the very harmful aspects of narcissism is the desire to bring about ruin. When I see that I'm not the only one who is great, I want to destroy the other. There is a concept called *narzisstische Wut*, narcissistic fury – I have a fantasy of omnipotence, and when something frustrates that fantasy, I want to destroy the whole world. I prefer the world not to exist so that it doesn't remind me of the limits of my power.

Another form of what I call true evil is cynicism. For me cynicism does not lie in the fact that someone doesn't believe in the existence of integrity or goodness and is certain that these are just outward appearances, that people are masquerading, that really everyone is alike and desires only power. Real cynicism is the conscious spoiling of goodness, when I, regarding others as naïve, exploit the goodness in them.

Marci: These two things seem potentially very connected: when someone disbelieves in the existence of goodness as such, that disbelief can easily become a justification for exploiting other people. I'm thinking of Konstantin Pobedonostsev, the nineteenth century advisor to Russian tsars who was the alleged model for Dostoevsky's Grand Inquisitor. Pobedonostsev rallied against democracy as "the great falsehood of our time"; he lamented the fact that the idea of popular sovereignty had taken hold so firmly since the French Revolution. A parliament would be pernicious because its members would only be guided by personal ambition; a free press would be worthless because journalists would write whatever was desirable to the person who paid the most. Pobedonostsev was rebelling against Enlightenment thought, but his rebellion was quite different from that of Fichte or Schelling or Dostoevsky. Pobedonostsev countered Enlightenment not with Romanticism, but with cynicism. I think of Vladislav Surkov a bit as a contemporary incarnation of Pobedonostsev – a postmodern version of cynicism laid bare.

And returning to sadism, Ivan Karamazov, just before he begins his tale of the Grand Inquisitor, forces his brother Alyosha to listen to stories of children being tortured. And Ivan says to Alyosha, "Indeed, people speak sometimes about the 'animal' cruelty of man, but that is terribly unjust and offensive to animals, no animal could ever be so cruel as a man, so artfully, so artistically cruel."

Jurko: True evil we can observe only, exclusively in connection with man. Animals are not in possession of this kind of evil, because they are not in possession of culture. Animals have only violence. An animal can kill another animal – kill, bite, slay with its horns – but no animal is capable of building a construction where a ball is suspended and the animal knows that when it stands on a string, the ball will drop and take a life. Only man is capable of that. And man is capable of that precisely because he is in possession of language.

Marci: And imagination.

Jurko: And imagination, yes. For me language is the condition for imagination. Verbal modality, for instance – something does not exist in physical reality, but in language it does. Modality is a way of thinking about what in reality is not, what is not *Faktizität*, but what *would be*.

Marci: Modality relates to the distinction that Jean-Paul Sartre describes as the *en-soi* versus the *pour-soi*. *En-soi*, the "in-itself" is *Faktizität*, what is and what has already been, what cannot be changed. And *pour-soi*, the "for-itself", is possibility, potentiality. For Sartre we, human beings, are free because we are not only *en-soi*, but also *pour-soi*, precisely this possibility of bringing about or becoming what is not – or is not yet – *Faktizität*, is our freedom.

Jurko: Modality opens the possibility of undertaking the *"what if"*. Because it's possible to think it, it's possible to do it. In this sense we do evil because we *can* do evil, because we can imagine it.

Marci: So in the absence of the subjunctive mood, there would be no imagination.

Jurko: This *what if* makes the distinction in jurisprudence between premeditated and unpremeditated murder so essential. Someone, in outrage, strikes someone and kills him, *nolens volens*. That's one thing. Whereas in the novels of Agatha Christie someone prepares for years, devising a plan of extermination. *This* is evil. This is evil bound up with our capabilities of fashioning, planning, supposing: *and if it were … what would be …*

Marci: I want to ask you about still another distinction. In spring 2022 you gave an interview in German where you said that what you felt towards the Russian soldiers was not hatred, but *Verachtung*, which in English would be "contempt". In March 2023 a chilling video circulated of a captured Ukrainian soldier smoking a cigarette. His Russian captors evidently had guns pointed at him. The Ukrainian soldier looked at them and said *"Slava Ukraini"* in an uncannily composed voice. Immediately after that the Russians shot him to death. What was in the eyes of that Ukrainian soldier was precisely *Verachtung*, it was an eerily calm, utter contempt.

From the point of view of psychoanalysis, are you able to understand those Russian soldiers?

Jurko: I am. And it's precisely because I'm able to understand them that they evoke in me *Verachtung*, not *Zorn*. I can hate someone whom I perceive as my equal. But someone whom I don't perceive as being equal on the plane of *Würde*, of dignity, I don't hate, but rather feel contempt for. This is very narcissistic, I'm aware of that.

Marci: I'm imagining Hannah Arendt sitting in the courtroom in Jerusalem in 1961, listening to Adolf Eichmann, and thinking that he's pathetic in his ordinary, banal obtuseness, in the pettiness of his concerns and self-interest, in his failure to think. When she published *Eichmann in Jerusalem*, people despised her. Readers interpreted her attitude towards Eichmann as an attempt to exonerate him. But this was a misunderstanding. For Arendt to conceive of Eichmann as demonic was to give him too much respect. That Eichmann didn't want to think for himself evoked in her only contempt.

Jurko: If someone goes along with the orders of a corrupt dictator just because he's afraid, or hopes to repay a loan, or to make money off of this war, or to have the chance to rob and plunder, or in the hopes of playing the role of master over someone — what feeling could this evoke in me, if not contempt?

Marci: With respect to those Russians who go off to kill people not knowing what for, I'll tell you a small anecdote. My kids were doing admissions interviews at a secondary school, and I was waiting for them in the lobby. Another mother was waiting there, too, she started chatting with me, and I said that visiting these different possible schools, I was struck by how they were all so much nicer than the school I had gone to, which was mediocre at best and a generally unpleasant place with quite a bit of physical violence. And she said that she understood what I meant, that the school she had gone to was horrible. I asked her where she had gone to school. In Moscow, she told me. Then I asked her to describe it to me in Russian, and she told me that every morning the teacher would come into the classroom and say to the students, *"Good morning, idiots!"* That stayed with me: if throughout your whole childhood and adolescence you hear every day that you're good for nothing, do you end up feeling that you're at all competent to think for yourself?

Jurko: Here is that terribly Russian paradox. It's long been known that megalomania is only the other side of a feeling of inadequacy. In the Russian case, though, this is egregiously conspicuous. They've always had a feeling of inferiority towards what they call "the West". Just for this reason they've always tried, on the one hand, to degrade and debase "the West", calling it decadent and impotent, and on the other hand, to be still mightier than the West, and ultimately to imitate it. This where the history of violence begins, precisely this *narzisstische Wut*, for seeing that they're not succeeding in being the way they imagine the West to be, they turn more and more to violence out of despair that they're unable to reach that standard. Maybe that standard is imaginary, chimerical, but even so, it's a reference point for them. This is also the effect of Putin, of Yeltsin, of the end of the Soviet Union and the hope that maybe now, finally, they can catch up with the West and bring about in their country liberal democracy, freedom, human rights. And once again this failed. And instead of trying to understand what went wrong, what happened, why it wasn't successful, the idea of betrayal emerged. *The West betrayed us.* This is what we were just talking about in relation to Trump – that people who believe they've been betrayed feel that now everything is permitted them.

Marci: This is truly glaring among Trump and his supporters: *ressentiment* in Nietzsche's sense and the feeling that everything is permissible.

Jurko: Russians' hatred towards Ukraine is a projection of the hatred they have for the West. But this hatred is even worse. In the first place, they somehow feel that Ukraine has decided to be "Western". And in the second place, they feel that the West has accepted Ukraine as its own, while rejecting them. And they feel: but we're worth more than some Ukrainians over there, for we were an empire, and *they* belonged to us. So why would you regard those pathetic people, and not us, as one of you?

Marci: And do Ukrainians feel accepted by the West?

Jurko: In fact no, they don't. And this is why the enormous number of questions plaguing Ukrainians now can be reduced to this one: *will the West betray us?*

Marci: In this sense, do Ukrainians feel themselves to be victims? That is, not only victims of Russia, but also victims of an absence of full acceptance by the West? Or do they now feel themselves to be the avant-garde of the West? Or both one and the other?

Jurko: Both one and the other. This is a very ambivalent country.

Marci: Victimhood is itself very complicated.

Jurko: Yes, very complicated. But it seems to me that Ukrainians' dignity and success lies in the fact that beginning from the first Maidan, with each subsequent Maidan and now with this war, we've been able to achieve something that had not been before, and so of course to feel like a victim, but not *only* a victim. A victim can elicit empathy and compassion, but victimhood can never, at least not over an extended period of time, evoke dignity. It's not by chance that the Maidan was the Revolution of Dignity. The concept of dignity became so fundamental because a victim lacks dignity.

Marci: That demand for dignity has now also taken the form of Ukrainians' refusal to appear publicly with anyone from Russia, regardless of who that person is.

Jurko: I can understand this expression of separation between ourselves and everything Russian, and why we will not sit on the podium next to even the most wonderful oppositionist, liberal, anti-Putinist, pro-Ukrainian writer. Not because I don't respect that person, but because through my rage and the violence done to me, I want us for the first time to be seen as separate. We do not even want to be compared to Russians. Because each comparison, which in German is called *Vergleich*, contains *Gleich*, "sameness", and from *Vergleich* to *Ausgleich*, comparison to equalization, is but one step. For once in our lives we want to be perceived not as the object of *Vergleich*, but as something unto ourselves.

That said, I think this cancelling is a very bad thing. On the contrary, I think we should now be studying Russian culture. We need to know it, and to know it deeply, so as to understand where this evil now directed at us comes from.

Marci: And how has this daily grappling with absolute evil, with this war, changed you?

Jurko: I fear it's changed me totally, but I'm not yet able to say how. The war changes not only us and everything, it also changes itself. When you ask me what the war has done to me, I'm not yet able to give an answer – precisely because the war is continually changing. For one thing, it's a fantasy that I'll be able to give an answer when everything ends. And for a second thing, the question has come too early, nothing has yet come to an end, nothing has yet been decided, everything is still unfolding.

Marci: Hegel's Owl of Minerva … Europe, after all, is also changing, it's also on the way, we don't know to where. German chancellor Olaf Scholz speaks about a *Zeitenwende*, but it seems to me that this turn is taking place too slowly from the German side. Scholz is still vacillating about whether to give Ukraine this or that weapon. Maybe the vacillation will end only when he becomes afraid that the war will come to Germany. It's apparent that Emmanuel Macron is now afraid. In my own country, unfortunately, we're not afraid enough.

Jurko: Yes, the fact that Americans are allowing Trump testifies to the fact that they don't fear the consequences. Someone like Trump should immediately evoke a feeling of danger. It's as if a lunatic, a psychopath, a murderer has escaped from prison – and the response should be "he needs to be returned to prison", not "we're enraptured by him".

Marci: That so many Americans are enraptured by him terrifies me. It's also apparent that Trump is in Putin's pocket. It's not certain why, what the source of the influence is, but it's clearly the case.

Jurko: It could be *kompromat*, although it could also just be that Trump is captivated by Putin in the sense of *"I like this guy!"* It could just be that they understand each other because they're alike. And as long as Putin takes his side, Trump will be captivated, but when Putin disappoints him, Trump could fall into *narzisstische Wut* and want to destroy the whole world …

Marci: Chto delat'? Would Freud have an answer for us as to what we can do?

Jurko: His answer, I think, would be *so ist es.*

———

Ausgleich, "equalization", was the term used for the 1867 compromise by which the Habsburg Empire became the Austro-Hungarian Dual Monarchy.

The original version of this conversation took place in person in the Podil district of Kyiv on 17 March 2024. Thank you to Dawid Kopik for transcribing the original Polish-language version. Thank you also to Victoria Smolkin for pointing me towards Pobedonostsev when I was preparing this seminar on the problem of evil. The quotation from *The Brothers Karamazov* is from the translation by Richard Pevear and Larissa Volokhonsky.

Marci Shore was born in 1972 in Pennsylvania and completed her BA at Stanford University, her MA at University of Toronto, and her Ph.D at Stanford University. She is Professor of History at Yale University and a regular Visiting Fellow at the Institut für die Wissenschaften vom Menschen in Vienna. Her research focuses on the intellectual history of twentieth and twenty-first century Central and Eastern Europe. She is the translator of Michał Głowiński's The Black Seasons *and the author of* Caviar and Ashes: A Warsaw Generation's Life and Death in Marxism, 1918-1968 *and* The Taste of Ashes: The Afterlife of Totalitarianism in Eastern Europe. *Her third book,* The Ukrainian Night: An Intimate History of Revolution, *was republished with a new preface in March 2024. Her articles and essays have appeared in* The New Yorker, Foreign Policy, Eurozine, The Atlantic, The Yale Review, The New York Review of Books, The Times Literary Supplement, The New York Times, *and* The Wall Street Journal. *In 2018 she received a Guggenheim Fellowship for the book project she is currently completing about phenomenology in East-Central Europe tentatively titled* Eyeglasses Floating in the Sky: Central European Encounters that Took Place while Searching for Truth.

Jurko Prochasko was born in 1970 in Ivano-Frankivsk in what was then the Ukrainian Soviet Socialist Republic and is now Ukraine. He studied German philology in Lviv. He is a literary translator, essayist, and psychoanalyst who trained in Austria. He has been a fellow at Wissenschaftskolleg in Berlin, the Institut für die Wissenschaften vom Menschen in Vienna, and various other institutions. He translates literature from German, Polish and Yiddish, including

Katja Petrowskaja's Vielleicht Esther, *as well as works by Joseph Roth, Kafka, Freud, Robert Musil, Jarosław Iwaszkiewicz and Debora Vogel.*

A SUITE OF POEMS ON THE HOLODOMOR

Sonia Jarema

Behind the criminal lens.

Author's Note: In these writings I have attempted to keep company with sorrow. It was a surprise to me that these poems came. They started as an absence in my unpublished novel Shaking the Tree *(shortlisted by Penguin Random House in the Write/Now Program, 2016); they are the diary of Bohdan, a perpetrator of the* Holodomor.

12 April 1933

Last night I walked down to the river, and as I passed between the trees the smell of crushed wild garlic rose and starburst flowers climbed the banks. And there in the river, the moon trembled. Silence snapped as figures appeared and bent down to gather the sheath-like leaves for green borscht. I raised the camera and looked through its lens. The women moved slowly, swaying; the earth was tugging them down. One of them stooped, put a flower in her mouth, as though eating fire, and a desperate sound escaped her lips. One by one the others followed suit. The eye of the camera opened for the longest time, and I prayed both that the picture would and wouldn't take. The women froze, but as they couldn't source the sound of the shutter they returned to the task of gathering, filling the baskets over their arms. Now and then one would stop, exhausted by the smallest exertion. My cheek on its bark felt the suffering the tree had borne and the grace of small fissures. The women left slowly, moving as though nearing the end of an arduous journey. I sat on a tree root and watched the water trip the moonlight, breaking it into a hundred crescents. The ripples of the river quickened, and the wood's eternal voice spoke the words, "Bohdan, there will be blood on your hands".

14 April 1933

Through the window I watched Baba
walk past a body on the roadside, her hands clasped
behind her back and her body tilted forward.

Saffron stains broke through the bandages
on her legs, her thickened ankles bound
like the apple tree my mama loved, a branch

of which a storm tried to take.
My hand itched for my camera but I felt the pricking
of a hundred hidden eyes so stopped myself.

At lunch Chovnyk offered to get me
developing chemicals. How can I tell him
I've no idea how to use them? He'll not allow me

to take photos of his daughter's wedding
and more than likely will take away my camera.
But God-willing, I can take a photo daily,

each film will last a month or so. Three films,
three months – some pictures will have to exist
only in my mind. Oh, my mind and what it sees!

My mama being dragged by her hair across
the living room floor, her heels digging into the rug.
I found Papa's belt on the floor – did he try

to take his life? I witnessed none of this
but my home afterward spoke to me in its disarray.
Last night I dreamt a tree was so full of crows

that its branches bowed under the weight.
As the wings lifted there was an almighty wrenching
and the dark earth gave up the roots.

I thought I could start afresh coming here.
On the way back from Kyiv, Mama would say,
"A village is a village — it never changes."

15 April 1933

I woke up, disquiet twisting my stomach. What I thought
was the tapping of birds' beaks on the windowpane was hail
intermittently striking the sill. I pulled myself out of the dip in
my mattress. Was that the door? False alarm. My landlady, the
schoolmistress, was not back. I prefer not to speak of her, as
she's bitter, vengeful and full of the joy of reporting on those
hiding grain. I think she would report me if she could, but
I'm a favourite with the village council. I'm untouchable, like
Mama and Papa. Not untouchable enough for this to be read.
I must always keep this diary on my person. Just now, in the
middle of the road a man reached into his pocket, smiled and
withdrew a carrot. Still smiling, he bit off the end. People fell
upon him and clawed his sleeve as he stuffed it back into his
pocket. They tore at him till the material gave way and ripped
open his trousers. Heads smacked in the struggle.

Into the cracks in the road blood ran. A young girl ran over
with a cup and held it to the gash in his head and before she
could drink from it, his hand swiped down, knocking it spinning. I framed a shot of a butterfly-shaped bloodstain on her
face but didn't release the shutter. This wasn't a picture I could
take. But in my mind, I've taken many more photos: the man's
trousers torn open like flayed flesh; the girl pressing the cup
to his wound; the carrot bright against a grey face.

2 May 1933

Praise be to God! Who knows what favours Chovnyk called
in but his friend, Hrehori, agreed to develop my films in his
darkroom. My pleasure soon subsided as Chovnyk lectured

me on the quota as yet unfulfilled. I looked around the barn,
sacks piled high, grain spilt and spoiling. "Tell me, why gather
more, when this lies rotting?" I searched his face but found
no trace of daylight breaking there. He spoke only of numbers,
instructing me, as he left, to count the sacks of grain and I
wondered if I dared to fabricate amounts. I took out my camera
and scanned the barn. One sack lay near the wall like a mother
with her back turned. On the white cloth a single grain lay
holding the shadow of its stalk. I captured the line the past
makes, the cleaving of the present and put the lens cap back
on my camera before I scooped up two handfuls of unspoilt
grain and poured into my pocket their tiny flames.

3 May 1933

Shame's a heavy mantle; today I took the last food
from a mother. Outside her house a small clump
of blonde hair lifted, caught on the catch of the gate,

just the right height to be her daughter's.
I took out my camera catching the moment it turned
into strands of pure light. I'd forgotten to change

the shutter speed and as I cursed the fact, a howl
from the mother curled in the air and something hard
hit the back of my head. I swallowed my pain

but Chovnyk strode back and cut her off
with the thunderclap of his hand. He really is the devil
and I am the devil too, sitting here with my belly full.

My landlady's cooked meat borscht followed by *holopchi*.
In the orchard the crowns of the apple trees have two seasons:
their lower half Winter-bare and upper Spring-blossom.

Tomorrow it all will be gone, eaten by the starving villagers.
I write while the candle flickers eating its way down,
pooling wax as I try to catch the horror and the beauty.

4 May 1933

After dinner, I delivered the figures
for goods requisitioned to Chovnyk's house.
His wife sat by the stove embroidering *holubi*,

on the *rushnyk* for sweet Solomiya's wedding.
She tilted her head, and smiled
before she bowed back into her task.

What power this woman must have to induce
Chovnyk to sanction this scorned tradition!
As I watched her needle work the linen

images of the *vyshyvanki* I had unearthed
back home flooded back. I had lifted a sleeve,
seeming to see people line up to pass through me.

I dropped the trapdoor on the blouses and shirts
catching the arm adorned with guelder flowers –
exposed for whoever next ransacked

my parents' house. Others no doubt came.
Sometimes I feel I shouldn't be alive –
that I'm a kind of ghost. Or is this what happens

when you live surrounded by strangers?
Shevchenko said this more elegantly, "my tears
[…] soak this foreign field. Water it day and night."

I, however, am exiled on my own land.
I handed over the papers, took the dark road
and shrank like the lights from the house.

6 May 1933

I tried to walk further than my feelings today
but they stretched so far ahead of me
there was no road I could travel to lose them.

The moon has a pinkish tinge as it looks
down on this peacetime war. I wish
my words would gallop like horses

and mark the field with shapes true and strong.
I miss those nights they would fly with a power
not of my making and barely touch me

before they sprang from the page to be read
later in amazement. Pacing, I haul
words in the sack of my stomach

and retch as they edge up, stopping my breath
when they make their painful way onto
the pages of this book Mama left me.

As I sip her absence, I am halted.
The village is quiet – its wings injured
and its nerves paralysed. These days are sluggish.

The cart comes every week; bodies thrown
onto its open back. Clinging to their dead,
stand a wailing mother or wife, or a man

with deep sobs wracking his body. And the driver
kicks and pushes them away, before he jumps up
and the uneven road reanimates the dead.

10 May 1933

Yesterday, it was Solomiya's wedding.
Chovnyk's face hauled a smile, all day.
I couldn't take all the photos I wanted:

A lozenge of honey on the floor.
Crowns placed on the couple's heads.
Branches, their leaves like birds

learning to fly. Rips in the sky, chocolates
thrown in the air by the bride;
children's arms reaching through

church railings for the sweets.
The sole of a young boy's foot
relieved by the white of his arch.

The legs of the chair as it falls.
The spaces on the dancefloor.
God help me if Chovnyk dislikes

the wedding photos! I wanted to be shot
of the films and when today he finally
took them along with my owns reels,

my mind cleared of a waking dream
in which I helped a figure up and Baba
pulled my arm down saying something like

wait or don't touch. I wanted to watch
my photos take their first breaths,
but Hrehori, will develop them alone.

The term Holodomor *(death by hunger, in Ukrainian) refers to the starvation of millions of Ukrainians in 1932–1933 as a result of Soviet policies. The Holodomor can be seen as the culmination of an assault by the Communist Party and Soviet State on the Ukrainian peasantry, who resisted Soviet policies. This assault occurred in the context of a campaign of intimidation and arrests of Ukrainian intellectuals, writers, artists, religious leaders, and political cadres, who were seen as a threat to Soviet ideological and state-building aspirations.*

Born in Luton, to Ukrainian parents, Sonia Jarema is a poet, writer, learning support assistant, self-employed gardener and mother of two. Her father worked on the production line at Vauxhall Motors and her mother sewed buttons on coats for Eastex. As a child she was obliged to memorise and recite Ukrainian poetry and either this started or fed her love of language and its inner music. When she began primary school she was unable to speak English, but gradually it took over as her main language.

Her poems have been published in Stand, The North, South Bank Poetry, Envoi *and* The Interpreter's House *as well as online and in anthologies. Her poetry pamphlet* Inside the Blue House *was published by Palewell Press in 2019. She how lives in Enfield, England.*

FOUR POEMS

—

Ciarán O'Rourke

Cannon fodder.

IN BRESLAU PRISON
Rosa Luxemburg, 1871-1919

Reddish black, and violet! Tell me more
about the lovely berry-bunch you picked
in Steglitz Park, the black, perhaps,
the elder berry, which hangs in thick
and heavy clusters, fanning down,
and the violet – it must have been
the common medlar, properly
a crushing red, but, at this late time
of year, too ripe, begun to rot, a violet tinge,
and leaves, no doubt, like myrtle,
punctiliously green, a leather-like
top-surface, rough beneath.
Oh, tell me more! In the courtyard
where I pace, the daily army trucks
arrive, piled up with haversacks
and tunics, from the front, a ragged war,
the bundles stiff with blood. The women here,
each waiting in her cell, together take
the tarnished fabrics, mend them all,
then send them back, repaired, for future use.
Last week, a truck came, slowly dragged
by buffaloes, not horses ... I never saw
such creatures, close enough to touch!
Black and bulky, mythic things, they peered
across the yard, big-eyed and ever-softening.
War trophies from Romania, the soldier said.

Difficult to snare, these animals, so fierce
was their habituated life, so lush, a flowing green,
their original terrain. They were, and had
been since their capture, mercilessly flogged,
the wildness beaten out, then yoked
to heavy loads – he grinned – and quickly
worked to death. You know, their gleaming hide
is near-proverbially tough, but the whip
had left a web. They stood, the buffaloes,
in stillness, dripping tiny droplets
on the stones; the one in front
looked like a weeping child severely
thrashed about the head, who cannot know
the why, nor how to slip away, the sheer
unending torture all there is. I went before him,
watched his pooling pupils sink, and thought,
with him, somehow, of deep Romania,
the meadows long ago, an easy
breath of wind, a distant dream (or
memory) to wash away the agony
of now, the broken blood that trickled
down his back. I reached a single finger
to his neck, and heard the ebb. When asked,
the soldier smiled again, and said,
the whipping stick a-dangle at his side:
nobody feels compassion, not today,
not even fellow men for men –
and nothing for the beasts.

THE SEVEN YEARS' WAR

In thirsting Bay, Bakool and Banadir
last year, at least four dozen, maybe more,

of the dislocated population
died for every day gone by, in crisis

and malaise – a fever-ridden region
cursed

to weather seven fallow seasons,
petitioning for rain,

in a brassy, broken polity,
ravenous for grain:

the smoking, far-away foray
of bellicose White Russia

on weltering Ukraine
has twisted to a trickle

all shipments to the Horn,
sowing hunger

in the bellies
of Somalis in the sun,

and nourishing migration,
cadaverous and glum.

Observers of the conflict
have witnessed every sin.

Among the *excess deaths*
forecasted

in the summer still to come,
half are famine-children,

withering and young,
and all

have grown accustomed
to living on the run.

THE ENVOY

A sandstone block, brackish brown,
with capillarous designs

carved in, has surfaced,
of a sudden, from the earth,

offering, though neither gift
nor prayer (but solidly, a wedge

of slowly travelled time),
the earliest example

of runic lettering – a signature
and capsule

of long-forgotten life – in lake-lit,
Southern Norway, ferrous

atmosphere a-gleam, where latterly
a mercenary

landed, in distress. Medvedev
(by name) had led

a killer pack
of hunters in Ukraine,

capturing combatants
with a bullet to the brain.

Deadened
by disaster, sickening,

in fright, the murder-
maddened officer

dashed across the ice,
braving treachery

and fire
for sanctuary and peace.

Having lived as *cannon fodder*
in the Russian war machine,

which designates destruction
for any men who disobey,

Medvedev is pleading
to be made a refugee.

Rapidly re-numbered, buried
on their knees, in battle

all subversives
were shot in twos and threes.

THE INNOCENT
Pieter Bruegel, 1566

Beyond the fray, in frozen light,
the blue geese yodel hoarsely,
careening toward the sun.

Lowly winter
burnishes the day: a little drift
of crows from tree to tree,

the snowed-on roofs
a tidy white, brightening
the bricks beneath

to red – a ruddy sheen.
At the brilliant
centre of the scene,

the Alban Duke, on horseback,
calmly waits, a glinting
troupe of lances at his beck,

for the careless carnage
round him to abate –
the newborns dead, his duty done,

the wailing, puckered villagers
abashed – and aftermath
to settle in its stead:

a sigh of vacant doorways,
under every
shaken gable, peace …

all this to come.
For now, in the sky
above his patient head,

the godly banner
dances in the breeze,
gold and rippled crimson,

as the massacre unfolds.

Ciarán O'Rourke was born in 1991 and took a degree in English and History at Trinity College, Dublin. He received a Masters in English and American Studies from Oxford in 2014, as well as a doctorate on William Carlos Williams at his alma mater in Dublin in 2019. A winner of the Lena Maguire / Cúirt New Irish Writing Award, the Westport Poetry Prize, and the Fish Poetry Prize, his first collection of poems, The Buried Breath, *was published by The Irish Pages Press in late 2018. His second collection,* Phantom Gang *(The Irish Pages Press), was published in 2022 and was shortlisted for The Swansea University Dylan Thomas Prize, a global award for writers under 40 in any genre. He currently lives in Dublin.*

DIES IRAE, DAY OF WRATH: MUSIC AND MUSICIANS AT WAR IN UKRAINE

———

Ed Vulliamy

With a little help from the Irish.

Andriy Khlyvnyuk – Ukraine's biggest rock star – bids the crowd in Drogheda to calm, between numbers. There's whooping applause for a hallmark number entitled *Naked King.* "The day you become a beggar / You'll value all you had / You'll fix everything you broke."

Khlyvnyuk fronts the country's most successful band: Boombox – sophisticated but no-nonsense rock and roll, catapulted onto the international stage by a collaboration with David Gilmour and Pink Floyd for a rendition of the Ukrainian patriotic anthem *"Chernova Kralnya"* – "Red Viburnum" – as "Hey Hey Rise Up". The band has been on and off the road for months now: a tour of Europe, North America, Europe again – now the banks of the Boyne.

Andriy invariably cues his songs in Ukrainian, to audiences mostly from home – rarely in the host language. But there's something palpable in the air tonight: Boombox have played to another level of commitment; there's a buzz, and bigger contingent than usual of curious local fans, Ireland having taken a higher proportion of Ukrainian refugees per capita than any other country apart from Poland.

Andriy clears his throat: "I'm sorry I'm not saying this in the Irish language, but we didn't learn that in school – so I'll say it in a language you understand. Thank you, Ireland, for having us here", and with emphasis: *"We all know that our countries share the same terrible story."* He didn't have to say anything else to raise a shiver up every spine. Its name during the 1840s was the Great Famine, and during the 1930s *Holodomor*; two attempts to exterminate an entire people through calculated hunger. A viscerally shared history: within a shared context of repression and defiance – much of the latter in arms, much of it with music.

Since the Russian occupations of 2014, and even more so the full-scale invasion of 2022, Ukraine has resisted with every fibre of society, irrespective of age, economic stratum, social, sexual or political identity. Ukraine has countered President Vladimir Putin's genocidal notion that neither it nor its culture exists, with an explosion of culture, by way of affirmation of what it calls нація, the nation as political and cultural entity.

Music has been to the fore in that attestation, a renaissance in classical, rock, folk, jazz and electronica – music at war, and musicians at war. When he is not touring and performing, Khlyvnyuk is fighting: with a police combat unit based on the Southern outskirts of Mykolaiv, towards Kherson, liberated in November 2022, but under constant threat and bombardment. Also in the fighting unit is Stanislav "Stas" Gurenko, a documentary filmmaker in peace time, now accompanying the band to make a film about its double life between fame and combat, stage and trenches.

We'd had a time of it across Europe, and especially in Ireland. In Frankfurt, the audience had spoken for itself, literally: Anhelina Chumak and her twelve- year-old daughter Yeva fled their home in Zarozhne in late February; "We're now far away, in a strange place", said Anhelina, "but when Boombox plays, it's like we're all together again, back home." "They pour out so much energy and love", said Andriy back at the hotel afterwards, "I have to look into their eyes", and Andriy's own eyes moisten. "We – the band – are not the important part of this now. *They* are."

Then off for a North American tour, after which: London, where Stas and I had strolled around Portobello and Notting Hill, visiting the address where Jimi Hendrix died on 18 September 1970 – on the street where I had been born. After both nights of playing at the Scala in Kings Cross, Andriy – for all the showmanship on stage – stood alone on a fire escape stairwell to smoke a cigarette. Then into the green room, a few photos with friends and fans, then the over into a corner to sit by himself, and consult the news from home.

The night before Drogheda, we'd all had pints of Guinness in Dublin, but in the van back to the capital after the gig, bassist Inna Nevoit talked about her daughter Yeva in Odesa, and problems of internet schooling, first Covid-19, now the war. This is life on the road: a long way from home, but home is never far; every centime and penny raised from these gigs goes to buy weapons. After the encore in Drogheda, Andriy had wished everyone: "a new day, a new dawn, and I hope a new life for all of you." Back in Kyiv, he prepares to return to the front, to fight for just that in Ukraine.

He does so with his inimitable, droll good humour: proudly showing a video of his patrol crew in combat fatigues on the front line, deploying a Punisher drone against the enemy. The video shows it unleashing a bomb on a

Russian tank, which it blows up. "I call it a Ukrainian parking ticket", Andriy laughs. "Your vehicle is illegally parked in our country!"

———

The first anniversary of the full-scale invasion was marked in Lviv, in February 2023, by two mighty performances at the magnificent neo-Renaissance, Hapsburg-era opera house. On the anniversary itself, a rendition of Verdi's terrifying *Messa da Requiem*, under the baton of Canadian-Ukrainian conductor Keri-Lynn Wilson. Verdi's *Requiem* is electrifying at the best of times, but tonight Wilson achieved something strangely cogent: the notion of "restrained Verdi" should be oxymoronic, but it turned out not to be, the opening *Kyrie* focused by uncanny understatement entirely appropriate for this occasion. Not for long, however: Verdi's unforgiving *Dies Irae* – Day of Wrath – erupted from Wilson's discreet sonority into a gale-force swirl of acceleration and deceleration. The front rows had been reserved for serving soldiers, whose uniforms made the foyer coat-check look like a barracks locker room. They watched, and listened, enthralled.

The following night, the Lviv Opera staged a vast work by Ukraine's greatest living composer, Yevhen Stankovych: *The Terrible Revenge*, based on the story by Nikolai Gogol, born in Poltava – then part of the Russian empire, now Ukraine. The libretto, by Stankovych, was a resetting for stage in Ukrainian of Gogol's original Russian prose. Here is a dark masterpiece of cruel but cathartic prescience, composed – and the production designed – before the Russian invasion. The story concerns the Antichrist, poisoning love and unleashing violence at an intimate level: he is also the father of the heroine, Katerina, whom he violates and murders. But it is also about the final defeat of this monster, hurled into an abyss by a young boy. "Now", wrote the composer in a programme note, "all of this resonates with our reality, and what is happening."

Stankovych's music has for decades been synonymous with Ukraine's cultural defiance of empire. In 1978, his oratorio/ballet *When the Fern Blooms*, went into dress rehearsal. The piece evoked the pagan ritual of Ivana Kupala night in early July, blending midsummer in the Julian calendar with courting and nuptial rites and bonfires. "It was so obviously Ukrainian", recalls Stankovych, "an expression of subjugated culture and its ancient rites. We had prepared everything – designed the sets, perfected the choreography, and rehearsed the music – the concert hall was booked. But gossip circulated, that this piece contained some show of Ukrainian liberty. So along came the KGB, and stopped the whole thing. The piece established a Ukrainian national identity, and that is what the government was afraid of." The work was eventually premiered in 2011, "after which I hope everyone who hears it understands where it comes from – deep Ukraine."

Stankovych's *Requiem for the Holodomor*, about the Ukrainian famine engineered by Joseph Stalin between 1932-3, was premiered in 1993, on the 60th anniversary of the calamity, and after Ukrainian independence. But, says the composer, "I had been working on it for years, while living in Canada. I think it was the first music to confront, express and commemorate the *Holodomor*." When we held this conversation in summer 2022, Stankovych was coy about "working on something large – music at war. It might take something from the Bible; large scale, tragic, something to say that Satan is still enjoying himself in the 21st century."

It is one thing to write a staged piece about war, with a set of apartment blocks collapsing after a missile attack, and quite another to do so from deep *within* a war, when that same set is for real beyond the theatre exit. This was October 2023, when the premiere of Stankovych's *Psalms of War* became the most important musical moment in Ukraine's cultural resistance to date. The piece is at once visceral, shattering and epic. "He is like a mid-20th century composer writing for our age", said the premiere's conductor, Ivan Cherednichenko.

Stankovych had begun work on this music after his grandchildren had fled their house in the Kyiv suburb of Bucha for the Western Carpathian region, before Bucha's occupation early on during the full-scale invasion (and scene of some of the most heinous war crimes), during which their home was destroyed. And then while undergoing surgery twice for his heart, and a further twice on his back. These personal ordeals palpably permeate the sonority, aura and impact. Conductor Cherednichenko lost both his parents to Russian war crimes on the same outskirts of Kyiv early in the war, and this indescribable loss inevitably infuses the playing he demands from his musicians – he, as well as the composer, speaks with this remarkable music. "It's very hard for Cherednichenko to conduct this", said Stankovych, "but what is an artist to do with such a situation, if not this?"

The mood, and its sonority, are established immediately. The first movement – entitled *Music for War* – is launched by martial timpani, rushing strings, a tolling bell, and wail of an air-raid siren on trombone: Ukraine's reality dramatised in sound. The brass leads an orchestral gallop pregnant with menace and the violence to come; searchlights scan the sky as the choir clambers to its positions on layered platforms made with what look like railway tracks, to give a sense of flight, and down into the lower level inevitably evocative of a bomb shelter. They carry wheelie bags, teddy bears, portable pet baskets and other quotidian items that have become icons of this war.

I put to Stankovych a question asked by TV reporters to Cherednichenko before the dress rehearsal, that it is too early to present such a piece to Ukrainians who may not want to experience their real-life trauma in a theatre – to inflict it upon them. Reverting to his diagonal laugh at almost everything, Stankovvch replies: "My piece, too early? Is the war too early? It's certainly here, it's hanging in the air. And my music would be too late after the war is over. This is not art for art's sake, this is art for when the windows are shaking and bed is jumping from another air raid. When it's all flying at you for real." And on the awful sound of air-raid sirens played on trombone, which the audience hears almost every night in reality? "It's not my fault there's a siren there, it's Vladimir Putin's fault! He put it there!"

Cherednichenko said: "there is an argument that this is not the right time for such a piece. But I think it is; a work like this can motivate and empower people, and ensure that we will never forget the feelings of this moment. There's a catharsis in this." He adds: "Stankovych is a composer of truth. All his major pieces have a huge dramatic narrative that stretches the soul, and this is one of them."

Stankovych had discussed ideas for a piece with the Director of the Lviv Opera, Vasyl Vovkun (a friend and collaborator over decades), and Volodymyr Sirenko, conductor of most of Stankovych's recent recorded music. But "I don't know what this piece is", he says. "It's not an opera; it's neither an oratorio nor a cantata. It's a synthesis, I suppose, of what we are feeling in this moment. We can only write what we feel – the meanings will come later … It just happened." "For me, it's more of a Requiem", says Vovkun, who wrote the libretto and staged the work. "A distillation of all our wars with Russia into this present one, and into this piece."

The second movement was added at Vovkun's urging, and sets a folk song of yore, "The Black Earth", about the burial of a Cossack warrior, for deep baritone, who begins his solo within the shelter's darkness before taking the stage, conjoined by the choir, building to a further onslaught of sound, both vocal and orchestral.

Once it passes, like another air raid, the third movement – an *adagio* of sorts – is cued by a ringing triangle and haunting four-note motif on flute, picked up as a five-note phrase by solo soprano from within the choir, again wordless, then conjoined *pianissimo* by the rest of the chorus. "It is a lullaby for children killed during the war", says Stankovych. "What words do you use when a child is killed? There are none."

The piece, like the war, is relentless, and denies repose. Each time the music tries to catch breath, reaches an orchestral plateau or settles into a cadence of cathartic respite – even when it is anxiously dissonant – that moment of reflection, is assailed by another brutal charge on kettledrum, hammer and anvil. Lyrical passages of yearning on strings are whipped out of their attempt at reprieve by crashing timpani. So there is this sense, as in life outside, that the attack – the missile, the drone – can arrive to kill at any moment.

The fourth and final movement is a setting of lines Stankovych selected from the Book of Psalms, mainly from Psalm 59, defiant in its Biblical promise of deliverance. But the beginning of the end, a heave in orchestra and choir, is not the usual "triumphal" ending promised by most war music: here, even the swell towards affirmation that hallmarks many a great finale is interrupted more than once by fusillades and aggressions. "In the middle of a war, there can only be a half-way towards the final chord", remarks Stankovych. "You'll notice that the four-note lullaby is there, but there can be no real 'ending' while the war still rages."

A group of soldiers was invited to the Lviv dress rehearsal, sitting along rows 14 and 15 of the stalls. As one of them put it afterwards: "We have come to the theatre to see reality."

———

The Ukrainian term "Faine Misto" translates roughly as "Cool City", and the music festival of that name, held last summer in Lviv, was an assertion of just that: several thousand young Ukrainians converging on buildings of a former red-brick industrial zone on the city outskirts. In one such space, Ukraine's most interesting folk group was engaged in something between a sound check and dress rehearsal. The first, because this is a tight three-part vocal female trio, and the harmonies have to be just right. The latter because this is also a show: the band is called Folkulaka – a play on the Ukrainian word for were-wolf, *Vovkulaka* – and the three ladies' neo-goth mascara, lace, leather and deep purple have to look as sharp as their voices sound. "Scary, but cute", as one of them, Sasha Kladbische, puts it. *Kladbische* means cemetery.

Two things are happening here, beneath the effervescent surface: the first is a deep rip-tide, delving into Ukrainian folkloric legend and ritual – and the second is another profound connection to Ireland.

On they come: Sasha to the right, bright eyes deep behind a black mask, beneath a black cap; at centre is Antonina Vinnyk with a garland of flowers around her long hair, and long red skirt; Tash Zolotarevska, seated at left with cello, long coloured platted locks, and a broad-brimmed witch's hat. They dive into their best-loved songs, "*Mavky Lisovy*", better known as "Hey Hoo!"

"Hey Hoo!" is about Mavky, defined in the Encyclopedia of Ukraine as "mythological female figures, tall, long-haired and sometimes naked ... the souls of girls who died an unnatural death", who "live in forests, caves or sheds"; they "love flowers – wear them in their hair, and plant flowers in the mountains, with which they lure men to their death. At Pentecost, they hold dances – accompanied by a demon playing a flute – and orgies."* Mavky feature in a famous drama by Lesia Ukrainka of 1918: *The Forest Song.*

For the crowd now packed into the former factory, the song captures this ancestry and lore: a whooping, swirling incantation, notes flying from Antonina's pipe; Tash's cello driving the dance: a group in the middle of the crowd forms a circle, whirling, spinning. "Farewell my boy / Today we ride / We don't know where / Where will we sleep tomorrow? / We are the forest Mavki."

A summer afternoon in Lviv has been transformed into a pagan rite. Alex, a computer programmer, explains how "this is all new to me – these myths and fairy tales. I'm loving this music, but more importantly, I'm learning my own culture."

The invocation of old applies directly to the present war. A song called "Fly, Falcon" opens *a cappella*, in tight but powerful harmony before taking the wing itself, with major lifts and soaring polyphony: it is about the bird – but also drones flying over no-man's land to target Russian lines. "Falcon, fly! / Across the wild meadow / Death stalks the fields / And the enemy is nigh / May your wings smother the foe / And set the hoards ablaze."

The music has depth, from the soil whence it comes, and gravitas comparable to Lankum's vision of how to interpret traditional Irish music; yet it is also saucy, giddy and fun. The encore is vivid evocation of pagan lore: "Stay, oak tree, oak tree, stay, stay stay ..." The circle in the crowd reforms, around and around, as though never supposed to stop.

Back in Kyiv, where the girls live, we meet to talk. Antonina runs her own music school, she explains, "at which I teach folk music to what is basically a tech generation. I tell them: these are the roots of who you are. This tradition is ancient, yet at the same time not so ancient: you can sing it as it was always sung, or you can bring it into the present, fuse the folksong with something else, to keep it alive. What matters is to both make it understood in the present, and to understand where it came from."

In that vein, she continues: "we shift words, and shift songs. We take a song that has existed often for centuries, and darken it, or brighten it. Dress it up in black robes, or make it funny. Or just sing it the way it is, but dressed as we are. If we wore traditional Vyshevanka, people would say: 'Oh how lovely' – but we look like this, and they wonder: 'What's going on?'"

"Until recently", says Sasha, "traditional Ukrainian folk was something for your grandmother or grandfather. But all that has changed. There's a generation of our age opening this box, fascinated by what's always been there in the villages, a world away. People with a way of life connected to the seasons: spring, harvest, Christmas. It's now also connected to the war: an exploration of our culture, especially folk culture – this is *metaphysical Ukraine*, if you like. There's a circle of young people serious about this music, and who've made it cool."

"For me", says Tasha, "most interesting are the winter songs. Everyone knows a carol called '*Shchedryk*' – but there are so many more: celebrations of Winter Solstice, other songs from other beliefs, mostly pagan." The strange video for one winter song, "*Dark Kodolka*", shows the girls wearing goat skulls and dragging a wrapped skeleton through snow, burning it and dancing in the blackened smoke.

"The premise", says Sasha, "is that everyone has their weakness when it comes to horror and the imagination. We're all afraid of werewolves, dead girls resurrected – things that are close, but afar; within you, but on another level – and you don't understand. They're your pagan roots, knocking against your window at night."

"This kind of music comes from the people and their story", says Tash, "just as Irish music comes from the people of Ireland. You cannot just sing it, you need to understand it. We have to get the technique right. We have to make it sound Ukrainian. But" – and here's the twist – "we also bring in a lot of Celtic and Irish parts, and harmony." Of course: it had been tapping one on the shoulder, from some musical subconscious, all along: a connection between that eternal circle of sound in Folkulaka, and the reels and jigs of Irish music, likewise without end.

It was my honour to host a small 69th birthday party in Kyiv, at a metal rock bar called Grails in the funky Podil district; along came Folkulaka, and sang the "Fields of Athenry" in English, then "*Siúil a Rún*" in Irish. Now we meet at Andrew's, an Irish pub nearby: these young women are immersed in Irish song, culture and politics, feeling, like Khlyvnyuk, that visceral connection between their country's heritage and struggle, and that of Ireland. Among the many spin-off bands in which they also play, one is called Torf, as in turf, with an entirely Irish repertoire, much of it sung in Irish. "When I was a little girl", says Antonina, "I heard Irish music on the radio and was immediately compelled. Something in it said: this is *my* music, this speaks to me – this is *music*; while the rest is just a show. I was only five or six years old. By 2008, there were Irish sessions in the pubs in Kyiv; musicians learning Irish instruments – fiddle, flute, bouzouki, bodhrán, tin whistles and Uilleann pipe – and playing them at jam sessions. I said: I can't play, but I can sing – and I did. And we ended up singing Ukrainian songs to Irish tunes and music."

Sasha explains: "During the early 2000s, a large number of our youth were fascinated by films about anything related to Ireland, the IRA or the Irish emigrants. Celtic bands such as Enya, Clannad and others were very popular, so '*Siúil a Rún*' was a well known song. People in our community studied Gaelic in college, so could tell us how to pronounce something we couldn't understand. I love '*Oro se do bheatha bhaile*', by both by The Dubliners and Sinéad."

Irish and Ukrainian music have much in common, argues Sasha; "essentially, the meaning is the same: they share the *Melos* – shared history, shared music. If we sing an old Ukrainian song to an Irish tune, it works, thematically, and chromatically. That's why we started playing Irish music – it underpins our own." "It's because", says Tash, "Irish music has a rebel soul, like ours. When we dig deeper into Irish music, we feel how close it all is to our own story – both expressed in music."

This is political, as well as folkloric. Sasha shows a photograph of what appears to be a rural IRA unit, in camouflage, with flag – Sasha wearing a paramilitary beret in the middle. It's a battle re-enactment group called Éire Nua "which had been simulating outfits and weapons of Ireland from the 8th to the 13th century" she explains, but opted to update their theme. "Some were Royal Irish Rangers, but I and others did not support the British crown, so we 'joined' the IRA. So, for several years me and my team-mates have been shooting at each other in competitions!" The photograph shows the IRA winning a battle re-enactment of 2008. But, adds Sasha, with a shiver: "Most of these people are now on the frontline, fighting for Ukraine."

It is not just folklore that Ukraine's musical renaissance brings from the past into the present moment, and establishment of *нація*. Some of the most important music in contemporary Ukraine calls on the great national poets of the 19th century, and more recent verse.

This is the endeavour of Ukraine's most compelling band – for what it is worth, I think they are the most innovative and artistically cogent new ensemble playing in the world at present. Pyrih i Batih is led by Marian Pyrozhok on vocals, playing his guitar with a technique entirely his own: using bamboo sticks as bows across the strings to achieve a hypnotic "drone" effect. He is accompanied by musicians from the Lviv National Opera orchestra: Yurii Hvostov on oboe, Kristov Vikov on bassoon, Markiian Turkanyk on violin, and Artem Kamenkov on double bass – plus Oleksandr Drachuk on percussion. In setting Ukrainian poetry from the past century and a half, Pyrih i Batih has a didactic, almost missionary, purpose: "We are pushing back against an imposed Russian culture which permeated our society: Pushkin, Tolstoy and all", says Pyrozhok. "They're not ours – what is ours is largely forgotten. This is a revival of the richness of who we are. If it's an educational moment for our audiences, good. But what we are trying to achieve is a few hours of delight and interest in something that belongs to them – to us all."

Pyrozhok receives me on a number of occasions: once at his basement apartment in the arty Old Depot neighbourhood of Lviv, with his grandfather's ammunition belt on the wall, filled with paintbrushes. Here, Pyrozhok explains why he plays this music during wartime. "Music doesn't change. Music is a constant, and does not remember. But we remember music, and during this war, music becomes an affirmation. We are working on a new Ukrainian music astride the classical and folk traditions, that resists Russian influence." The "project", as Pyrozhok calls it, "is based on poetry, and blending the sound of Ukrainian language with musical chromatics. It sounds paradoxical: that you have to convey your language through music, but that's what is happening. I'm trying to find a way of setting work by Ukrainian poets who were persecuted or killed by Russia, to chromatically appropriate music."

The venues at which Pyrih i Batih play are as various as their music is elusive: home base is the Dzyga club in Lviv, started up during the 1980s by a group from the city's Vyvykh arts festivals, for "music, avant-garde happenings, theatre and installations", as Pyrozhok recalls. The band recently returned from a tour of the East, including Kharkiv; they played at the funeral of the writer and activist Viktoriia Amelina, killed in Kramatorsk last year; they starred at the Lviv international book forum, playing in a cellar beneath the famous puppet theatre.

I also caught them at the Velna exhibition area on the outskirts of Kyiv, on a sweltering August afternoon, playing a benefit for the Azov Regiment, a militia fighting under command of the armed forces. Here, the music begins with a hypnotic setting of a poem by Bohdan Ihor Antonich, whose verse makes up the best part of the band's latest, wonderful double album, *Green*. This poem, "Spring", is recited in song by Pyrozhok's deep voice, surfing atop mellifluous musical progressions by this strangely beautiful collection of instruments – flurries on oboe and bassoon – until they reach a glorious melody and cadence at the end of each stanza: "Antonich grows and the grass grows / As the alder trees turn green. / Oh, bend down, bend low just a little / And you will hear the most secret words of all / As the grass grows."

Pyrozhok sent me a photograph taken in 1923 of the principal poets whose work he sets from the so-called "Executed Renaissance", mostly in Kharkiv. The explosion of verse during the 1920s and early '30s was, literally, "executed": Pyrozhok marked, with a red circle, the eight out of fourteen poets in the photo either shot or perished in the Gulag, plus that of Mykola Khvylovyi, who committed public suicide in protest against the repression, and whose poem "Why This Gloom?" is set, marvellously, in song: "The shadows disappear / The evening is blue / And bloody…"

Next comes *Cemetery of Souls* – setting a poem by the most important Ukrainian post-war poet, Vasyl Stus. Stus joined the opposition to the Soviet regime during the 1960s, was arrested in 1972, and served time in labour camps. He was rearrested before the 1980 Moscow Olympics, and sent to the infamous Perm-36 camp near Kucshino, where he went on hunger strike and died in September 1985, under unknown circumstances – either starved or murdered. Seven other prisoners in the camp were killed between 1980 and 1987, of which three others were, like Stus, members of the dissident Ukrainian Helsinki Group. *Cemetery of Souls* is sung as invocation with an extended instrumental coda; a spell is cast over the people gathered. "All around me is a cemetery of souls / In the white cemetery of the people." At the end, there's a painful but pregnant silence before anyone dares applaud.

The music is beyond – and defies – "genre", to use that infuriating word. It draws on folk rhythms and jazz chromatics, but has classical origins

— "academic" as the Ukrainians say. Inevitable, perhaps, given the make-up of the band: inflections of Leos Janáček and Bohuslav Martinů, but above all citations from the composer with whom Pyrozhok is estimably obsessed: J. S. Bach. There's an arrangement of Mykola Leontovych's traditional "Shchedryk", but with a coda based on Procol Harum's "A Whiter Shade of Pale", with its quotations from Bach's Orchestral Suite No. 3.

Finally, Taras Shevchenko — Ukraine's iconic national poet: mainmast of the romantic, revolutionary mid-nineteenth-century cultural uprising against Russia. His verse is set to an articulate tribute to Bach: "My Thoughts" to the lovely opening *Vivace* in D Minor to the Double Violin Concerto, written in 1730: "Why are you on paper / In sad rows? / Why didn't the wind scatter you / In the steppe, like dust? / Why didn't the disaster put you to sleep? / Like a child? / Because you were born to laugh at the world / Watered with tears..."

Marian had been, he said, "a rock and roll fan like everyone else, listening to Velvet Underground and Nick Drake, when I basically fell in love with academic music. Borrowing and buying vinyl LPs of Renaissance and baroque music, from polyphonic Gesualdo, through to Telemann and Bach — also contemporary academic music." At the same time, Pyrozhok was studying poetry, especially the Executed Renaissance, "and I suppose I had this idea: to connect the Renaissance that came to fruition in Europe, and that which was executed in Ukraine — to revive the poetry with songs based on music from the real Renaissance."

How come bamboo sticks? "I was just sitting at home, staring at a Chinese painting on my wall, framed by bamboo sticks. I wondered... and disassembled the frame to make two 'bows' for my guitar." Pyrozhok shows me a wooden box, with his selection of bamboos, each carefully and differently treated with "a solvent of resin and turpentine". The ensuing "drone" is a final, singular touch to the band's remarkable, and remarkably original, sonority. Outside, an air raid siren wails across the oncoming night. Pyrozhok stays put in his apartment and accompanies it — or it accompanies him — with Shevchenko's "My Thoughts": "It's like a prayer to me", whispers Pyrozhok when it's over, "or perhaps a Requiem Mass!"

———

BoomBox's military encampment in Mykolaiv lies along a road running South towards Kherson, in the Inhulavska district, named after one of the two great rivers that converge in the city. The house lies behind a metal gate, which Stas Gurenko opens: a warm and strange greeting, after the hotel bar in Dublin only weeks ago.

It had been quite a day: during early morning, a missile landed loud and close, four blocks from my hotel. The deafening detonations of an H-22 guided missile and two drones, which had penetrated the air defences of this former shipbuilding city, to land in Admiralska Street. They destroyed a row of buildings: a hotel, an unoccupied property, plus retail and residential buildings. An elderly man had been killed, and 19 were injured, including a baby and an infant aged three. By morning, the inimitable stench of charred masonry hung in the humid air.

"Well here we are", says Stas, requesting that shoes be removed and left at the door. He gives a guided tour of the premises – and the instruments played by "Andriy's other band" – not guitar, bass or keyboards, but a pile of body armour and a machine gun. In the "commander's quarters" – Andriy's room – a PK machine gun, cleaned and oiled. In the "blue collar quarters" upstairs jokes Stas, clothes horses are hung with helmets, body armour, radios, and machine guns. At the front of the ground floor, curtains drawn, is the arsenal of sorts. The First Person View (FPV) "suicide drone" is a metal cross on legs; several of them hang from the walls, and are piled up on shelves, along the with gadgetry required to launch and fly them. Stas demonstrates how various items of ammunition fit to the underside: a stunted steel bomb with a pink tip, others with explosives painted white.

The Punisher is a fixed-wing glider, "reusable", which looks like a black Tintin rocket and carries bigger loads, in longer, plastic cartridges. In one big box are a pair of black Punisher fuselages with a design in white on their wings: a Ukrainian trident atop crossbones, a customised Jolly Roger. "We're under the command of the Armed Forces of Ukraine", says Stas of the complex chain of command that does and doesn't control this unit, "but we like to think of ourselves as pirates." Stas shows his tattoo of the same design (the following day, I got one too).

The sweltering night will soon draw in, close and humid after the thunderstorms; a low, pale sun sinks over the shrubbery, and a tabby cat sleeps and stretches on a bench press. "This is an entirely new kind of warfare we're fighting", says Stas. "It's radio-electronic warfare that guides the actual battle on the ground. The major military powers have advanced technology, but most American and British doctrine, and almost all of its recent experience, has been counter-insurgency. What we are doing is using that technology, but pitched *against* a major army, on our own ground. Most of the time we feel like the fucking Taliban!"

"We used to do at least five Punisher and drone flights a day – now it's more like two. We need more and more, because they're sending 3,000 drones a month against us. Faced with such a powerful enemy, you have to think: what's he going to do next? What's the next counter-measure that we'll have to counter? In drone warfare, you have always to think a step ahead. For every one drone we have, they have ten. They make them industrially in bit batches or get them from the Iranians; we buy them with money from touring. To beat them, we have to outsmart them."

The Russians "have a lot of military grade cameras with a range of 10km, along a road across the river. These help guide missiles to a target, and can intercept the movements of our troops. So we destroy the cameras, and that gives our military at least two weeks free passage along that road. Obviously we're also hitting tanks, vehicles and artillery." The famous Ukrainian parking tickets – "Yes, exactly".

A vehicle pulls up beyond the metal gate, and here comes the rest of the drone crew: Andriy covered in camouflage and sweat, holding his helmet: and the warmest of greetings. "Don't hug me, I'm dripping!" I don't care. "Let me get out of this shit, have a shower ..." Here too are Miroslav, a former marine from Los Angeles; Zhenya, a sniper; Serhii, a military veteran; and Kolya, a volunteer.

Once out on the veranda, Andriy wears shorts and a Johnny Cash t-shirt he bought on tour in Los Angeles. "This is how we've lived for the last year. And we're very privileged – a lot of our people are spending the night in trenches. We had an apartment in town, reserved for police and military guys, but it worried the neighbours – they feared they might be targets, so we came here."

Andriy and Stas are just back from the tour, and Andriy usually likes to open a conversation with chat about rock and roll, or the world out there. But here and now, he picks up the theme already under discussion. "This is the first war of drones", he says. "It's about who learns faster, who is smarter. You have to do it that way. There is no way to win this war with just a rifle on your shoulder." However, he adds, "sometimes we do take RPGs they've left behind when they escape from us. And we give them back: hey there, you lost your RPG, we found it for you – have it back! Boom."

He says of the small arsenal indoors: "We offer good value for money. We're spending $6-700 per drone", he says, "right up to the enemy's front line. It's a good, cheap way to kill Russians. Every time I sing a song, I can buy between

30 and 50 of these. But of course", he adds, picking up from where Stas laid off: "you know where this drone warfare strategy came from? Fucking ISIS!"

"These 16 months", says Andriy, "have taken me from being afraid to go on the first line, to being bored on the second line. I have to be where the fighting is, and to do it our way." Andriy explains what "our way" means. "Not long ago, we were in action with a group of special forces from America and Britain. These were good guys, and we appreciate their help very much. But they don't quite get it. They use an interesting combination of words: they say we cannot fight with 'an unacceptable level of risk', and we laughed. 'Do you have air support?' they ask. No, we said. 'Do you have an evacuation cover?' No, I answered. 'Then what are you doing here?' They asked. 'We are going to attack the enemy', we said. They say we cannot operate on the basis of 'unacceptable risk'. And we say: I'm sorry, that does not translate into Ukrainian. For us, there is no such thing. We are Apaches, fighting for our survival. We are not here to fight in Afghanistan or Iraq, and then go home. We are at home."

He makes his point by discussing soldiers he has encountered: "There's a guy, he's a sniper from the 59th Brigade. He got shot up and lost his arm. But he carried his badly wounded comrade over his shoulders for 15 kilometres, to safety. We do this stuff ourselves – there was no 'cover' or 'evacuation plan'. His skin was totally blue." By contrast: "look at the kind of soldiers the Russians are. Last night, they hit a grain store in Odesa, ready to ship grain to people in Africa. How many people will go hungry because of what they've done?"

Á propos: it's soon time for dinner, and Andriy goes inside, to the stove. Customised flags line the kitchen walls. One has a pastiche of Leonardo's *Last Supper:* the Christ figure a skeleton wearing military garb and helmet, with a machine gun and other weapons laid out on the table. The disciples are dead-robotic soldiers, like on a heavy metal album. "Sometimes we go for a grill", says Andriy, "but mostly we cook for ourselves." It's his turn this evening.

The crew gathers for servings of meat, beans, fries and delicious, strong goat's cheese made by Kolya's mother, to whom the company accordingly raises a toast of Coca-Cola Zero. There's animated conversation, bordering on anger. There's a company, "a fucking *Ukrainian* company", says Andriy, from which the crew buys Punisher glider-drones, but which refuses to repair them because they have been modified for military action. "We've done $850,000-worth of fucking business with this company. Did anyone tell them there's a war on?" Conversation barely drifts from war; it's as though the world out there – of touring, playing, fans – were like a dream from which we've now awoken. "When we leave to perform or take a break", says Andriy, "there's that major part of me, of us, that just wants to come back here as soon as possible. We call this our vacation."

Stas drove me back to town, and my hotel. "God, I could kill a beer", he confessed. "But I can't. It's not easy, and we're a strange group of people, thrown together like this. We didn't know each other at all before, apart from Andriy and me, and now we're sleeping, eating and working together 24/7, fighting a fucking war! Tomorrow, we're going to get a fucking camera that's causing our boys a load of trouble. I'll keep you informed." Next evening, he sends a video: direct hit. We see the drone approach the mast, close in, look the camera right in the eye ... and WHAM! "No signal."

The following night, the crew is out on the back terrace, with rain beating down on the canvas canopy. There's a stark contrast to the animation of 48 hours ago; a cloud hangs over the company even heavier than those above. The Russian enemy had located the boys' forward Punisher launch position and fired a salvo of mortars. They missed, but narrowly. "We had to move, quick – and we're lucky to be back here this evening", says Andriy, direct and severe.

In a few days time, there'll be an occasion in London that illustrates international solidarity with Ukraine at its most creative. The veteran idol of Ukrainian football, Andrey Shevchenko, who played for Dynamo Kyiv, AC Milan and Chelsea, has – with the captain of the Ukrainian national side Oleksandr Zinchenko then of Everton FC – organised a "Game4Ukraine" at Stamford Bridge, between two all-star teams of retired and current players. We joke about Chelsea trying to "clean up their act after being owned by [Russian oligarch] Roman Abramovich after twenty years!" There will be a musical show at half time, and BoomBox are invited to perform; Gilmour may join them. With what drop-jawed pride and excitement Andriy recounted, during one of our early meetings, his call from Gilmour, wanting to collaborate for "Hey Hey Rise Up". Tonight, though, news of a further collaboration takes second place to the day's mortar attack. "I spoke to David today", says Andriy. "About playing at this football game. I said I wasn't sure. Look: we have a lot of work to do there. I want to take out those fuckers who nearly killed us today. Instead: we've got to rehearse, go all the way through Poland to get fucking visas, fly to London, go to a hotel, *just for one song*? We'll be good boys, and we'll have to do a soundcheck, but it won't be our soundcheck, it'll be shitty sound in a stadium. And afterwards, they'll offer me a Limoncello in the fucking corporate hospitality suite, and tell us how wonderful we are, and" – he winces – "photos photos, more fucking photos. Just for one song?! All I want to do is stay here and kill Russians!"

Stas is vexed, grappling with some problem on his laptop, which of course isn't on his laptop, it's somewhere on the front line. The sky clears, and a low, fat, red sun hangs over the horizon and the river; a pale tangerine light wraps the steaming eventide and sodden land. "I realise", Andriy thinks aloud, "that this, down here in Mykolaiv, is another life. It's different even than Kyiv, another world. It's like World War One. There's the world, here's the battlefield. And after that mortar attack, tomorrow will be a very busy day."

*Volodymyr Kubijovyc, ed. *Encyclopedia of Ukraine*, University of Toronto Press, 1994 (Vol III).

Ed Vulliamy is a British-born, Irish-Welsh journalist and writer. He was born (1954) and raised in London, and attended Hertford College, Oxford, won an Open Scholarship, wrote a thesis on the Northern Irish Troubles, and graduated in Politics and Philosophy. He became a journalist and wrote for The Guardian *and* The Observer *for many years. Amongst the numerous regions he has covered during his career were Ireland (1970s-1980s), Bosnia (1990s-2000s), and the United States and Mexico at the same time (1990s and 2000s). He is the author of five books, more recently* Amexica: War along the Borderline *(2010),* The War Is Dead, Long Live the War: Bosnia: The Reckoning *(2012),* When Words Fail: A Life With Music, War and Peace *(2018).*

His discovery with British television reporter Penny Marshall of the notorious Serb concentration camps of Omarska and Trnopolje in Bosnia — followed by their graphic accounts of the conditions of the prisoners — led to the documentary Omarska's Survivors: Bosnia 1992, *and is widely credited with contributing to the establishment of the International Criminal Tribunal for the Former Yugoslavia in The Hague. He became the first journalist since the Nuremberg Trials to testify at an international war crimes tribunal, appearing for the prosecution in ten trials at the ICTY, including those of the Bosnian Serb leaders Radovan Karadžic and General Ratko Mladić. For his work in Bosnia, Italy, the US and Iraq, he won a James Cameron Award and An Amnesty International Media Award, and has been named International Reporter of the Year twice. In 2016, after 31 years, he left the staff of* The Guardian *and* The Observer *to become a full-time author, journalist and film-researcher — but continues to work regularly as a reporter for both newspapers and Guardian Films.*

AG CUIMHNÍU AR AN ÚCRÁIN
I MACHAIRE RABHARTAIGH

Do Tatiana agus Patrick Breslin

Cathal Ó Searcaigh

(1)

Tchím bodógaí mara
i mbéal na toinne
is spéir an mhurlais
os cionn Innis Bó Finne.

Os mo choinne, tráigh
mhíngheal shoilseach:
Sna dumhaigh, tá uabhair
fáis sa mhuiríneach.

Tá an treathlach mhór
ina shuí go rí-dheas
ag móradh a Íomhá féin
sa tsáile gormghlas.

Síocháin agus suaimhneas
fa mhuir is fa thír,
chan ionann is an Úcráin
mar a bhfuil ár go síor.

Ár agus slad oíche is lá!
Crá croí domh a gcás,
an doirteadh fola, a mbailte
á ndíothú is a mbás.

(2)

As uaigh réabtha i mo chroí
éiríonn na cnámharlaigh;
Iad scallta, feannta ó fhéith
is ó fheoil, saighdiúrí

A bhásaigh san ár, sa phláigh,
sa deargadh fola i mBucha,
i Mariapol, i Zaparizhzhia
agus i gcraos Ifrinn Baghmut.

Iad ag súil nach gníomh in aisce
a bhí ina mbás; an cath tréan
a throid siad ar son fuascailt a dtíre
ón leatrom agus ón léan.

Faraoir, ar an uair chinniúnach seo,
níl agam ach focla gan bhrí
le teangaidh a thabhairt dá n-iobairt,
na stócaigh seo a cuireadh ó chrích

i réabadh piléar, i roiseadh pleascán
ar ármhá catha sa Úcráin.
Caidé a thig liom a dhéanamh ach á dtaisí
á adhlacadh i bfód mo dháin?

(3)

Tráth den tsaol, bhí siad ann,
Iadsan a bhíodh ag maíomh
as réabhlóid na Sóivéide, as Lenin,
as cinniúnt ghlórmhar na Rúise.
Dá mba á dtoil é, is cinnte
go n-ardóidh an Bratach Dearg
ar cheann-cheathrúna na hEorpa.
B'fhada leo go mbeadh soiscéal na Sóivéide:

an tréad seachas an duine is slua-dhearcadh an Stáit,
a bhuanú go fada agus go leitheadach.
An bholscaireacht bhithiúnta sin is an bhréag
a d'fhágfadh muid i ngeimhlí go h-éag.

Tráth den tsaol, bhí siad ann,
iadsan a chreid go diagánta
gur slánú an tsaoil a bhí i Lenin
is gur Parthas na coitiantachta
a bhí i dtiarnas fada Stalin.
Is cé gur loisc Jan Palach é féin ina bheatha
i bPrague ag achainí ar an tsaol
le scréad ghéibhinneach a bháis
gan géilleadh do réimeas na Sóivéide,
níor loic ar a n-iontaoibh siúd.
Sa bholscaireacht bhithiúnta sin agus sa bhréag
a d'fhagfadh muid i ngeimhlí go h-éag.

(4)

Is fada ó chum mé
aon dán le haiteas.
Tá aighneas is achrann
ag cur smál ar mo dhóchas.

Idir an lag agus an lom
siúlaim amach sa tsruth.
Tá mé ar thóir mo dháin
sa raic agus sa bhruth.

Tá ré dhorcha chugainn
mar a bhíothas á thuar.
Ar an traígh fholamh is an lá
ag dul ó sholas, tá sé fuar, fuar.

THINKING OF UKRAINE
IN MACHAIRE RABHARTAIGH

For Tatiana and Patrick Breslin

———

Cathal Ó Searcaigh

(1)

Seaweed lies thrown
at the edge of the tide
and over Innis Bó Finne
floats a mackerel sky.

Before me, a smooth
lime-white strand.
In the dunes, a rampant
growth of marram grass.

A cormorant, its wings
spread regally wide,
stands admiring its reflection
in the blue-green tide.

Calmness, tranquillity,
over land, over water,
far, far from Ukraine's
unremitting slaughter.

Endless killing, scorched earth!
The heart is breaking
for broken, bloodstained homes,
for death, for displacement.

(2)

From a desecrated grave in my heart
the skeletons arise;
scorched, stripped of flesh
and tendon, soldiers

Who died in war, in plague
and carnage in Bucha,
in Mariupol, in Zaparizhia
and in the hellfire of Bakhmut.

They trust their death
was not in vain; the hard struggle
to lift up their country
from oppression, from suffering.

But at this fateful moment
I have only inadequate words
to give voice to their sacrifice,
the youths who were destroyed

by ripping bullets, by rending bombs
on battlefields in Ukraine.
Under the earth of my poem
I will lay their remains.

(3)

There were those, they had their time,
those who celebrated
the Soviet revolution, celebrated Lenin,
celebrated Russia's glorious destiny.
Had they got their way,
the Red Flag would have flown
over Europe's capitals.
They yearned for the Soviet gospel,

the herd over the individual and the groupthink of the state,
to be set in stone far and wide.
That evil propaganda and the lie
that would make a bondage of our lives.

There were those, they had their time,
those who had faith
in Lenin as the world's redeemer
and that Stalin's long reign
was a paradise for the masses.
And although Jan Palach immolated himself
in Prague, imploring the world
with the fearful cry of his death
not to surrender to Soviet rule,
they never wavered in their loyalty.
To that twisted propaganda, to the lie
that would mean slavery for life.

(4)

It seems forever since I took
pleasure in writing a poem.
Hostilities and conflict
have corroded all my hopes.

Desolate, despairing,
I walk through high tide,
scrambling for a poem
in what it leaves behind.

The dark time is on us
that has been foretold.
The empty shore, as daylight
diminishes, is cold, cold.

Translated, from the Irish, by Paddy Bushe.

Cathal Ó Searcaigh was born and grew up on a hill farm in Mín an Leá, Gort an Choirce, an Irish-speaking glen and Gaeltacht community in the northwest of County Donegal. The author of 20 volumes of poetry, three plays and four works of prose in Irish, as well as five books in English, he is a leading figure in the remarkable renaissance of Irish-language writing in our time. He is a member of Aosdána, and continues to live on the home ground of his parents.

Paddy Bushe was born in Dublin in 1948, and now lives in Waterville, Co. Kerry. He writes in both Irish and English, and has published nine collections of poetry, most recently To Ring in Silence: New and Selected Poems *(The Dedalus Press, 2008), a bilingual volume, and* My Lord Buddha of Carraig Eánna *(The Dedalus Press, 2012).*

IF A TRANSLATION FALLS IN AN EMPTY LIBRARY, DOES IT MAKE A SOUND?

WAR AND TRANSLATION

———

Iaroslava Strikha

Double deadlines.

Every European culture, of course, is at its core a translation culture. That might be easy to overlook in the current anglophone literary landscape, which may trick the readers into believing that translations are a fancy accessory rather than a load-bearing structure, an Instagrammable monochrome cover rather than an integral part of your library. But dig deeper into the soil of any European culture, and you'll hit the unavoidable skeleton of translated classical antiquity and the Bible at its foundations. That said, translations are much harder to overlook in postcolonial cultures. It has become a common-place in translation studies that translation, broadly understood, is an essential paradigm for colonized cultures that were not lucky enough to have acquired statehood early on. Existing in the fraught liminal space between the coloniz-ing and colonized culture, explaining and justifying the persecuted culture to the powerful establishment, and otherwise playing the game of literary history in nightmare mode, practitioners of colonial and postcolonial cultures function as translators whether they had set out to do so or not. This is true of Ukrainian culture, among others. As the prominent Ukrainian playwright Mykola Kulish (1892-1937) – ironically, one of the very few Ukrainian writers of his generation to have never dabbled in literary translation – scathingly quipped in the 1920s, we are a nation of hicks and translators. Certainly there are far worse things to be.

The role of an unwitting translator, smuggling in exotic cadences and peddling forbidden cultural wares in a repressive cultural climate, stuck to nearly every writer at the earlier stages of Ukrainian literary history, whether they chose to write in Ukrainian or in Russian. The most notable example would be Nikolai Gogol (1809-1852), best known under the Russified version of his name as a Russian writer (the Ukrainian version of his name is Mykola Hohol; ongoing discussions about whether his role in coining useful imagery for the Russian imperial ideology make his reappropriation as a Ukrainian writer possible or desirable can be vitriolic, if entertaining, if you enjoy recreational bloodbaths). His earlier works, collected under the title *Evenings on a Farm Near Dikanka*, are steeped in Ukrainian folk culture, and it is this cultural pedigree, I would argue, that made Gogol rely heavily on the literary device of *skaz*, or an imitation of an oral narration. Writing from within the fold of the culture that was treated alternately as an ethnographic curio or as a sign of dangerous political resistance by the Russian Empire, Gogol, like many other writers, felt the need for a safety net of a mediating presence of a folksy narrator, a naive country bumpkin who could not be more different from the real author, a sophisticated urbanite with an immaculate grasp of literary techniques. In this, he was far from unique in the nineteenth-century Ukrainian literary landscape, which had more masks than the Carnival of Venice. Even if the aesthetic and linguistic choice to develop a Ukrainian literature did not come with an explicit ethical and political anti-imperial choice, even if Ukrainian culture was being translated into terms legible within the Russian imperial mainstream, writers often felt the need to speak within quotation marks, from the point of view of "the folk" rather than themselves, as a ventriloquist, ethnographer or indeed a translator.

Far from being consigned to earlier stages of Ukrainian literary history, an act of self-translation as a method for constructing one's cultural identity has become a prominent plot point in contemporary Ukrainian literature since the Russo-Ukrainian war began in 2014. Russian military aggression made many hyphenated identities less tenable, as can be attested by the literary trajectory of Volodymyr Rafeyenko, a writer born in Donetsk, in the east of Ukraine, who started his literary career as a Russian-language novelist published in Russia. Despite winning some acclaim in the Russian literary market, including the prestigious Russian Prize in 2010 and 2012 and the New Literature Prize in 2014, he chose to switch to writing in Ukrainian in response to the Russian propaganda that cited "the defence of Russian speakers" as justification for the Russian occupation of his home town. Forced to flee the occupied Donetsk in 2014, he said that the Russian propaganda made him feel like "simultaneously a victim and a pretext of the war". His first Ukrainian-language (or, rather, bilingual) novel, *Mondegreen* (2019), explores how the transition from the monolingual Russian-language space to a more culturally and linguistically diverse mindset grants access to new plots and narrative modes. The novel's protagonist is, like the author, an internally displaced person trying to make a home in both a new city and a new language, weaving a new life out of quotations and misquotations from very different sources, befriending folk tale characters and mediating between eras and genres driven by the free-floating associative linguistic logic familiar to everyone who's just beginning to learn a new language.

Of course, older and more recent books that feature a portrait of narrator as a young (self-) translator are not the only translations happening in Ukrainian literary history. From the very earliest days, translations *sensu stricto* had played an integral part in creating a land of our own, a Ukraine that became an established literary fact well before it had a chance to become a political fact. Translations create a shared space of dialogue, but they are also often the space of struggle for independence, a way for the subaltern to strike back and affirm the rights and potential of their culture. The imperial culture had the whole repressive apparatus at its back, complete with the army, the police and the ability to put its opponents in mass graves. The other side had writing, and the writing had to be seductively beautiful to convert its readers to a more dangerous but also more exciting future. The fact that we are still here to fight, translate and talk about our favourite books in Ukrainian to anyone who doesn't run away fast enough is testament that it was, and it did.

The repressive apparatus of the Russian Empire saw translations into Ukrainian as a deeply subversive activity from the very beginning. The Valuev Circular of 1863, a secret decree of the Minister of Internal Affairs of the Russian Empire Pyotr Valuev, who famously maintained that "a separate Little Russian language never existed, doesn't exist, and couldn't exist", banned most publications in Ukrainian. The decree was prompted by the translation of the New Testament submitted for approval to the Most Holy Synod, to which General Governor of Kyiv Nikolai Annenkov noted, "Having translated the Bible into Little Russian dialect, proponents of the Little Russian party would get the Little Russian language, so to speak, recognized as independent, and they won't stop at that and, highlighting the independence of their language, will demand autonomy for Little Russia." While his faith in the efficacy of bans proved misguided, his faith in the power of translations was not.

Aside from fighting for national self-determination, translators into Ukrainian were also working to develop culture as an inclusive diverse venture where a public of different faiths and ethnicities could develop a sense of empathy and solidarity against the repressive regime. When the first Ukrainian-language theatre opened its doors in Kyiv in 1907, after decades of bans, its director Mykola Sadovsky thought it important to start their first season with a staging of the Ukrainian translation of Evgeny Chirikov's

The Jews, a drama about the Kishinev Pogrom of 1903. A theatre critic wrote that, despite certain artistic shortcomings, "The play is important because it fosters deep love for the suffering nation … and an outrage against the regime that allows predatory abuse of innocent victims. And outrage is the first step towards actions to destroy the evil." By the time when the Ukrainian theatre was shut down as part of the reactionary measures introduced at the beginning of World War I, it had successfully staged Ukrainian translations of many classical Yiddish-language plays, including Sholem Asch's *God of Vengeance*. When that play was staged on Broadway in 1923, the cast was arrested for public indecency because of a lesbian seduction scene. Ukrainian viewers in 1908 were more open-minded, even if the staging did cause backlash from the monarchist Russian ultra-nationalist Black Hundreds that claimed that the play aimed to "awaken separatism in the Little Russian people following the Jewish example." A Yiddish-language anti-religious lesbian drama playing a part in the awakening Ukrainian national aspirations is certainly an endearing thought, and not as absurd as it might seem at first glance: after all, the anti-colonial undermining of hierarchies often went hand-in-hand with undermining patriarchal norms.

Compared to our heroic predecessors, contemporary Ukrainian translators are extremely privileged. We have a state to protect us: a state that earlier generations of Ukrainian writers and translators wrote into existence, no less. Regular missile attacks notwithstanding, we are free to translate whatever we choose, from the latest spicy BookTok phenomena to the venerable classics. And how is translating A.S. Byatt, Susan Sontag or Julian Barnes when a Russian missile strikes a couple blocks away from your place different from translating them when one doesn't? Having done both, I consider myself a bit of an expert. Being a reader of war literature, I felt as reasonably well-prepared as one can ever be for the heavy bovine shudder that your house makes before it, and you, settle back into calm realization: this one wasn't meant for you. (As Victoria Amelina, a Ukrainian writer killed by a Russian missile in the summer of 2023, wrote in her poem, "Air-raid sirens across the country / It feels like everyone is brought out / For execution […] This time not you; all clear"; transl. by Anatoly Kudryavitsky). What no war memoir or fiction had adequately prepared me for is the fact that normal life will continue, and rolling electricity cuts or kamikaze drones don't abstain you from meeting your deadlines and don't wipe away the joy of finding the best synonym for the sentence you are working on. What changes is a sense of a double deadline, especially nagging when you work on hefty novels with longer production cycles: will your publishing house, your readers, your colleagues and your country exist by the time you manage to complete the translation? I wish these were idle questions.

On the one hand, the Ukrainian cultural scene has been undergoing a very unlikely boom. After a deep slump in the first months of the full-scale invasion, the book market rebounded. The costs of book production might be soaring, but so are the print runs and the lists of titles. The central street of Kyiv is flanked on either end with two exhibition spaces hosting large shows of Ukrainian artists, with lines of viewers stretching across half the block, and if you want to take a rest, there's a convenient new bookshop midway between them. It's called Sens (Ukrainian word for *meaning*), complete with Guardians of Meaning signs on the uniforms of their guards. Of course, you'll need to be lucky to find a seat in their café area, because it's usually filled to bursting at all times. During a missile attack, you are supposed to stay behind two walls. If you look at the crowds in bookshops, you might assume that everybody's building the second wall of books.

This stubborn insistence on enjoying fine art and fine literature, while endearing, may also seem a bit surreal in its precariousness. At the time of writing, in the winter and spring of 2024, the US Congress has not passed a decision to send further military aid to Ukraine, with the Republicans holding Ukraine's survival hostage to their electoral campaign. While Ukraine's European allies have been both ramping up production and finding caches of ammunition to buy for Ukraine, they cannot fully compensate for the US stalling. Depleting supplies of ammunition for Western air defence systems make the country more vulnerable to regular cruise and ballistic missile attacks. At present, approximately 80% of Ukraine's power-generating facilities had been destroyed by Russian air strikes. Most relevant to the future of book publishing in Ukraine is the fact that the Zmiiv Thermal Power Plant, which supplies energy to the Kharkiv Region, was destroyed by a Russian missile on 22 March 2024.

Kharkiv, a city with a rich literary history and the pre-war population of over a million (slightly more than Dublin city and its suburbs), has been a centre of book printing for decades. Severe electricity shortages in the city, where rolling electricity cuts last hours, have forced printing presses to either work night shifts not to overload the scant power supply, or to purchase fuel-powered generators. These emergency measures mean that the Ukrainian publishing scene is facing unpredictable printing delays, from several weeks to up to two months, and sky-rocketing prices due to higher production costs. Printing presses also become targets of Russian missile attacks, either calculated to quash Ukrainian culture or designed as mindless acts of terror: sending an imprecise anti-ship missile into a dense urban area means that sooner or later a printing press, too, will get hit. The most recent attack on a printing press working with several children's publishers occurred on 20 March 2024. In this atmosphere of gathering gloom, translating sometimes feels like racing against time. I'm a fast translator, but a missile is faster, so I keep asking myself if I will manage to complete my work before we are knocked off the grid.

Of course, electricity cuts are not the worst possible scenario. If military support doesn't come, the front might crumble catastrophically. In that case, Europe faces a crisis far greater: many millions more refugees, authoritarians worldwide emboldened by the democratic world's complacency. For Ukrainians, the threat is more direct: if genocidal rhetoric coming from Russian state-run TV channels is to be believed, everybody involved in culture production will have no land to call our own except the mass grave in which we'll be buried. We have reasons to believe that threat. Oleksandr Kysliuk, the Ukrainian translator of Aristotle's *Politics* and Xenophon's *Anabasis*, was shot by Russians in the occupied Irpin on 5 March 2022. Volodymyr Vakulenko, a children's writer and translator who ended up under the Russian occupation in the Kharkiv Region, disappeared and was discovered in Grave 319 in a mass burial site outside the city of Izium. The collective democratic world might still rally to help Ukraine to protect ourselves and the rule-based world order. If it doesn't, my main question as a translator is, *if a translation falls inside an empty library, does it make a sound?*

And while we are here and our metaphorical library is very crowded indeed, we make as much noise as possible. As we held the book launch of my translation of *Regarding the Pain of Others* by Susan Sontag in early March 2024, more than a hundred readers braved the unseasonal snow and cold to cram into the industrial loft-style space of Sens Bookshop. A friend jokes that the crowd is buying up books for the inevitable electricity cuts, when less screen time would mean more reading time. We are surrounded by shelves upon shelves of books in Ukrainian, both translated and original, and I find myself envying the translators and readers in other countries who will discover our vibrant and daring literature, one of the best-kept but exciting literary secrets on the continent. Our translators, past and present, have been instrumental to nurturing these literary woods. Now many of them are setting their literary pursuits aside to join the Armed Forces in Ukraine and defend the space where our culture is possible. The list includes but is not limited to Yevhen Lir, the Ukrainian translator of Robert W. Chambers, David Lynch and Aleister Crowley, who had fundraised and delivered 300 cars to the army before enlisting; Anna Sorochynska, the translator of the autobiography of Theodore Roosevelt; and Ostap Ukrainets, the translator of David Mitchell, H.P. Lovecraft and Szczepan Twardoch, among others. This article, like all our literary adventures, is only possible due to the efforts of Ukrainian men and women, including translators, who are currently writing our history.

Iaroslava Strikha (born in Kyiv in 1988) is a literary translator and critic based in Kyiv. She holds a PhD in Slavic Languages and Literatures from Harvard University. Her translation credits include Walden *by Henry David Thoreau,* Maus *by Art Spiegelman,* Shosha *by Isaac Bashevis Singer,* Life After Life *and* God in Ruins *by Kate Atkinson,* Ways of Seeing *by John Berger,* England, England *by Julian Barnes,* The Children's Book *by A.S. Byatt and* Regarding the Pain of Others *by Susan Sontag, among other texts. She's currently translating* Possession *by A.S. Byatt. Her translation of* Behind the Scenes at the Museum *by Kate Atkinson received the Best Book Award of the Lviv Book Forum in the Best Book in Translation category in 2018.*

WAR, FAITH, AND COFFEE:
A WEEK WITH KYIV'S POETS

—

Amelia Glaser

A belief in living, against all odds.

My hotel in Kyiv had a café area with colorful porcelain teddy bears balanced precariously on built-in bookshelves. There was no barista, but if you flagged down a hotel worker, they would bring you a decent cappuccino from the restaurant. It seemed an odd backdrop for Pavlo Vyshybaba, a tall man in his 30s with military fatigues, a thick beard and deep blue eyes, but he had just arrived from the front, and this was the only time and place we could meet. "I am not an elitist about poetry", Pavlo told me when we sat down to our coffee. His sixty-four thousand followers on Facebook include teenagers and fellow soldiers, hairdressers and schoolteachers from across Ukraine and beyond, who respond, collectively, to his poems with thousands of likes and shares. A poem he posted in March 2022, shortly after Russia's full-scale invasion of Ukraine, modifies the common Ukrainian Easter greeting, "Christ has risen, Glorify him".

> Five a.m. Kyiv time
> in the black sky, a fire
> from a star or downed missiles
> a Nation's born, glorify it.

Poetry and war in Ukraine are not irreconcilable. As Ukraine gives birth to a new national identity, poets have glorified this birth. And they are defining something like a new faith. "My poems should be legible to people who don't know anything about poetry", Pavlo tells me. "I sometimes read them aloud to the guys in my platoon. Some of them try writing, too." Originally from Kramatorsk, in Ukraine's war-torn Donbas, Vyshybaba was a journalist and eco-activist before joining the army following the full scale invasion in 2022. He campaigned against fur-production in Ukraine, and founded a vegan restaurant. Like many writers from Eastern Ukraine, Vyshybaba made a complete switch from his native Russian to writing in Ukrainian during the early stages of the Donbas war. A lot of Pavlo's Facebook posts are fundraisers to help wounded soldiers or to raise money for his battalion. Occasionally a selfie features Vyshybaba on the frontlines cuddling a cat. The proceeds for his popular recent collection go to the Ukrainian defense.

We needed coffee that morning. The night before, Russia bombarded the city with 32 long range and ballistic missiles, and the city's air defense shot all of them down. Kyiv has far better defense resources than the rest of the country. Jessica Zychowicz, the director of Ukraine's Fulbright program, texted to ask how I was doing after the long night in a bomb shelter. "There's a saying", she wrote, "Kyiv is not a city that drinks tea." While poetry cannot shoot down missiles, the week I spent in Kyiv gave me the strong impression that poets in Ukraine are helping to buoy the nation, both in its cities and on its frontlines. As the nation's leaders worked to convince the world to support their physical defense of self-determination, the Ukrainian poets I met in Kyiv (mostly in the city's vibrant cafes, over strong coffee) spoke to me about finding a new language, about the values Ukraine is coming to stand for, and about keeping faith in a time of war.

There is a very real sense that poetry in Ukraine has gone to war. This year's prestigious Shevchenko Prize for poetry was shared by two poets who have been fighting on the front, Yaryna Chornohuz and Dmytro Lazutkin. Serhiy Zhadan, the well known Kharkiv poet and rock musician, recently joined the National Guard. The young poet and soldier Artur Dron just published his first book of poems. Elizaveta Zharikova, a poet and musician who was wounded in action last summer, has continued to publish and make music while recovering.

In mid-September 2022, Ukraine retook the city of Balakliya, which had been occupied by Russian troops for six months. A video went viral showing three soldiers stood in front of a billboard bearing the Russian flag that read, "We are with Russia! One people!" One soldier climbed up to pull down the flag. In doing so, he revealed a picture of the Ukrainian poet Taras Shevchenko and an excerpt from the 1848 epic poem "The Caucasus", which had been covered by the Russian poster. It ends with the words,

> The truth is with you, glory is with you
> And a sacred will!

The video concludes with an image of the Romantic Ukrainian bard dressed in the 21st century uniform of the Ukrainian army.

The nighttime missile attacks are terrifying, but during the day, Kyiv is full of a palpable creativity and will to live. A billboard on the nearby Palace of Sport advertises an upcoming stadium reading by Serhiy Zhadan. New book-store-cafés boast contemporary Ukrainian literature sections that seem to have doubled since the full-scale invasion. Musicians playing in a park harmonized, as though intentionally, with an air raid siren. At the PEN Ukraine writers club, the poet Yaryna Chornohuz, who has been fighting in a reconnaissance battalion since 2020, discussed Milan Kundera with a panel of translators and cultural critics. The PEN Center, in addition to its artwork, books, and stylishly designed space for readings, boasts a Russian missile, which a group brought back from one of its many missions to transport supplies and put on literary events in Eastern Ukraine.

"War and art are completely different", Chornohuz said when we met for coffee the following day. "Art is a form of imitation. War demands truth. But poetry about combat allows you to step back, to reflect." Chornohuz, who is 28 years old, enlisted in 2019, and went to the frontline in 2020. Her book, *[dasein: in defence of presence]*, is inspired by the question of actively being in the world.

> a voice won't go out if it knows how to be
> there's a soldier girl in every woman
> who will have to pass through the dark alone
> and all help is unnecessary
> and all shoulders are redundant
> and all the burden is for two hands alone
> and all loves are lived and left
> and all the solitude is yours
> and the world's whole night is like one sun for one life

"When the war is over", Chornohuz tells me, "I'd like to study philosophy." Her war poems explore the possibility of a true subjecthood. How does one become a subject in the world? Through the insistence on freedom, even against all odds, she suggests. In another poem, Chornohuz writes:

> i want to sing, while I still can,
> of freedom,
> for which, after endless years
> of combat

it would seem,
there's no room left

What does it mean to fight for presence? To fight for the ability to be a subject? Hannah Arendt, in *The Human Condition*, writes, "Only sheer violence is mute, and for this reason violence alone can never be great."[1] Poetry is a way of holding onto humanity in a time of war. Of ensuring that this fight to defend Ukraine's sovereignty is not a war of sheer violence, but a war for subjecthood. Chornohuz shared the Shevchenko prize with Dmytro Lazutkin, a poet and journalist in his mid-forties who has also been fighting on the front, and was recently appointed spokesperson for Ukraine's Defense Ministry.

Lazutkin's new book, *Zakladka*, is his tenth, and literally translates to "placeholder". But the book cover is designed such that the word is broken into its three syllables, suggesting an alternate reading: "*za kladka*" or "stone by stone". The book opens with a poem about spring, transience and faith:

in frost-covered March or in April
when stars are like gashes from knives
find the words someone needs,
find the words – while everyone's alive

Lazutkin has worked on musical projects from hip-hop to an oratorio, and many of his poems follow a strong meter and rhyme, but with unexpected variants, lending themselves to vocal performance. In another poem, Lazutkin writes of a bombed-out school. The students were evacuated, but the school has been defiled:

in the geography classroom
hang shreds
of a tattered world map

The bookstores in Kyiv are full. On display, however, are constant reminders of the fallen. The children's writer Volodymyr Vakulenko was killed during the large massacres of towns occupied by Russia in early 2022. PEN Ukraine has published a collection that includes his poetry, as well as his "Diary of an occupation". Vakulenko, realizing he may not survive, buried the diary beside a cherry tree. Following the liberation of the town, and the confirmation that Vakulenko had been killed, the celebrated young novelist Viktoria Amelina unearthed the diary with the help of Vakulenko's heartbroken father. "My worst fear is coming true", Amelina wrote in the preface.

> "I'm in the middle of a new Executed Renaissance. Like in the 1930s, they're killing Ukrainian artists, manuscripts are vanishing, memory's being erased. It seems as though the times are getting mixed up and frozen as we wait for some kind of solution: I'm combing the Sobodan soil not only in search of the notes of one of our own, but for all the lost Ukrainian literature: the second half of Khvylovy's [novel] *The Woodcocks*, Kulish's plays, Stus's last poems, diaries from the Holodomor, the old Ukrainian prints burnt in the Kyiv library in 1964. All our losses, from the old prints to Volodymyr's diary seem like one big text that no one will read..."[2]

Amelina's preface is dated June 3, 2023. A month later, she was killed by a missile that hit a pizzeria in Kramatorsk.

Alongside Vakulenko's diary, the bookstores in Kyiv displayed *Poems from the battlement [Virshi z biinytsi]*, a poetry collection by Maksym Kryvtsov that came not long before the poet was killed in action in early 2024. The poems are darkly ironic, sometimes prophetically fatalistic.

> When will a rocket
> finally kill me?
> When will a grad
> Burn me up?
>
> I'll smoke this world
> like a cigarette,
>
> I jump into my sleeping bag,
> Pull off my socks
> And write to you on Telegram:
> Everything's fine.[3]

After Victoria Amelina died, Kryvtsov posted to his Facebook page, "the Russians have again taken the life of a wonderful person."[4] The chain of writers mourning one another is heartbreaking. Those who remain to defend and rebuild the country have a strong sense of survivor guilt. Despite and because of these deaths, poetry keeps emerging from Ukrainian soil. "It's important for me to show that even after a genocide, we can remain human", Kateryna Kalytko told me. "Here is a shelling and something else happened over there. Here (forgive me!) someone was killed. Everything keeps getting interrupted and stitched back together. The seams are all visible." Kalytko spoke to me about the guilt she felt when in 2014, during the Revolution of Dignity, snipers opened fire on on Kyiv's Maidan, killing over 100 unarmed protesters. "I was on the Maidan then, and I still blame myself for surviving when they died. This survivor's guilt intensifies each time something happens. That pizzeria, where Victoria Amelina was killed – I ate there three weeks earlier."

Poetry is a way of asserting agency, even if it's by meditating on physical destruction, even as tens of thousands have been killed. A tattered world map. The tormented soil. These material products of war are personified in contemporary poetry. Kateryna Kalytko's 2023 book, *The order of the silent (Orden movchal-nyts')*, won the Shevchenko prize last year. In one poem Kalytko writes in the voice of the earth:

Ось що скаже земля, коли знову зійдеш на цю твердь –
навіть коли вона чорна груднева твань:
можеш від мене втекти, можеш у мене померти,
та найважливіші історії – завжди про подолання;
тільки й життя, що по той бік твоїх страхів,
тільки й притулку – груддя,
що до ніг налипає.

This is what the earth will say, when you step onto terra firma again –
even if it's black December murk:
you can run from me, you can die on me,
and the most important stories are always about persevering;
and life is only what's beyond your fears;
and the only shelter is the bosom
that sticks to your feet.

The war in Donbas came on the heels of Ukraine's 2013-2014 Revolution of Dignity. Many Ukrainians view this large protest movement, when tens of thousands of Ukrainians occupied their city centers, as the beginning of a new chapter in Ukrainian nationhood. The protest, initially in response to former president Viktor Yanukovych's reversal of a planned agreement with the European Union, became a much broader expression of frustration with corruption, and especially with the former government's adherence to Kremlin policy. "The Revolution of Dignity was a love story", Kalytko said. "People began to understand they were subjects. And they had to find a new language for this. So we've been writing poetry to rebuild this language."

The cover of Kalytko's book, *The order of the silent* is illustrated by the painter Kateryna Kosyanenko, whose exhibit of war paintings I viewed at the Kyiv Cave Monstery. It is a series of large oil paintings in the style of Orthodox Christian icons, but with contemporary themes. A group of people are depicted huddling in a basement in Kyiv. Kosianenko and the curator Victor Gyshchuk wanted to be sure I understood the reference: the subjects of the painting are framed, in their basement shelter, like saints in an Orthodox icon. She is suggesting that they did not come out again. They are now in the afterlife, still waiting for victory. In another painting, people welcome the liberation of a city. The faces are typical faces from icons, but they are wearing tennis shoes and sweatshirts, carrying cell phones. One boy in a hoodie looks disarmingly like my own 10-year-old son. (When I left, Kosianenko gave me a magnet depicting this child.)

Could it be that poetry and art are forming a new religion? "People need a system of rituals", the poet Dasha Suzdalova said. "They need some kind of belief system." Suzdalova shifted to writing in Ukrainian after the 2022 full-scale invasion. She peppers her poems with emojis and references to social media. Her poems often describe a kind of secular new faith:

> the sky had no plans to collapse
> on the street as evening approached

What does it mean to reinvent – or at least reconceptualize – faith? When former president Petro Poroshenko ran for reelection in 2019, his platform was "Army, language, faith". For Poroshenko, "faith" referred specifically to the Ukrainian church, which the former president hoped to permanently separate from the Moscow church. This happened in May of 2022, following Russia's full-scale invasion. But the faith that poets are defining is something different. It has more to do with optimism in the country's future. Language in Ukraine has also changed since the start of the war. Since 2014, many Ukrainians have actively reinvented their language, shifting from Russian to embrace Ukrainian. When I apologized for my grammar mistakes, people sometimes smiled and admitted they were still working on their Ukrainian, too. And native Ukrainian speakers have had to find words for a new reality. The poet and radio journalist Olena Huseinova described a breakdown of language when war first erupted in the Donetsk and Luhansk regions in 2014. "It seemed there were no words left – only fragments that rolled around in your mouth like stones", Olena said.

The poet Iya Kiva, too, has compared language to a mouthful of stones. In a 2021 poem, Kiva writes:

> a frozen sea of people rolls stones around its mouth
> this dead language of the time we will turn to
> when the wind cuts the thread of life like a flower

Language has been reinvented by the emotions of war, but also by the vocabulary of war. Halyna Kruk writes of thermal sensors and night-vision devices, which are designed to track animals in the wild, and allow soldiers to detect the presence of enemy forces:

> taking aim, you must remember
> human warmth is special –
> it can kill

Although many Ukrainians – particularly parents of young children – have understandably left the country to seek safety and stability, those who remain are documenting the country's difficult passage into something new. There is a willful commitment to living, despite widespread death. To some outside Ukraine, this bravery looks reckless.

How can this one non-Nato country hold back the strongest army in Europe? But Ukrainians realize that their choice is between reckless bravery and losing a country they have fought hard to build. During my final day in Kyiv, I listened as Admiral Rob Bauer told his Ukrainian audience, "pessimists don't win wars". As for explaining their continued optimism to the rest of the world – this is where Ukrainian poets come in. Olena Huseinova sums this up simply in a poem about making coffee:

> I didn't go down to the basement
> in the morning I made coffee
> in a Turkish ibrik
> on the gas stove

Huseinova ends the poem by describing pouring the coffee into a:

> translucent white cup
> like a shell
> brand new
> right out of a box
> for better times

Unpacking a new cup to drink coffee during an air raid requires an act of faith. This isn't the kind of faith you find in a church. It is a belief in living, against all odds.

Amelia Glaser is Professor of Literature at the University of California, San Diego, where she teaches courses in Slavic literature, Jewish literature, and translation studies. She is the author of Jews and Ukrainians in Russia's Literary Borderlands *(Northwestern University Press, 2012), and* Songs in Dark Times: Yiddish Poetry of Struggle from Scottsboro to Palestine *(Harvard University Press, 2020). She is the editor of* Stories of Khmelnytsky: Competing Literary Legacies of the 1648 Ukrainian Cossack Uprising *(Stanford University Press, 2015) and, with Steven Lee,* Comintern Aesthetics *(University of Toronto Press, 2020). Her translations, from Ukrainian, Russian, and Yiddish, include* Proletpen: America's Rebel Yiddish Poets *(University of Wisconsin Press, 2005) and, with Yuliya Ilchuk, Halyna Kruk's* A Crash Course in Molotov cocktails *(Arrowsmith, 2023), which was shortlisted for the prestigious 2024 Griffin Poetry Prize. She is currently writing a book about contemporary Ukrainian poetry.*

NOTES

1. Hannah Arendt, *The Human Condition* 26.

2. Viktoria Amelina, "Istoriiq odniei peremohy", in Volodymyr Vakulenko-K, *Ia peretvoriuius-... Shchodennyk okupatsii. Vybrani virshi* (Kharkiv: Vivat, 2024) 7-23, 10

3. Maksym Kryvtsov, "Koly uzhe mene", *Virshi z biinytsi*, (Kyiv: Nash format, 2024) 164.

4. Maksym Kryvtsov, Facebook post (https://www.facebook.com/permalink. php?story_fbid=pfbid0q3x12WhMuTAZkRfsDwG9Z8vxNuwPBC8Yx-sMAwLTsbxxLrKCWtDyHyyH37PEdft6Al&id=100011994764563)

SHARING THE DARKNESS

for Dr. Baha Alashqar, of Odesa and Gaza

———

Carolyn Forché

Scrims of memory.

24 February 2022. I wake with a start at midnight. A nightbird striking the window? A bat in the eaves? Maybe someone in the theater of my sleep gave me a nudge – someone I don't know in waking life. It is cloudy and warm this night, so the waning moon isn't visible through the window beside me, nor the bright star Antares to the right of it. There is no wind. There have been no sharp knocks on the door as I seem to hear sometimes in my sleep, and no imaginary bell. A stillness has descended on everything: the pile of books on the bedside table, the water glass lit from within, and across the room, a gallery of people looking out from their photographs as if through windows in the past. Nothing moves. *Something has happened*, is what the darkness says. It had to do with the maps I had been studying in recent days, with the drawings of tanks and the arrows pointing at Ukraine. At one time, such as in Beirut years earlier, I would have reached for the Grundig shortwave radio and spun the dial through frequencies of music, language, and white noise. Now I reach for my cell phone and begin to scroll, tenting the light with a bedsheet so as not to disturb my husband's sleep. At first the world seems quiet. Kyrgyzstan's President has signed a decree banning the slaughter of cattle during funerals. Anti-war protesters have gathered outside the Russian Embassy in Berlin. Singapore reports a record number of Covid cases. I solve the Wordle puzzle and the mini-Crossword, and then I play the game of guessing how many words can be made from the same seven letters, using the same single letter in each of them. I learn that it will rain tomorrow. I hear the water heater turn on then off again. Car lights from the road pass over the walls. Maybe in the distance a racoon is opening a garbage can. It is all very normal, but something bothers the mind. *This has to do with the war that is coming* is what the darkness is saying, and it is right. The country on the map is now ringed by battalions and tanks, convoys with their missiles pointing at the clouds. The Russian military forces are arrayed along the borders of Russia, Belarus and occupied Crimea.

The air raid sirens sound just after dawn in Kyiv, and some minutes later in Lviv. Blasts are heard in the cities of Dnipro, Mariupol, Kramatorsk and Odesa. This has to do with a city near the sea, *city of wheat and light, city of limestone soft enough to cut with a hatchet*, as I had written in a poem about Odesa. Poems sometimes whisper in the dark like this. They appear in the dark like lights when the eyes are closed. Within hours, I would know what woke me up. In Kyiv it was already morning and it was clear that a full-scale war against the people of Ukraine had begun, a war to destroy kindergartens and libraries, theaters, farmer's markets, hospitals, filling stations; a war on universities and maternity wards, factories and shopping malls, apartment blocks and playgrounds, a war on a language spoken for centuries, on the history of a people, on folk songs and dances, fairy tales, literature, and food; a war, as I saw it, upon *an opera house, a madhouse, a ghost church with wind for its choir / where two things were esteemed: literature and ships, poetry and the sea.* These lines are from a poem I wrote for the Ukrainian-born poet Ilya Kaminsky after we traveled to Odesa two decades ago, when it seemed possible and even restorative for him to go back, to see once again the city of his childhood, the city he left with his mother and father in the years just after the collapse of the former Soviet Union.

This was not my first trip to that part of the world. A decade earlier, I had driven through Belarus toward Ukraine to document the conditions of people living in the exclusion zones surrounding the damaged reactor at Chernobyl: the elderly people who refused to leave, and refugees from the war in Chechnya, who found safety in the peace and quiet of the place. In memory, the giant blue cabbages growing in their radiated gardens are visible through a scrim of acacia trees lining the streets of Odesa. The passage of time has caused these journeys to happen all at once, the images flickering like photographs in a chaotic slide show. Ilya and I are walking in the cold wind toward the Potemkin steps when he interrupts this reverie by playfully inviting me to dance, as suggested by the title of his first volume of poems, *Dancing in Odessa*. And so we waltz down Prymorskyi Boulevard, and later, over a samovar of black tea in the Hotel Londonskya, he confides that emigration is death. "You must die when you board the plane and walk into your resurrection as you disembark in the new land. If you are unable to do this, you remain a corpse. I'm not sure I can say now that emigration is a good thing."

That trip was the first of many for him. He even went back during the war, in part to visit his ailing uncle, to bring whatever aid and comfort he could to his relatives and friends, the poets he had come to know in the decades since that first journey, poets he had been translating and publishing, and now was trying somehow to rescue, in whatever way he could. Most Ukrainian poets had chosen to stay behind when millions of women, children, and elderly men boarded the trains, piled into cars, or walked to the country's borders. Like everyone else in the west, I was confined in my knowledge of this exodus to photographs and video footage: arms reaching through train windows, crowded platforms, children in snowsuits, house cats and small dogs tucked into winter jackets, roller boards, rucksacks, wheelchairs. Some had packed believing they would only be away a short time. I wondered what they had chosen to bring with them and tried not to think about all they had left behind. I did, however, understand that the images before me did not transmit how cold it was, how raw the air, how painful the boots and shoes, did not convey the desperate hope for a toilet, a sip of water, a place to dry out the mittens and socks. In the photographs, the black smoke pouring from burning apartment blocks doesn't sting the eyes or burn the throat; there is no stench of cordite and no overpowering petroleum odor of war.

Soon after the invasion began, the writer Askold Melnyczuk asked me to join a Zoom gathering of Ukrainian poets, sponsored by the PEN-American Center. Despite our far-flung locations, in the computer screen, it was as if we were all in the same apartment house, looking out from our different windows. In Ukraine, it was already dark. The mood in our dimly lit poetry building was solemn. Vasyl Makhno was in New York, Ostap Slyvynsky and Halyna Kruk were in Lviv, Oksana Lutsyshyna in Austin, Texas; Iryna Shuvalova in Beijing, and Oksana Zabuzhko tried to join us from Warsaw, but was unable to get the technology on her borrowed computer to work. Askold welcomed us. There were greetings and sad smiles, shrugs and knowing looks. I knew that I would share a poem I wrote for Ilya, titled "Exile", but in the hours leading up to our meeting, I also composed a message in the form of a poem, an urgent message written quickly and read in its raw state. In the days that followed, the message was published, translated into Ukrainian, and letter-pressed as a broadside in both languages against a field of sunflowers.

If there is ink

If there is ink for this hour if there is
something to say to write that would
send the tanks the convoys and transports
into reverse on the roads they have rutted
send them back to the borders they crossed
send them back, and the hours too that have passed
since dawn on the twenty-fourth day of the second month
send those hours with them, and the enemy
soldiers dragging with them their crematorium
and the corpses of their fellow soldiers they have left
behind and their own wounded send them back if there is ink
if there is something to write that would raise the cities
from the ruins the apartment blocks hospitals schools
that would put the cities back as they were
I would give everything to fill my pen with it

This was before Mariupol was razed to the ground, before its theater was bombed, killing six hundred people who had taken refuge within it; before the discovery of the torture chambers and the corpses of Bucha; the aerial bombing of Vinnytsia, Chernihiv, Kyiv, and Izium, a litany of cities and towns; the siege of the steelworks; a child photographed lying dead beside a baby carriage; a mother in labor carried on a litter from a burning maternity ward. It was possible in those first weeks and months to imagine myself to be following "the news", especially by reading *The Kyiv Independent*, just as it was possible to hope that the sanctions would work, that the courage of a besieged people could prevail against despotic aggression, that the largest land war in Europe in almost seventy years would not end in thermonuclear war; that Ukraine would somehow survive this onslaught against significant odds. After all, hadn't the Russian warship been sunk off the coast of Snake Island? Hadn't the farmer's tractor towed the broken tank out of a field? Didn't they put these images on postage stamps? The warship and the trac-tor-towed tank?

I lie in the dark most nights, aware that at that very moment, on the other side of the world, a rocket had struck a power plant and the lights had gone out. And then I was lying again on a basement floor in Beirut many years ago, listening to the thunderous shelling of Ras Beirut from the Maronite east. Almost every journalist posted to Beirut was in that hotel basement, along with a handful of people from neighboring apartments. There were thirty or so of us. Beside me was a young Lebanese girl lying under her coat, whispering to me about her life, and wondering if there would be anything left in the morning. "Of course, there will be", I reassured her, "they can't destroy everything." However, the truth was that yes, they could. I feared that our building would be hit and we would be crushed beneath it. "We have to sleep", I said to the girl. In the morning, we will wake up, and it would be over. I said things like that until she fell asleep, and then I lay there, staying awake to keep the world intact. That is how one thinks in a makeshift shelter under bombardment.

As I scroll through photographs taken in Kherson or Nikopol, I remember not only the stench, but the deafening sounds of detonated ordnance, acrid dust and debris, the screeching of metal on metal, the coughing of the mortars and shattering of glass. In the morning, the streets of Ras Beirut were covered with broken windows, green, jagged scraps that made it look as though the streets were iced. It was hard to walk. And there is so much else one can forget: how for hours or even days nothing happens, and it seems safe to come out because after all it is necessary to find food and water, to prepare meals and wash up, to think about where to go next. I remember the young boy who every day ran from doorway to doorway with a tall stack of pita bread he balanced like plates in a circus act. He sometimes had to dodge rifle-fire, but he never dropped the bread, and people watching from a slight distance cheered him on as if he might not die at any moment, as if this were an extreme sport.

Sometimes in the early hours, I discover my friend, Edward, awake in Odesa. He is on Facebook's Messenger. I ask him if he is somewhere safe, in a shelter or basement. "No", he replies. Then: "Around 20:00 hours, two heavy shots sounded right next door to our house. It was our defense firing. I now live not far from the restaurant where you and I dined. My wife and three animals. I do not lose heart. We are not afraid." Then: "A few hours ago there were ten shots, very loud, so my head ached but we are not discouraged. We think it will be over soon." Later: "In Odesa there were several volleys from the sea and the air. In the city for a long time a siren and a distant bombardment were heard. My wife and I and our three pets – Santa, Puma, and Charlie – are calm and confident in our victory. We are waiting for the end of the war. Thank you for being with us."

October, 2023. I begin texting, sometimes through the night, with a doctor who had taken shelter, first in the hospitals where he worked, and later in a white tent pitched in a city of tents in Gaza. He texts me about his work, tending to the wounded and maimed. He texts about sickness and disease, lack of food, lack of water, lack of medicine and medical supplies. He sends photographs and videos taken on his phone, and he tells me about his bombed house, his uprooted olive groves, his family, and the beautiful life they once lived in Gaza. His Ukrainian wife, whom he met while studying medicine in Odesa, had already been evacuated by the Ukrainian government, together with their five children. But without Ukrainian citizenship himself, the doctor had been unable to join them. When aerial bombardment of Odesa intensified, his wife and children fled again, taking refuge in Germany. I had begun working with a small group of friends in the United States and Egypt, who were helping people to cross the border at Rafah, and that is how the doctor was able to reach Cairo, where he is now enduring the very long wait for an appointment at the German embassy to plead for a visa to visit his family. He texts photos his wife sends him from Germany: his children in snowsuits, the littlest in a carriage. He sends a video someone took of him as he extracted a coin from the esophagus of a starving child.

11 April 2024. The genocidal wars against the people of Ukraine and Gaza continue through the sleep of all who still live in safety. Lying awake at night I insist to myself that yes, this is happening again now, in the heart of Europe and in Palestine. What the Polish poet Czesław Miłosz wrote is true: "If a thing exists in one place, it will exist everywhere." There is nothing that cannot happen, nothing impossible where humanity is concerned. War is an old story. As for human survival and so-called civilization, there are no guarantees. In our times, everything senses that an end might come, that annihilation is possible.

We know that war destroys language, as it destroys everything within its zone of prosecution. Under conditions of such extremity, language is wounded, fragmented, cratered. It is put to military use in the creation of euphemisms that have become all the more sinister with the advance of technology. What is happening before our eyes is not "warfare" but a "military operation". Mass murder is "ethnic cleansing". In Ukraine and Gaza, there are no "shortages" of food, water, and medicine. These are deliberately withheld as a weapon of war. We say the "fighting began" as if on its own, and not in response to an order. We "come under" attack as if positioning ourselves by our own volition. While firing rockets at apartment houses, we speak of the civilian dead as "collateral damage" so as not to admit that we are intentionally killing noncombatants. War does not begin as a sudden occurrence, like an automobile accident. Preparations are made and can be seen from a long way off, like a storm on a horizon. Yet against this destruction, poetry is written in the midst of war and in its aftermath. As might be imagined, many of these poems do not survive. They disappear into the pockets of corpses and the drawers of demolished desks. The poems that do survive often have a strange tone: ominous and pleading, as urgent as an SOS or *m'aidez* sent into the night from a damaged ship. These poems are often addressed to the future, like messages in a bottle (Paul Celan) or to those who live in safety beyond the war zone. In reading poems as witness, we read all that the poet endured, all that she saw, felt, tasted, and smelled. These are reports from the human soul, from the depths of being – not factual dispatches such as would appear in newspapers, but "facts of art", attesting to the truth of the human experience. The poet writes as if making an incision in consciousness. At the site of this wound, language breaks, becomes tentative, interrogational, kaleidoscopic. But it endures. In the words of Paul Celan at Bremen: "One thing remained attainable, close, and unlost amidst all the losses: language. Language was not lost, in spite of all that happened. But it had to go through its own responselessness, go through horrible silences, go through the thousand darknesses of death-bringing speech."

According to Milosz, "the poetic act changes with the amount of back-ground reality embraced by the poet's consciousness." Awareness of that background reality demands vigilance, this very wakefulness in the dark, and is sustained through the faculty of the empathetic imagination, by our ability to respond to hidden forces, to disturbances in the cosmos, the way horses run back and forth across a pasture before a storm, or migratory birds sense an early winter. The background reality for those who live far from the war zone is the war itself. It shares the darkness with us, the moment of night.

One of America's most celebrated poets, Carolyn Forché (born 1950) is the author five books of poems, most recently In the Lateness of the World, *a finalist for the Pulitzer Prize in 2021. Her works also include translations, anthologies, and a memoir. She is a professor at Georgetown University in Washington, D.C.*

TWO POEMS

——

Chris Agee

The easy West.

Yellow cat's-cradles

of the old gantries
in the dawn's
sulphury blue
a twinkling easyjet
preparing to land
behind a row of poplars
silhouetted
as if a besom-broom
blown out of the East
from the Ukrainian drama
where history has
hardly ended

And Davos
be aware
and be apprised
with your Faustus
of capital
running amok
and wreaking
its havoc
the mass
ethicalized
here too
may yet arise
like a Luther or Brecht
to defenestrate
banksters and oligarchs

in a collective
catharsis
to roll the tumbril
for your shameless
self-indulgences

says at least
this easy passenger

Belfast-Glasgow, 22-25 February 2014

(from Blue Sandbar Moon: a micro-epic, *by Chris Agee, The Irish Pages Press, 2018.)*

PUTIN

is a fly feeding on death and carrion;
                    like those, say,
Alighting on the high-rise apartments,
                or high-hanging garnet grenades
Of pomegranates split open, their once
Rosy-fingered flesh now
              spilling their seed
Into blackened rot and waste,
              not far
From the terrace's classic *onlooker.*

              Or those Others,
                no golden horde,
Buzzing around the fermenting or even raisined
                  dead
Grape-clusters, in a last frenzy of life overhead.
To no great purpose:
             they will be laid waste and to rest
Within a week or a month.
           For them, now,
There will be no winter campaign.

October 2022, Žrnovo, Croatia

Chris Agee is a poet, essayist, photographer, editor and publisher. He was born in San Francisco on a US Navy hospital ship and grew up in Massachusetts, New York and Rhode Island. After high school at Phillips Academy Andover and a year in Aix-en-Provence, France, he attended Harvard University and since graduation has lived in Ireland. His third collection of poems, Next to Nothing *(Salt, 2008), was shortlisted in Britain for the 2009 Ted Hughes Award for New Work in Poetry, and its sequel,* Blue Sandbar Moon *(The Irish Pages Press), appeared in 2018. He is the Editor of* Irish Pages *and The Irish Pages Press, and edited* Balkan Essays *(The Irish Pages Press, 2016), the sixth volume of Hubert Butler's essays, published simultaneously in Croatian by the Zagreb publishing house Fraktura. His "poetic work of non-fiction" on the former President,* Trump Rant *(The Irish Pages Press), was published in 2021. He lives in Belfast, and divides his time between Ireland, Scotland and Croatia.*

AN EMIGRANT'S TALE

——

Natalya Korniyenko

House of being — and roads to safety.

War began to appear in my dreams long before 24 February 2022. Jets exploding in the air, the enemy army swarming the streets of my city, me saving my
children from a murky river or running up and down the ruins of houses like
in an airsoft tournament to escape mortal danger.

In one of the most chilling dreams, enemy soldiers appear in the yard
of the church I frequented as a young girl, and one shoots me. I feel the
bullet pierce my body in the area of my heart, launching a countdown in
my mind: ten, nine, eight, seven ... I understand that this is all a dream, but
for some reason I believe that unless I manage to wake up by the end of the
countdown, this is where I will forever remain: in the dream, outside reality.
This is what my mom once taught me: when in a dream, never walk towards
the light at the end of the tunnel and never take the hand of the dead; if you
do, the otherworld may pull you in, and you will never wake up. That time, I
managed to rip myself out of the clutches of the nightmare at the last second.
I woke up with my heart pounding, but the sense of meeting the people who
wanted me dead lingered.

On the eve of the full-scale invasion, I can picture this clearly. I meet
a Russian soldier face to face, and he sees it all in my eyes: my distaste, my
unwillingness to obey, my inability to pretend to be somebody I'm not even
if that's what it takes to survive. I grew up in a Ukrainian-speaking family
and hadn't ever switched to Russian. At first I felt no need to, and then it
became my principled position not to switch to the language of the country
that had spent centuries trying to destroy my native language, Ukrainian,
through imposing bans and regulations and instilling an inferiority complex
in its speakers. "Language is the house of being", wrote Heidegger. And now
a Russian soldier was headed for my land to rob me of it all: of my home, of
my language and of my very being. This is why I knew that, even in mortal
danger, I wouldn't be able to contain my emotions and make myself beg in
Russian: not to save my life, not to persuade the invader not to hurt me or
my children. It was my sense of responsibility for my children's safety and

213

psychological well-being that drove me to decide to leave Kyiv days before the full-scale invasion.

I didn't want to believe that the invasion was coming. I followed the news as Russia began to amass an army along the Ukrainian border starting in the autumn of 2021. I read reports of Western intelligence agencies and of Ukrainian analysts. Whenever I met with friends, we discussed our fears and anxieties, considered the possible new developments and calculated risks. All the while, the Ukrainian government had been trying to calm down the public and asking citizens not to spread panic; as late as January 2022, a month before the full-scale invasion, President Zelensky promised Ukrainians peaceful picnics during the May holidays.

That is why I was telling myself that we would be back within a week as I was packing my car three days before the invasion. We would celebrate my daughter's birthday, have a change of scenery and come back in no time. I made a point of bringing just one backpack per person: the bare necessities, our documents and some cash. My children grabbed random toys, and we left our home not to see it again to this day.

We stayed the night at a hotel to take a rest on our way to my parents'. I forced myself to watch a snippet of Putin's televised address, and it wasn't until that moment that I realized what was at stake. "The final solution of the Ukrainian question" could only mean one thing: Russians wanted to destroy us as a nation, as a state. In the mind of the brutal Russian dictator, we had to stop existing. Much like his imperial predecessors, he aimed not just to conquer our land, but also to destroy everything Ukrainian, including our language, our culture and our identity, as well as to physically destroy us, our parents and our children.

On February 23, we celebrated my daughter's birthday. I felt the catastrophe approach with every cell of my body but made the last staggering efforts to give my baby a fun day. That night, my kids went to bed with the questions that spelled the end of their childhood. "Mom, show us the main bad guy (Putin)." "Mom, are the clouds in Russia evil?" "Mom, why is Russia so big? Why do they want war?" "Mom, are the bad guys already attacking, or are they lying in wait?" "Mom, what about our poor people?"

On the morning of February 24, I was woken by a text from my kids' kindergarten: the nanny wrote that, given the situation, the kindergarten would remain closed. In the scant seconds before I opened the news-feed, I already knew that the irreversible had happened. In another second, I would read about missile attacks on Kyiv, Kharkiv, Ivano-Frankivsk and other Ukrainian cities, and feel a yawning chasm, colder and darker than the deepest and darkest abyss, somewhere in my belly, in the place from which my children came and that had always felt like a symbol of safety, peace and comfort to me.

I woke up my mother: "Mom, the war has begun." We switched on the TV to follow, day by day and hour by hour, the advance of the Russian army and the heroic resistance of Ukrainians, to see enemy tanks, destroyed homes, slaughtered civilians and captured POWs.

Watching and reading the news was all that I could do at that stage. That, and take my kids to the basement gym doubling as a bomb shelter or to our tiny bathroom to hide during air raid alarms. I didn't have the energy to cook, to take walks with the kids or to help my journalist colleagues to spread the news. The word I'd use to describe my state at the time is impotence. "Mom, don't think about the bad things, think about the good", my son would try to console me, but good thoughts just wouldn't come. During every air raid alert (in Ukrainian, "alert" and "anxiety" are cognates), I imagined a missile hitting our house and burying us under the rubble.

I don't remember when I first started to think about fleeing abroad. In conversations with my friends and loved ones, the thought loomed ever clearer. It seemed to be the only thing I could do at the moment: to take my kids to a place where no missile would reach them. I'd been considering Poland, where my sister had been living for a couple of years by then, and Ireland, where my friend from college lived. Quite a while ago, before my kids were born and seven years before the great war, my ex-husband and I visited my friend in Ireland. We chose the wrong season for the trip. It was late autumn, so I remembered the country as the land of constant rain, chilly homes, medieval castles decorated for Halloween, the cold Guinness and the unintelligible Joyce. Since it was out of season, every place we visited (Dublin, Tullamore, Galway, the Cliffs of Moher and the Aran Islands) seemed nearly deserted. We seemed to be the only tourists interested in exploring Ireland at that time. Choosing between Poland, already filled to bursting with Ukrainian refugees, and Ireland, I asked my friend, "Do you ever get any sunshine?" The friend just laughed.

We decided to go with another college friend, also a single mom. During peacetime, the trip would have taken no more than a couple of hours. During the war, with the Ukrainian airspace closed to civilian aviation and with colossal waiting lines at the border, we scheduled three days for the trip.

"*Zdravstvuite*", the Polish border guard greeted us courteously in Russian at the pedestrian border point of Rava-Ruska/Hrebenne. Strange as it was to hear Russian from a Polish border guard, he must have believed that this language was convenient or even preferable for us. It was far from the last time when I would have to explain that Ukrainians have their own language, and that Ukrainian was not identical to Russian; in fact, it is closer lexically to Polish than to Russian. But I didn't have it in me to explain the linguistic nuances to the Polish border guard. The long trip and the unknown awaited.

Poles were the first to rush to help Ukrainians. As early as in January 2022, the Polish government announced that it was preparing to admit at least one million Ukrainian refugees. I found the announcement absurd at the time. I couldn't imagine Ukrainians being forced to flee their homeland *en masse*. Moreover, I could never imagine myself becoming a refugee. At that time, I did not yet know what a war of extermination looked like.

We felt the Polish kindness and willingness to help from the very first moment. Polish soup from a volunteer tent at the border will forever remain a symbol of their kindness for me. "Mom, why are the Poles so kind? Why are they helping us? If the Russians attack Poland, will we help them too?"

"When did you first feel that you were safe?" a Ukrainian scholar studying the health and mental well-being of Ukrainian refugees in Ireland would ask me later. I immediately answered that that was at Dublin airport, when a welcoming elderly Irish border officer brought my children colouring books and coloured markers. Later he carefully packed the markers into a branded pencil case and gifted them to my kids.

Our road to Ireland wasn't easy. First we had to get from the Polish-Ukrainian border to Warsaw and spend a night at the refugee centre. It was a giant windowless hangar with long rows of camp-cots to accommodate two thousand refugees. As the prominent contemporary Ukrainian writer Yurii Andrukhovych once wrote, it had "just enough light not to be able to sleep or read, just the right level of light to hang yourself." I was too afraid to sleep and feared that my children would be abducted to beg in the streets somewhere on the outskirts of Warsaw. On the way, my friend caught Covid, and my children and I caught stomach flu. Despite all that, after we were taken from a reception centre in Dublin to our accommodation outside Galway, I felt that *now* we would be alright.

"It's the Lviv of Ireland", a Ukrainian friend joked later, and Galway did indeed remind me of Lviv with its touristy streets, splendid architecture, churches, cultural atmosphere and swarms of students. Moreover, the similarities between Ukraine and Ireland are not limited to just these two cities: more and more parallels crop up when I least expect them. I see glimpses of the familiar in old houses under thatched roofs, in hollyhocks blossoming by the porches, in our shared love for hearty food, in the propensity for gossip. "Ireland is the Galicia of Western Europe", I like to joke now.

The parallels between our two countries are much more essential and run deeper than landscapes. The Irish keep telling us: "We have very similar histories"; "We understand you well"; "Ireland will always stand by the victim". They welcomed us with open arms after Russia's full-scale invasion of Ukraine with the cordiality and kindness driven not just by human empathy but also by the genetic memory of solidarity with those facing the historical challenges that they themselves had once faced. The personal stories of the Irish, the stories of their families and friends, allusions and hints dropped in conversations is what brings us closer and gives us a sense of unity. We may speak different languages, but we understand one another better than anyone. Delving deeper into Irish history, I find myself facing the same motifs that we encounter in Ukrainian history: colonization, centuries of fighting for independence, bans on our languages and cultures, famines, physical extermination and migrations.

Looking at the National Famine Memorial in Westport, "The Coffin Ship", I'm thinking about the millions of Irish that perished during the Great Famine. I'm also thinking about millions of Ukrainians that perished in the Holodomor, an artificial famine of 1932-33 organized by the Soviet authorities. I'm also thinking about millions of Irish who had been forced to emigrate from Ireland in different eras. I'm thinking about their motifs, feelings and roads to safety. I'm also thinking about millions of Ukrainians who have been forced to emigrate or were forcibly deported from Ukraine over the years.

My children and I belong to the latest wave of the Ukrainian emigration caused by the Russian invasion. I still find it hard to believe and accept this. I'm still fighting the sense of forced displacement and hopelessness. I was lucky not to encounter a Russian soldier face to face, but the invaders still managed to chase me out of my home and country. Here, in Ireland, nearly two thousand miles away from home, I often think, "Who am I? What did I manage to save in the calamity of war and forced emigration? What did I manage to snatch out of the hands of a Russian soldier and bring with me?" I brought my language, that language that I always had and that makes me *me*.

Translated, from the Ukrainian, by Iaroslava Strikha.

Natalya Korniyenko is a Ukrainian journalist and editor, born in Stryi, Lviv region, in 1985. She graduated from the Ivan Franko National University of Lviv, Department of Ukrainian Philology, where she received a Master's Degree. She has worked as a journalist and editor at The Ukrainian Week, *and at 5.ua (online), as an analyst at the Ukrainian Book Institute, and as PR director of the Book Space Festival. For the past 10 years, she has been working with* Chytomo, *the largest independent media outlet covering publishing and contemporary literature and culture in Ukraine. She has coordinated the "EmptyChairPeople" online media project, which covered stories from Crimean Tatar citizen-journalists who became political prisoners during Russia's occupation of Crimea. Since June 2022, she has worked as a coordinator and interviewer for the "Words and Bullets" online media project, a series of interviews with Ukrainian writers and journalists who have become soldiers or volunteers during the Russo-Ukrainian War. A collection of 24 of these interviews will be published as a book soon. In March 2022, she moved from Kyiv to Ireland with her two children due to the war. She is now based in Galway.*

FORCED COMPARISONS

—

Daniel Colm Simpson

Falling conkers.

Last week I travelled to Ukraine for the first time since Russia's full-scale invasion. I had lived in Kyiv on and off in short bouts since 2014. Whenever my life lacked direction, and I needed a couple of months to think away from home, I would go to Ukraine. I spoke fluent Russian and passable Ukrainian and had a circle of local friends. Each visit would involve leisurely walks around Kyiv's many parks, accompanied by conversations which seemed to pierce much deeper than what I was used to. Maybe it was my philosophical Russian-speaking alter ego, but I felt I could be more myself in Ukraine.

I expected things to feel different now that Ukraine is at war – I thought there might be a palpable change in the air, perhaps a heaviness which can't quite be described. Instead, I found myself entering the same city I had loved before. Cafés, restaurants, and bars were fully packed; patrons spilled onto the streets outside. Parents took their children out to play. The sandy banks of the Dnipro River were packed with sunbathers. You could still pay to bungee jump off a bridge near *Hydropark*. There was a cycling competition at the *Velotrek*. And, for some inexplicable reason, the city was full of Boy Scouts, sweat running down their ironed shirts.

At night things were different. Parties were moved forward to daytime, and all businesses closed at 10:00 p.m. Curfew started at midnight. The Russians were at least "nice enough" to keep most of their air raids to curfew hours. From around 1:00 a.m. to 6:00 a.m., there was always a chance that rockets and drones would be blowing up in the sky above. No one seemed worried, though: the air defence systems, including the American-supplied Patriot, were so reliable that even on the worst nights, Kyiv mostly ended up with a few non-fatal shrapnel injuries in areas of the city close to critical infrastructure. Most of my friends didn't even take heed of sirens anymore: "We saw an explosion over that building on Wednesday night", Yurii said, smoking on the balcony of the 20th floor, "I woke up that time. I don't wake up to sirens anymore, just explosions." He showed me on a cloud wisp where the rockets had been.

My yoga teacher, Irina, smiled: "Danya, there's no need to worry. We're under an umbrella." The word she used for umbrella — *zontik* — was so cute and childish that I couldn't help but picture her tucking me into bed. Later, when the sirens were playing and I could hear the odd, whale-like sound of the defence systems in the distance as I diligently hid behind two walls in the hallway, I would repeat that refrain to myself: *my pod zontikom, we're under an umbrella.*

When I returned home and described Ukraine to my family, everything I said would elicit a story of the Troubles. "Oh, that's what it was like when I worked at the bank", my dad said, "they'd put bombs in the city centre all the time, and I just carried on. You had to go to work."

"Ah, sure it sounds like the good old days", my mum said, "the IRA used to run through our house or there'd be shooting outside, and I still had to put Cathy to bed."

In a way, they were right. The strange everydayness of conflict in Kyiv did seem to resemble Northern Ireland in the 1970s and 1980s. I pondered the consequences of the kind of chronic stress which results from rarely being in immediate danger but constantly knowing that if you are unlucky, you might die. I wondered whether that would produce similar results down the line in Ukraine. Would there be an epidemic of depression and anxiety? Would doctors prescribe pills without looking the past in the face? Would people feel they had no justification for being depressed? It is plausible that a Ukrainian who manages to escape the worst of the war might use the same excuses we use in Northern Ireland: "Sure, we all went through it. It's not like I can point out some specific event or trauma. I can't be depressed. I wasn't on a frontline. I'm not special. None of us are special."

I shared my trip with my colleagues at a writer's group. Here too within several minutes we were all "reminiscing" about the Troubles. A lady told of how she felt at entering Derry after Bloody Sunday — it was a city changed overnight, the air suddenly leaden with fear — and yet at the same time life soon returned to normal.

"The people outside are often more uneasy than the people in the midst of it", said another member, referring to her family abroad. This too was a common motif I heard from friends in Kyiv, many of whom said their friends seeking refuge in Europe were more worried for them than they themselves.

Kyiv is now hundreds of miles from the frontline. It is a refuge for many Ukrainians. Nonetheless, the dynamics of the war are such that at any given time all Ukrainians can be mentally thrust to the frontline; to horrors so vast and incomprehensible that I feel the comparison to our "low-intensity, chronic" Troubles becomes awkward. One of the songs that plays on the radio talks about "keeping you in a pocket by my heart", referring to a girlfriend keeping her phone close to her chest so she can receive texts from her boyfriend on the frontline; another song begs for release "just to go home for Easter", even though there "aren't as many chairs around the table".

Irina worries about her husband serving in the army who regularly "sees death", despite his advanced age and lack of training. As we sit in an Indian restaurant staring at an exotic turtle, she urges me to accept my own mortality: "Danya, it's the only thing that we all know is inevitable. War and death are natural parts of life. Sooner or later, you need to come to terms with it. And when you're not afraid anymore, you'll feel free. Maybe that's one of the things you might learn on this trip." Later that day, another friend tells me how one of her colleagues had walked into the office and announced that an acquaintance's husband had been shot in the head. The air was sucked out of the room.

One morning I go to the hairdresser's. I tell my barber, Ihor, where I am from, and that I'm here to meet my colleagues and close friends. I say that the first night of my visit was one of the worst air raids in some weeks. We talk about a superstition that on their first night in Kyiv, visitors often get a "good show". He tells me that in May of last year he was walking to work when he got involved in a strike. He had to go to the hospital for severe injuries, particularly his leg. "At least my moustache was still in the same place", he joked at the time. I asked Ihor whether he was less or more afraid of the air sirens now. "You get used to it, of course", he says, "although I'd be lying if I said I still don't get a rush of adrenaline sometimes."

Later, I walk with my dear friend Valera under yellowing leaves as conkers fall from above. On the day of my departure, Valera writes me a letter thanking me for coming to Ukraine:

"Chestnuts seem to fall onto passer-by's heads by chance, just like many events in our life. Even though you and I have known each other for less time than the average age of a chestnut tree in Kyiv, these years have shown me that we are true friends ... My inner voice tells me that you'll manage to avoid encounters with conkers, and, even if it is nature's will that they do fall, you'll be able to manage. You can always rely on me."

As my bus queues at the border to cross into Poland, an air raid siren goes off. Even here – in the far west of the country, now about a thousand kilometres from the front line – the sky will never truly be safe. The other passengers on the bus don't react. They have Telegram channels that tell them from where and in which direction the threat is flying; the exact model of the Russian rocket, drone, and its carrier; approximately what time the threat might arrive; and whether it's an immediate risk. Yet most of the messages go unread. There's no point getting worked up.

One passenger, however, is on the phone with her friend. She had come to visit Ukraine briefly, having fled in 2022. She describes the rush of adrenaline at hearing her first air raid sirens a few days ago and the strange sensation as people calmly walk past as she runs to a shelter. "They're all used to it now", she says, "and they told me to get used to it too." Somehow, I find the outrage and the panic in her voice to be more natural than the indifference of my fellow passengers. I wonder what my parents would think.

———

I wrote this text in September 2023. It was a response to the forced comparisons that were thrust upon me by my friends and family back home. I suppose, it was natural that they would see parallels with the Troubles. All humans are solipsists, to one degree or another. This text no longer sits comfortably with me. In the last month, Russian attacks in Kyiv have intensified. The room for comparisons to our beloved "chronic stress" has shrunk.

That September Summer is now a mirage. The kilometres to Kyiv have increased. I rarely hear from my friends – when they do write, they advise me not to return: "We'll see each other when this is over. When we're pensioners."

I visited in a fairly safe window; things aren't predictable anymore. As promised Western weapons fail to materialise, hope has been suspended. A colleague told me that things were so "loud" that she ducked away from her windows for the first time since the beginning of the war. Sometimes I turn on the air alerts on my phone. Bizarrely, the English language version announces the end of an air alert with the Starwarsian maxim "may the force be with you". I'm not sure how that makes me feel. Like many people now, I'm not sure how I feel about anything.

Kyiv
September 2023
Babyne lito

Born in 1994 in Limavady, Co Derry, Daniel Colm Simpson is a Russian interpreter, researcher and journalist. He received a BA in Russian and German and a Triple MA Erasmus Mundus (Political Science, Eurasian Studies and International Relations), both from the University of Cambridge. His creative work deals with themes of alienation and de-realisation, and he is currently working on an interview-based travelogue entitled Wrong Kind of Irish, *whereby he speaks, for example, with Northern unionists identifying as Irish, children of migrants, and others who feel alienated due to queerness and neurodivergence. He is also working on research projects involving public opinion in the occupied areas of Ukraine and peacebuilding in Nigeria.*

KUINDZHI

—

Alannah Millar

A picture of imperialism.

Museums in Russia always seemed to leave me with a headache. I would wander out the exit with the balls of my feet tingling in pain, and my hand reaching down into my pocket, searching for an ibuprofen. Alongside it, I'd pull out a tattered piece of paper, with a list of museums written on it, ticking one off.

The Winter Palace was the worst of the offenders. I left not just slightly dehydrated and bleary-eyed, but with a migraine, my sight embroidered with coloured splotches that seemed to pulsate.

The Russian approach to art collecting was similar to their taste in dill. Dill was stronger, more intense, than the distantly related variants I had tried back in Belfast. In the same way, Russian art collecting was masterpiece after masterpiece after masterpiece; it all blurred into a transcendental fever dream of high art. It horded works: Michelangelo, Rubens, van Dycks, Monet, Renoir, Degas, and rather demurely, only two Raphaels. And that was only one floor.

The Faberge Museum was no better, taking a Goldilocks approach. If the encrusted golden eggs were too obvious, perhaps the visitor would enjoy the stately palace the museum was housed in. If not, perhaps an exhibition of Dalí's best works would pique the interest of those with a more modern palate. One of them had to be just right.

Surprisingly, the Russian Museum was not top of the list. Perhaps this was because of its relative restraint. The walls were shockingly white – I had become rather accustomed to gold piping along the corners of the room like an *amuse-bouche*.

My friend and I had needlessly worried about our foreign Covid vaccines, which were widely rejected by Russian officialdom, but seemed to placate the blank gaze of the one guard on duty. He didn't even bother with the handheld metal detector, which was already being used to prop up his phone.

Having seen our passports were a different colour than the Russian garnet, he asked where we were from, but it seemed to be more of a reflex than out of any genuine interest. My answer of *Irish*, having handed him my British passport, seemed to do little to bring him out of his stupor. I felt rather put out by this guard's complete lack of interest; I had always had a much bigger reaction back home. I normally had to pick and choose, not being able to have my cake and eat it too. People had even outright rejected both before, deeming me utterly alien. I was too British to be Irish, and too Irish to be British, the paradoxical child of hundreds of years of history.

He didn't even ask about my Irish passport which was tucked safely away just in case I lost my British one which contained my visa. British citizens were allowed into Russia during Covid, the Irish were not. I didn't quite know what the Irish had done to Russia to make them think we were more infectious than the rest of Europe, but my dual citizenship had certainly come to my rescue.

As we entered the gallery, Russian folk figures danced and swirled before me – bogatyrs, holy fools, the fire bird. Landscapes were interrupted not by Milanese architecture, but by onion domes. Russian Orthodox saints replaced Celtic crosses and a rather imperious statue of Catherine the Great peered down at me, uncannily similar to a statue of Queen Victoria that I regularly walked past in Belfast.

I slipped through the museum. Names like Vasily, Anatoly, and Nikolai marked the walls and my eyes glided along them – the Matthews, Johns, and Lukes of Cyrillic. It was easier to read Russian names in Cyrillic than the Western alternative. They lost their signifiers somehow in the transliteration. I couldn't attach meaning to them like I could back home. I didn't know what side of the community the names were on when written in Cyrillic.

Something neon flashed in the corner of my eye and I faltered as the gallery quietened. It was a chartreuse moon, glittering out at me, incandescent as if lit from within. Unconsciously, my body moved closer as if in orbit. The light from the Moon bounced off clouds surrounding it and reflected on the river below, framing it almost. The river was unearthly still; the earth appeared to be holding its breath. Drawing close, my eyes strained to see through the blackness of the rest of the canvas. I had to squint to see the rest of the picture, animals and landscape smothered in a blanket of darkness.

Moving back again, to take in in its fullness, I glanced at the information to the left of the picture. *Night on the River Dnieper.* A landscape of rural Russia then, I presumed. But the name attached to the photo took me a minute to work through. Куинджи. My mouth and eyes stumbled over each phonetic, spelling it out slowly in my head, repeating it over and over until I could piece it all together fluently. Kuindzhi. One of the more unusual names in the gallery but given that it was "The Russian Museum" I hazarded a guess of its origin.

I left the museum empty-handed, having been unable to find a replica of the picture after flicking through the postcards in the museum giftshop. I looked online as well for prints, but they never quite seemed to capture the piece properly. The Moon lost its luminescence and seemed to wither in reproduction. I thought it would be more offensive to have such a bad replica than none at all and so I clicked off each webpage.

———

When I left Russia after the full-scale invasion of Ukraine, I kept coming back to that painting. My phone had lots of pictures of art that had enthralled me in the gallery and that flicker of attraction had died. But I regularly came back to the Kuindzhi piece.

I didn't show anybody the painting though, given the circumstances. The words that came out of my mouth became jumbled – what attempted to flatter a painting ended up sounding like I was excusing the brutal invasion of Ukraine. I heard a discussion of landscape painting, and the person on the receiving end heard a Putin sympathiser. The painting became muddied, complicit in Russia's recent illegality, trampled on by Russian soldiers.

As the war raged on, my Russian classes at university pivoted significantly. Gone were the classes on the golden age of Russian literature and history classes tracing the lineage of the Romanovs. Now, I studied Russian corruption, misinformation, and lack of legislation. It reminded me of when the building I had taken tutorials in during first year, had been stripped of its namesake when I returned for second year, because of his worrying historic comments on race.

I didn't think about that neon moon for months, but my hand stopped scrolling abruptly one day when a piece that was undeniably Kuindzhi came up on my newsfeed. It was a classic skyscape of his, a vermillion sunset I had seen across dozens of his works.

The painting wasn't standing alone however, suspended on the wall. Nor was it encased in glass. Instead, it was frameless, its white canvas edges laid bare with grubby dirt-flecked hands gripping it tightly. A man in soldier's garb held the painting, with a self-satisfied smirk. The flag on his arm was Russian.

Only then did my eyes lower to read the headline, announcing the Russian looting of precious Ukrainian artwork. Art in Ukrainian galleries had been taken by Russian soldiers for "safe-keeping" and was being transferred to Russian-occupied Ukraine. The cynic in me doubted the abilities of these burly Russian soldiers to masquerade as art conservators; they were hardly used to dainty work. Surely some pieces must have been damaged in transit.

Quite why Kuindzhi had been brought into this mess, though, I couldn't understand. But as I read on, a ball of dread seized my body up. The art museum in Mariupol that had been looted was named after Kuindzhi. Much as we had George Best International Airport in Belfast, it dawned on me that the art centre had been named after not just an icon, but a local icon. Kuindzhi was not Russian – he had been born in Mariupol, Ukraine.

My brain itched as I read, as if an ink pen was scribbling out the information in my head. Or perhaps rewriting. The river Dnieper was not in fact in Russia, but one of the key arteries in Ukraine's heartland. Nor was it the Dnieper, but the Dnipro. Kuindzhi's work did not depict Russian landscapes, but Crimean and Ukrainian.

Some of my own understanding was not wholly inaccurate, but parentheses were added in as I read to add much needed context. Kuindzhi had spent the latter part of his life in Russia (having grown up in Ukraine and only leaving for art school). Ukraine was a part of the Russian Empire during Kuindzhi's lifetime (but still held its own regional identity, culture, and language).

The breadth and gravity of my own misinformation left me on shaky ground. Kuindzhi was not, as I had initially presumed, a Russian name, but Ukrainian.

I had always thought such lies and misinformation were easy to distinguish, crudely dismissing the Russian population who blindly trusted blatant lies pumped out by state-owned media. But that was because I already had a basis of information that gave an alternative truth – my own English language media to distinguish lies from the truth. When I had no prior knowledge, I was not as sharp at distinguishing misinformation as I had previously assumed. It had just nestled into my subconscious, an assumed truth. It had slunk in unnoticed.

Wikipedia, ever faithful, also turned out to fail me. Even the Ukrainian and Russian Wikipedias could not agree to cooperate with each other when it came to Kuindzhi. Ukrainian Wikipedia claimed Kuindzhi had been born in 1841, citing a Ukrainian birth certificate. On the other hand, Russian Wikipedia disputed the existence of a birth certificate at all, estimating him to have been born in 1842.

Regardless, the guard in the Russian Museum would have certainly let Kuindzhi in with a Russian passport. Whether or not Kuindzhi would have said he was Ukrainian though, remains to be seen. While I was not Irish or British enough to constitute a citizen, and therefore counted as a half citizen of each, it seemed that Kuindzhi was both too Russian and too Ukrainian. Two unwilling participants in a contestation of identity, land, and sovereignty begun years before either of us were born. I wondered if Kuindzhi would have been a hun or a taig.

His most famous piece, *Ukrainian Night*, depicts a small rural idyll – a small cluster of houses lit against a dark backdrop of night. It is peaceful – the people in those houses are not crouching in bomb shelters, or experiencing blackouts.

Mariupol, Kuindzhi's birthplace has been decimated by Russia. It looks nothing like the Ukraine in Kuindzhi's artwork. There is a sense of safety in the solid walls of Kuindzhi's oil cottages. There is no safety in photos that come out of Mariupol now – entire apartment blocks have been made uninhabitable. While the pictures on the news show empty towns, much like the unpopulated pieces by Kuindzhi, there is no quiet in these photos. No peace.

NOTES

Bridge over the River Dnipro is permanently housed in the Russian Museum in St Petersburg.

Most of Kuindzhi's artwork is currently permanently housed in Russian state museums, including his most famous work *Ukrainian Night*. In 2019, celebrating Kuindzhi's 175th birthday (according to Russian calculations), the Tretyakov Gallery in Moscow brought together over 200 pieces of Kuindzhi's work from various other Russian museums.

The Kuindzhi Art Museum in Mariupol was destroyed on 21 March 2022 in a Russian airstrike. Kuindzhi's great nephew Serhiy Danilov was killed in the same airstrike.

At the time of this writing, the looted paintings, including Kuindzhi's *Red Sunset Over the Dnipro*, have not been seen since they were taken from Mariupol for "safe-keeping" in Russian-occupied Donetsk.

Arkhip Kuindzhi was born in Mariupol, in modern-day Ukraine. Kuindzhi's exact date of birth is highly contested though it is believed he was born in either 1841 or 1842. Both of Kuindzhi's parents died when he was very young and so he was forced to work from the age of six, receiving only a rudimentary education initially, until he began painting under the tutelage of Ivan Konstantinovich Aivazovsky in Crimea. From 1868, Kuindzhi moved to

St Petersburg, studying at the St Petersburg Academy of Arts. He was highly praised for his work during his lifetime, enjoying the patronage of Pavel Tretyakov, whose collection of Russian art now forms the basis of Moscow's Tretyakov Gallery. In 1878, he exhibited his work at the World Exhibition in Paris to much acclaim. At the height of his fame, in 1882, Kuindzhi secluded himself from society for twenty years, choosing to spend time shut away in his St Petersburg studio or on his property in Crimea. He died in 1910 from pneumonia. Much of Kuindzhi's work still resides in Russia today, including "Night on the River Dnipro", which can be found in St Petersburg's Russian Museum.

Alannah Millar was born in 2000 in England to Northern Irish parents but moved back to Ireland as a young child. She studied Russian Studies and English Literature at the University of Edinburgh and is now doing an MA in International Peace Studies at Trinity College Dublin, specialising in Russian Foreign Policy and the War in Ukraine. In 2021, Alannah moved to St Petersburg to study Russian but departed immediately after Russia launched its full-scale invasion of Ukraine. She now works as a journalist for Russian opposition newspaper Novaya Gazeta Europe *and as an advisor for WAVE Trauma Centre. She currently lives in Belfast and is completing her thesis.*

DEAR LARISA SHEPITKO,

———

Mark Cousins

The baton of detachment.

I'm an Irish-Scottish filmmaker. I saw your film *Wings* years ago, at the beginning of the twenty-first century and loved it. The solitude of the retired pilot, the way you show her memories, her self-doubt. I wanted to know more about you.

Decades later, though I've met people like Lynda Myles who knew you, I still want to know more. I'm sitting in an airport in Belfast in Northern Ireland, waiting for a flight. I always think of you and *Wings* and loneliness in airports. I usually travel alone, and so my mind wanders, or wonders. It's wandering now. Can I kill some time by writing to you? (My Ukrainian friend Polya Moshenska tells me that you have exactly the same "killing" time phrase in your language.)

Where to start? Maybe with the ending of your war movie *The Ascent*? I'm not sure I've seen many things like it in the whole history of cinema. I show it often and each time I cry. As you know, Boris Plotnikov's Soviet soldier has been captured by the Nazis and — it slowly dawns on us — is to be murdered by hanging. Snowy Belarus, and your shots gradually, and with dread, zoom in to the faces of the onlookers, the Nazis, to Boris as he starts to look more haunted, more Christ-like. Alfred Schnittke's music builds like *Das Rheingold*, layering the horror, the crawl to the atrocity. A boy cries, Boris seems to be transfigured, like a Guido Reni painting.

The scene's a gale of feeling, and I'm sure you're proud of it, but as I picture it here in this airport on a Thursday afternoon, can I tell you some things? The Soviet Union was dissolved on 26 December 1991, Russia invaded the Crimea on 20 February 2014, and the East of your home country on 24 February 2022.

These things happened decades after you died in your car accident, but I'm guessing that, as a Ukrainian who believed in the Soviet Union to a certain degree, but whose work was censored by it, these invasions would split you in two? Your earliest memories are of World War Two, and the Red Army at its best did indeed help defeat Nazism, but I know that by the time you made your first student film in 1956, Stalin had died, Khrushchev had asked questions about the barbarism of the previous years and the cautious Soviet introspection that ensued allowed you to begin to make cinema.

Seventy years later, it's hard to see Russian introspection. Many of its citizens support the invasions. My question to you – to myself – is how such changes would have affected your filmmaking. Most of the people in Ukraine have found common purpose in their hatred of Russia's violent land-grab. They are decolonising. This would chime with you in some ways because your movies are often about detached people – the retired pilot in *Wings* seems outside her times, the soldiers in *The Ascent* are part of an army but alone too, the doctor in *You and Me* (one of your greatest films) has out of body experiences. You weren't a natural joiner-upper were you? You were a lone wolf, and such people are sceptics away-from-the-numbers. That's where I want to be.

I've been appalled by Russia's murderous invasion of your country and I've seen how Ukraine has responded. Statues of Pushkin are being taken down because he has been used to tell a story of Russian exceptionalism. Such stories debase. The great soul of mother Russia is grating now. Maybe it grated for you decades ago.

So the detachment is right, and the detachment in your films is looking mature in new ways. I wish you were here in this airport, however, to help me understand where the detachment might go. Ukraine further disconnects from the control of its invader, and here in Northern Ireland, in a more minor way, we had to take some distance from the colonial story told by the British State. We are not an outcrop, simply grateful for the influence of a superior culture. But a friend of mine recently told me that some of his friends think Catherine the Great was as bad as Hitler.

The fog of war, the fury of killing, etc., but this is surely wrong. If we detach so completely, then don't we under-imagine our own humanity? There are Soviet scenes in your films, but it looks to me like you were neither naive nor cynical. As you travelled internationally (our mutual friend in Berkeley, Tom Luddy, told me a lot about you, and I think was in love with you), you saw that it was harder for women in capitalist countries to make a career as a filmmaker.

So how far do we detach, Larisa? How much does Ukraine rid itself of Russian culture? How much does the North of Ireland emphasise its non-Britishness? When a country like Scotland rightly objects to un-democratic impositions from the UK's London government, where might that lead?

One of your tutors was your fellow Ukrainian Alexander Dovzhenko. He, too, leant her shoulder to the Soviet wheel. In your years with him, I wonder were there ever moments when you distinguished between your Ukrainian and Soviet selves? Or is that not even a good question? His films *Zvenigora*, *Arsenal* and *Earth*, which came at the end of the silent era in cinema, are as great as yours, and also interested in poetics and loss. What did you talk about in bars in Moscow in the 1950s, when he was past your best, when you were approaching yours?

Did you have a sense of the baton passing from him to you, the baton of detachment?

My flight is delayed, Larisa. I might film something to kill time. Lynda Myles says that many people who met you fell in love with you. I suspect that I would have been one of the many.

After your tragic death, your husband made a lovely short tribute to you. It's on something called "YouTube".

You are remembered.

Mark

This essay appears in Mark Cousins' latest book, Dear Orson Welles & Other Essays, *published by The Irish Pages Press in 2024.*

A globally acclaimed Scottish-Irish director, writer and wanderer, Mark Cousins was born in 1965, raised in Northern Ireland during the Troubles, and has lived in Scotland since the early 1980s. His 24 feature-length films (as well as 30 short films) and 40 hours of television — including The Story of Film: An Odyssey, What is This Film Called Love?, Life May Be, A Story of Children and Film, Atomic, Stockholm My Love, I Am Belfast *and* The Eyes of Orson Welles — *have premiered in Cannes, Berlin, Sundance and Venice film festivals and have won the Prix Italia, a Peabody, the Persistence of Vision Award in San Francisco, the Maverick Award in Dublin, the Stanley Kubrick Award, and the European Film Academy Award for Innovative Storytelling as well as many other prizes. He has filmed in Iraq, Sarajevo during the siege, Iran, Mexico, across Asia and in America and Europe.*

Mark Cousins is also the author of six books, including the acclaimed The Story of Film *(Pavilion Books, 2004),* Imagining Reality: The Faber Book of Documentary *(Faber and Faber, 1996),* Widescreen: Watching. Real. People. Elsewhere *(Wallflower Press, 2008) and* The Story of Looking *(Canongate Books, 2017). His most recent volume is* Dear Orson Welles & Other Essays, *published in 2024 by The Irish Pages Press. He continues to live in Edinburgh.*

POEM

———

Peter Balakian

THINKING OF UKRAINE (MARCH '22)

There is the shadow of Mandelstam again.
Goat tongues nailed to fences.

The dog barks, the wind carries it.
There is the Potemkin burning the waves.

Molotov cocktails. Putin's Drones. The dazed
faces of children under glass.

The sky is pomegranate and the howling stones
howl in the mouths of wolves.

Kyiv, Lviv, Kharkiv. We watch the smashed —
homes and buildings and onion domes.

Night blows mastic across the Black Sea.
There is the human chain.

The cross of Saint Sophia kisses the sun.
Fires burn in the pockets of nuns.

Everything in Donetsk is muscle and improv —
love and guns and dear.

Parajanov is in prison again for making
a film about Ukraine. Tanks cut the border.

A child is cut in half by mortar.
There is the human chain.

My grandfather is boarding a ship
again for points West.

The maternity hospital in Mariupol —
is fire, glass, cut heads.

There is Satan again offering his pay
for the mouths of children.

Pregnant women navigate the rubble.
A boy blown up on his mother;

Women pass their infants through a fence.
The hands of sisters cross the Polish border.

The dictator's face vanishes into broken
glass. There is the human chain.

Peter Balakian (born 1951) is an Armenian-American poet, prose writer, and scholar. He is the author of many books including Ozone Journal *(winner of the Pulitzer Prize for Poetry),* Black Dog of Fate *(winner of the PEN/Albrand Award for Memoir), and* The Burning Tigris: The Armenian Genocide and America's Response, *a New York Times Best Seller and winner of the Raphael Lemkin Prize. He is Donald M and Constance H Rebar Professor of the Humanities at Colgate University, in Hamilton, New York.*

THE NORMALIZATION OF EVIL: HOW TO DEFEND HUMAN RIGHTS AND FREEDOM IN THE TWENTY-FIRST CENTURY?

Oleksandra Matviichuk

Freedom, solidarity, love – and ordinary people.

I am a human rights lawyer. For many years I have been applying the law to defend people and human dignity. Now I am in a situation where the law does not work.

10 years ago, millions of people in Ukraine peacefully participated in the Revolution of Dignity and the authoritarian regime collapsed. We got a chance to build a country where the rights of everybody are protected, government is accountable, courts are independent, and police do not beat students who are peacefully demonstrating. In order to stop us on this path, 10 years ago, Russia started a war, occupied Crimea and Donbas, and two years ago expanded this war to a full-scale invasion. Because Putin is not afraid of NATO. Putin is afraid of the idea of freedom.

Russian troops are destroying residential buildings, churches, schools, museums and hospitals. They are shooting at the evacuation corridors. They are torturing people in filtration camps. They are forcibly taking Ukrainian children to Russia. They ban the Ukrainian language and culture. They are abducting, robbing, raping and killing in the occupied territories. The entire UN system of peace and security cannot stop it.

We have faced an unprecedented number of war crimes. We have united efforts with dozens of regional organisations and built a national network of documenters throughout the country. Working together, we have recorded more than 72,000 episodes of war crimes.

Russia uses war crimes as a method of warfare. Russia tries to break people's resistance and occupy the country with the tool which I call the immense pain of the civilian population. We are documenting more than just violations of the Geneva or Hague Conventions. We are documenting human pain.

This is a story of the 10-year-old boy Ilya Matviyenko from Mariupol. When Russian troops surrounded the city, they did not allow the International Committee of the Red Cross to evacuate civilians. Hence, Ilya and his mother

Nataliya hid in the basement of their house from the Russian shelling. Like many people in the city, they melted snow to have water and made fires to cook at least some food. When the supplies ran out, they were forced to go out and consequently they became exposed to shelling. His mother was wounded in her head, and the boy's leg was torn. With the last of her strength, the mother dragged her son to a friend's apartment. There was no medical assistance. The Russians had already destroyed the maternity hospital and the entire medical infrastructure in Mariupol. That is why in the apartment they laid down on the couch and just hugged each other. They were lying like that for several hours. Ilya told my colleague that his mother died and froze right in his arms.

I have one question. How will people, in the twenty-first century, defend human beings, their lives, their freedom and their dignity? Can we rely on the law – or does only brutal force matter?

It is important to understand this not only for people in Ukraine, Syria, China, Iran, Nicaragua or Sudan. The answer to this question determines our common future.

I don't know what historians in the future will call this historical period. The world order, based on the UN Charter and international law, is collapsing before our eyes. The international peace and security system established after the Second World War provided unjustified indulgences for certain countries. It did not cope well with global challenges before, but now it is stalling and reproducing ritualistic movements. The work of the Security Council is paralyzed. We have entered a period of turbulence, and now fires will occur more and more frequently in different parts of the world because the international wiring is faulty and sparks are everywhere.

We are dealing with the formation of an entire authoritarian bloc. I live in Kyiv, and my native city, like thousands of other Ukrainian cities, is being shelled not only by Russian missiles but also by Iranian drones. China is helping Russia circumvent sanctions and import technologies critical to warfare. North Korea sent Russia more than a million artillery shells. Syria votes at the UN General Assembly in support of Russia. These regimes that captured power in their countries feature a crucial commonality. All of them have the same idea of what a human being is.

Authoritarian leaders consider people as objects of control and deny them rights and freedoms. Democracies consider people, their rights and freedoms to be of the highest value. There is no way to negotiate this. The existence of the free world always threatens dictatorships with the loss of power. Because human beings inherently have a desire for freedom.

Therefore, when we talk about Russia's war against Ukraine, we are not talking about a war between two states. This is a war between two systems – authoritarianism and democracy. Russia wants to convince the entire world that freedom, democracy and human rights are fake values. Because they do not protect anyone in war. Russia wants to convince people that a state with a powerful military potential and nuclear weapons can break the world order, dictate its rules to the international community and even forcibly change internationally recognized borders.

If Russia succeeds, it will encourage authoritarian leaders in various parts of the world to do the same. So democratic governments will be forced to invest money not in education, health care, culture or business development, not in solving global problems such as climate change or social inequality, but in weapons. We will witness an increase in the number of nuclear states, the emergence of robotic armies and new weapons of mass destruction. If Russia succeeds and this scenario comes true, we will find ourselves in a world that will be dangerous for everyone without exception.

Unpunished evil grows. The Russian military committed terrible crimes in Chechnya, Moldova, Georgia, Syria, Mali, Libya, other countries of the world. They have never been punished for it. They believe they can do whatever they want.

I talked to hundreds of people who survived Russian captivity. They've told how they were beaten, raped, packed into wooden boxes, electrically shocked through their genitalia, and their fingers were cut, their nails were torn away, their knees were drilled, they were compelled to write with their own blood. One woman told me how her eye was dug out with a spoon.

There is no legitimate reason for doing this. There is also no military necessity for it. Russians did these horrific things only because they could.

If we want to prevent wars we have to punish states and their leaders who start such wars. Because all the atrocities which we are documenting stem from the leadership's decisions to start the war. In the whole history of humankind, we have only one precedent of punishment for the crime of aggression. It was the Nuremberg Trials.

We still look at the world through the lens of the Nuremberg Trials, where Nazi war criminals were tried only after the Nazi regime had collapsed. But we are living in a new century. Justice should not depend on how and when the war ends. Justice must not wait. The global approach to war crimes justice needs to be changed. We must establish a special tribunal now and hold Putin, Lukashenko and other war criminals accountable.

War turns people into numbers. The scale of war crimes grows so fast that it becomes impossible to tell all the stories. But I will tell you one.

This is the story of 62-year-old civilian Oleksandr Shelipov. He was killed by the Russian military near his own house. The tragedy received huge media coverage only because it was the first court trial since the full-scale invasion. In the court, his wife Kateryna shared that her husband was an ordinary farmer, but he was her whole universe and now she's lost everything.

People are not numbers. We must ensure justice for all, regardless of who the victims are, their social position, the type and level of cruelty they've endured, and whether or not international organizations or media are interested in their case. We must return people their names. Because the life of each person matters.

People in Ukraine want peace much more than anyone else. But peace does not come when the country which was invaded stops fighting. That is not peace, that's occupation. Occupation is just another form of war.

Occupation is not just changing the national flag from one to another. Occupation means torture, enforced disappearances, rape, mass deportations, forced adoption of your children, erasure of your identity, filtration camps and mass graves.

Russia is using terror against civilians to keep the occupied territories subdued. The Russian military and special services are physically eliminating active people on the ground – priests, mayors, journalists, volunteers, environmentalists, teachers, artists and entrepreneurs. People under occupation have no way to protect their rights, their freedom, their property, their lives, and their loved ones.

The occupation does not reduce human suffering, it simply makes it invisible. When the Ukrainian army released the Kharkiv region, mass graves were found in the forest near Izium. The murdered children's writer Volodymyr Vakulenko was found in an identified grave under number 319. He wrote beautiful stories for children and entire generations grew up with his *Daddy's book*. During the Russian occupation, Volodymyr disappeared. His family hoped to the last that he was alive and, like thousands of other people, was in Russian captivity. It is difficult for them to accept the results of the identification.

We can't leave people alone in the occupied territories, exposed to torture and death. People's lives cannot be a "political compromise". Sustainable peace is the freedom to live without fear of violence and to have long-term prospects. Calls for Ukraine to stop defending itself and to satisfy Russia's imperial appetites are not just wrong. They are immoral.

When the international community deal with wars there is a great temptation to avoid solving difficult problems, hoping that they will just vanish. But the truth is that they only get worse. If we don't stop Putin in Ukraine, Russia will go further. Whether we are brave enough to admit it or not, European countries are safe only because Ukrainians are still fighting.

The problem is not only that the freedom space in authoritarian countries has narrowed to the size of a prison cell. The problem is that even in developed democracies, forces calling into question the Universal Declaration of Human Rights are gaining weight.

There are reasons for this. The coming generations replaced those ones that survived the Second World War. They have inherited democracy from their parents. They have begun to take rights and freedoms for granted. They have become consumers of values. They perceive freedom as choosing between cheeses in the supermarket. Therefore, they are ready to exchange freedom for economic benefits, promises of security or personal comfort.

Yet, the truth is that freedom is very fragile. Human rights are not attained once and forever. We must defend our values. It is the determination to act that defines a society that has a future.

I have been working with the law for many years, and I know for sure that if you cannot rely on legal mechanisms, you can always rely on people. We are used to thinking in categories of states and interstate organizations. But ordinary people have much more impact than they can even imagine.

Immediately after the invasion, international organizations evacuated their personnel, and so it was ordinary people in Ukraine who supported those in the combat zone, who took people out of ruined cities, who helped them to survive under artillery fire, who rescued people trapped under the rubble of residential buildings, who broke through the encirclement to deliver humanitarian aid.

Ordinary people started to do extraordinary things. And then it became obvious that ordinary people fighting for their freedom and human dignity are stronger than the whole Russian military machine. That ordinary people can change the history quicker than UN intervention.

I would never wish anyone to go through this experience. Nevertheless, these dramatic times provide us with an opportunity to reveal the best in us – to be courageous, to fight for freedom, to take the burden of responsibility, to make difficult but right choices, to help each other. Now more than ever, we keenly feel what it means to be a human.

Despite everything, the story of Ukraine is a life-affirming story. Because it is in dramatic times that hope is born. When someone tries to take away freedom, it begins to speak powerfully through every person.

There are many things that have no limitation in national borders. Freedom is one of them. As well as human solidarity. We live in a very interconnected world. Only the spread of freedom makes our world safer.

Oleksandra Viacheslavivna Matviichuk is a Ukrainian human rights lawyer and civil society leader based in Kyiv. She heads the non-profit organization Centre for Civil Liberties (founded in 2007) and is a campaigner for democratic reforms in her country and the OSCE region. Since October 2022, she has been Vice-President of the International Federation for Human Rights, based in Paris. The Centre for Civil Liberties was awarded the 2022 Nobel Peace Prize, jointly with Ales Bialiatski (the Belarusian pro-democrcy activist and prisoner of conscience) and the Russian organization Memorial. This was the first Nobel Prize awarded to a Ukrainian citizen or organization.

THE AGE OF THE REFUGEE: NOTES ON THE WARS IN THE FORMER YUGOSLAVIA AND UKRAINE

Christopher Merrill

Following the Milosević-Tuđman playbook.

At dinner on the night of Bill Clinton's presidential inauguration in 1993, in a restaurant in Skopje, (North) Macedonia, an American diplomat attached to the Organization for Security and Cooperation in Europe (OCSE) remarked, "Anyone in refugee work will have no trouble getting a job for the next twenty or thirty years" – a prediction repeatedly borne out by the flows of refugees fleeing conflicts in the Balkans, Somalia, Rwanda, Afghanistan, Iraq, Syria, Eritrea, Democratic Republic of Congo, Central African Republic, Sudan and South Sudan, Myanmar, and Ukraine. More than one hundred and ten million people have been forcibly displaced from their homes in recent years, one third of whom are considered refugees. There is indeed no shortage of work for humanitarians today.

Nor is there a shortage of bad actors seeking to take advantage of chaos in the international order. The Russian invasion and occupation of Crimea and parts of the Luhansk and Donetsk regions of Ukraine followed the playbook perfected by Slobodan Milošević and Franjo Tuđman, presidents of Serbia and Croatia, respectively, in dismembering Yugoslavia, the tragic consequences of which I explored in a pair of books, *The Old Bridge: The Third Balkan War and the Age of the Refugee* (Milkweed Editions, 1996) and *Only the Nails Remain: Scenes from the Balkan Wars* (Rowman & Littlefield, 1999). What shocked the conscience in 1992 – concentration camps and mass graves, ethnic cleansing and rape as a tool of war, the siege of Sarajevo, which would become the longest in modern history, beginning just eight years after the city hosted the Winter Olympics – would be repeated, eerily for journalists, humanitarians, and observers of the Balkan wars, when on 24 February 2022 Vladimir Putin launched a full-scale attack on Ukraine.

"The war the Ukrainians face every day is the most devastating element of a coordinated effort to bring down democracies", notes the historian Timothy Snyder. This autocratic alliance of Russia, North Korea, Iran, and China, bolstered by right-wing governments in Hungary, Slovakia, Turkey, as well as Donald Trump and his Republican minions in Congress, poses the gravest threat to democratic societies since the advent of World War II and the end of the Cold War – an inflection point in world affairs, comparable to the immediate aftermath of the bombing of Hiroshima and Nagasaki in 1945 and the dismantling of the Berlin Wall in 1989. What assistance the United States and its allies provide to Ukraine, in the forms of weaponry, intelligence, financial support, military and political advice, strategy and tactics, may determine whether the democratic backsliding that has defined the last decade of international relations will continue or be reversed. What happened during the Wars of Succession in the Former Yugoslavia might help to guide our thinking about the West's obligations to Ukraine. No telling how this will turn out.

———

One rainy morning on a cultural diplomacy mission to Ukraine, in December 2015, not long after the Revolution of Dignity, I toured the memorial in Kyiv's central square to the protesters killed in the Maidan massacre – 108 men and women posthumously awarded the title, "Hero of Ukraine", and known collectively as the Heavenly Hundred. Their protest against President Viktor Yanukovych's decision not to sign the European Union-Ukraine Association Agreement, choosing instead to forge closer ties with Russia, turned violent when special riot police opened fire on the barricaded occupation camp established on the Maidan. The large photographs of the dead arranged in a line along the street were a vivid reminder of the bloodshed that marked Ukraine's third attempt to chart its own path forward after the dissolution of the Soviet Union, the first being its proclamation of independence on 24 August 1991, which was approved by 92 percent of Ukrainian voters in a subsequent referendum on 1 December 1991; the second was the 2004 Orange Revolution, which was inspired by accusations of election rigging that handed the presidency to Yanukovych, whose name would become familiar to Americans after the arrest of Paul Manafort on multiple charges arising from his work on Yanukovych's behalf before the pro-Russian president was overthrown in the Revolution of Dignity, precipitating Putin's decision to invade eastern Ukraine and occupy Crimea. For independence is the *bête noir* of authoritarians everywhere.

The siege of Sarajevo, which began on 6 April 1992, was perhaps inevitable once the government of Bosnia and Hercegovina, following the lead of Slovenia and Croatia, declared its independence from Yugoslavia. What haunts me from my journeys to the besieged city, apart from the suffering and terror that Sarajevans daily experienced, was the indifference displayed by many governments and their citizens toward the victims of war crimes documented by journalists, humanitarians, and diplomats. It never failed to surprise me, while visiting friends in Europe and America, on domestic and international flights, at parties and writers' conferences, how difficult it was to convince others that Bosnians deserved our sympathy and support, military as well as humanitarian.

I was hardly alone in despairing over the fact that the criminal siege of Sarajevo did not inspire the Western powers to lift the UN-mandated arms embargo on the ragtag Bosnian army and strike the Serbian forces occupying nearly two-thirds of Bosnian territory – the proposed so-called "lift and strike" policy that many pundits and politicians in the West had invoked to *justify* their refusal to act. One morning after a press conference in Sarajevo, for example, the Pulitzer-Prize winning journalist John Burns told me two things that would shape my thinking about the war: 1) "This story", he said, gesturing toward the mountains rising above the city, from which Serbian forces attacked civilians with impunity, "writes itself." And 2) *The New York Times*, which regularly published his stories on its front page, often above the fold, had commissioned a survey of its readers, only 19 percent of whom read his stories; if the most sophisticated American news consumers had little interest in the first European war since World War II, what hope was there for the outgunned Bosnians to garner support in the White House to implement lift and strike? The Clinton administration's failure to protect Bosnia until the summer of 1995, when Serbs massacred 8,000 men and boys in Srebrenica, finds a contemporary echo in the sizable number of GOP congressmen who refuse to approve arms sales to Ukraine. For political cowardice is always an equal opportunity employer. But the stakes are higher now than they were in the 1990s, when the Russian Federation that arose from the ashes of the Soviet Union was weak, corrupt, and impoverished, not to mention incapable of securing significant economic and military assistance from other countries.

We live in what George Steiner called "the age of the refugee", the social and economic fallout from which can harden the heart and inure us to the pain of others, accentuating political divisions even as governments are under increasing pressure to strengthen democratic institutions and ensure the well-being of all their citizens. "The Axis of Upheaval" is the term of art coined by Andrea Kendall-Taylor and Richard Fontaine to describe the coordinating efforts of China, Iran, and North Korea to support Russia's war on Ukraine and overturn "the principles, rules, and institutions that underlie the prevailing international system" (*Foreign Affairs*, 23 April 2024). And refugees are the most visible representatives of upheaval, which has come to define the age more than the end of history the political theorist Francis Fukuyama predicted for the aftermath of the Cold War.

———

"The past is never dead", William Faulkner wrote in *Requiem for a Nun*. "It's not even past." This was what often came to mind during the three-month-long Russian siege of Mariupol, a Ukrainian city on the coast of the Sea of Azov that fell to Russian forces in May 2022. The stories of Ukrainian valor under Russian shelling reminded me of the courage displayed by many Sarajevans during the siege; also the ingenuity of writers and artists who discovered reserves of strength and determination, despite the losses they endured. Thus an old woman invited me into her apartment to see her frescoes, which covered the walls with images of what she most missed – the sun; her husband, killed at the start of the war; fruits and vegetables, tea and sugar, a box of muesli; a jungle scene from a Kipling novel, which she had burned to cook a meal; her daughter and granddaughter, who were living in a refugee camp in the Netherlands – as well as a portrait of the Buddha, who in her view had no use for the nationalists who had destroyed everything she loved.

In a 2020 BBC documentary *Russia: The Empire Strikes Back*, Steve Rosenberg observed that "Russia's idea is to be the grand spoiler in the world." Consider Hungary in 1956, Czechoslovakia in 1968, Afghanistan in 1979, Georgia in 2008, Ukraine in 2014 and again in 2022 – Russian imperial designs are a constant in modern history. What the Franco-Czech novelist Milan Kundera wrote about the brutal end of the Prague Spring – "enraged by the country's insolent self-emancipation, the Russians invaded with half a million soldiers" – continues to be true. "Dictators are perishable", Kundera wrote in his penultimate novel, *Ignorance*. "Russia is eternal." This I learned when I undertook a series of cultural diplomacy missions to Russia, first as a member of the U.S.-Russia Bilateral Presidential Commission, which was created in 2009 to reset relations between the historic enemies and abandoned after Russia invaded Ukraine, and then in my role as Director of the International Writing Program. I traveled to Moscow and St. Petersburg, Smolensk and Tula, Krasnoyarsk and Yekaterinburg, lecturing on Joseph Brodsky, Walt Whitman, travel writing, war reportage, and the creative process, scarcely thinking about the war in Ukraine until a Russian writer-friend told me a story about her hairdresser, who told her that Putin's decision to occupy Crimea had filled her with such pride that her breasts grew a full size – which may help to explain why Putin has maintained the support of the vast majority of his citizens for a war that has left some 450,000 dead or wounded Russian soldiers.

On a walk through the Katyn War Cemetery, in a forest outside Smolensk, where mass graves containing the remains of nearly 4,500 Polish military officers from the Kozelsk prisoner of war camp were exhumed in 1990, along with 6,500 Russian victims of the Great Purges in the 1930s, I wondered how to gauge the depths of suffering integral to these bloodlands. Like any practitioner of cultural exchanges, I was mindful of the limits of what I might understand about the tragic fate of those memorialized. Yet all I could think about was the crash of the airplane carrying Polish President Lech Kaczyński, his wife, and 87 politicians and high-ranking military officers here on 10 April 2010 to celebrate the 70th anniversary of the Katyn massacre. The plane went down in dense fog on its final approach to the Smolensk Air Base, killing everybody aboard and launching conspiracy theories about the cause of the accident – which have not abated. Russian authorities removed the Polish flag from the memorial in June 2022, while members of the Duma began to call for the complex to be destroyed. Revisionist historians were hellbent on promoting the view that Nazis had carried out the Katyn massacre, which was patently false. But it turns out that in the hands of skilled propagandists the truth can become fungible.

———

The news of Jared Kushner's lucrative real estate deals in Belgrade, Serbia and the Albanian island of Sazan brought to mind an afternoon by the Adriatic Sea in 1995, on a cultural diplomacy mission to Albania. I was swimming in sight of the island, which in the Communist era had been a naval base, joking with another writer about the fashionable resorts that we imagined might one day line this coast, unaware that Serbian paramilitaries under the command of General Ratko Mladić were about to execute all the men and boys in Srebrenica. It was later reported that a photograph on the front page of *The New York Times* of a young woman who had hanged herself in the woods outside of town, hoping to avoid being raped and killed at the hands of the Serbs, prompted Vice President Al Gore's daughter, Karenna, to ask him why the administration was not doing more to end the bloodshed. "At that moment the decision crystallized to make the U.S. bombing threat a real one. 'We've got to try something,' the President concluded. Giving war a chance helped push all sides to the peace table in Dayton" (*Time*, 16 May 1999). An air campaign followed, and in a few short weeks the war was all but over – something that could have happened years earlier, if only the Western Powers had not dithered. This same dynamic delayed for six months the approval of funding in the U.S. House of Representatives for arms to be sent to Ukraine, causing the needless deaths of thousands of Ukrainians, the destruction of countless factories, museums, libraries, and schools, and the steady loss of U.S. influence across the world.

My last wartime trip to the Balkans was in December 1995, just after the Bosnian, Croatian, and Serbian leaders had signed the Dayton Peace Accords. The first stop was the village of Jasenovac, the site of the third largest concentration and extermination camp in World War II, where upwards of 100,000 Serbs, Jews, Roma, Croatian intelligentsia, and Bosnian Muslims were killed by the Nazi-aligned Ustaša regime. Sixty miles southeast of the Croatian capital of Zagreb, Jasenovac is infamous for the viciousness of its executioners, who used knives, hammers, and axes to kill the prisoners they did not shoot. The art gallerist I was traveling with did not want to be there, arguing that Croats were fed up with Serbian nationalists justifying their warmaking on Croatian crimes from long ago. "You know, you can't feel guilty forever", she said.

Meantime NATO peacekeeping forces were preparing to deploy to Bosnia. I spent a day in Županje, Croatia, watching hundreds of American tanks, Bradley armored vehicles, and Humvees cross the Sava River on the largest pontoon bridge erected by the U.S. military since the spanning of the Rhine in World War II. What an impressive display of firepower this was – the continuous roar of the vehicles could be heard from miles away – after years of Western indecision. In late August, after a Serbian shell killed 37 people in the Sarajevo Market, NATO launched waves of air raids on Serbian command-and-control centers, fuel depots, and ammunition dumps, coupled with thirteen Tomahawk cruise missiles, which prompted the Serbs to withdraw their forces from their positions above the capital and begin to negotiate the terms of the Dayton Peace Accords. When I arrived in Sarajevo the Serbs were digging up their dead and moving to Serbian enclaves outside the city or to Belgrade to start over. I struck up a conversation with a British officer, who would work with American forces to train Bosnian soldiers. "You have to admire these people", he said of the Bosnians. "They didn't just lay down and die. They defended themselves well. After all, they had no choice." The same could be said of the Ukrainians, who have no choice but to fight.

Christopher Merrill has published eight collections of poetry, including Watch Fire, *for which he received the Lavan Younger Poets Award from the Academy of American Poets, and* On the Road to Lviv; *many edited volumes and translations; and six books of nonfiction, among them,* Only the Nails Remain: Scenes from the Balkan Wars, Things of the Hidden God: Journey to the Holy Mountain, *and* Self-Portrait with Dogwood. *His writings have been translated into nearly 40 languages; his journalism appears widely; and his honours include a Chevalier des Arts et des Lettres from the French government, numerous translation awards, and fellowships from the John Simon Guggenheim Memorial and Ingram Merrill Foundations. As director of the International Writing Program at the University of Iowa since 2000, Merrill has conducted cultural diplomacy missions to more than 50 countries. He served on the U.S. National Commission for UNESCO from 2011-2018, and in April 2012 President Barack Obama appointed him to the National Council on the Humanities.*

JUST WAR

—

David Rieff

What one is good at.

Life, in Kierkegaards's great phrase, can only be understood retrospectively but must be lived prospectively. Looking back at my own life, it seems to me that I began the thirty-two years that took me from middle age to old age as a witness to one just war – Bosnia – and have entered my seventies as a witness to a second, Ukraine. I turned forty in the fall of 1992, watching with other journalists the evacuations of prisoners from Trnopolje, one of the archipelago of concentration camps the Serbs had established in Northern Bosnia over the course of that summer, but were then shutting down. And I have passed much of my seventieth and now of my seventy-first as well in a second just war – Ukraine.

Of course, when I arrived in Bosnia in the late summer of 1992, so ignorant of the place that in my pitch to *The New Yorker Magazine*, which first sent me there, I alluded to wanting to report on "ethnic cleaning", I would not have described it in this way. While I soon came to believe, both from what I experienced and from what I was able to learn about the background to the conflict, that the morality of the war was clear – that the Bosnians were the victims and the Serbs, and, to a lesser extent, and more ambiguously, the Croats, the victimizers – I did not yet have the language with which to justify that belief in any intellectually and philosophically serious sense. That language I only engaged with seriously in the mid/late-nineties, after the Bosnian War had come to its shabby conclusion, when I began to read Catholic Just War Theory, which, at least for anyone who is not a Pacifist, stands the most profound moral argument about war for those who believe wars are sometimes necessary.

Simply put, Just War Theory, which derives from both the writing of St Augustine and St Thomas Aquinas holds that for a war to be just, two principles must be fully met. The first, known as *just ad bellum*, holds that a war must have a just cause, while the second requirement, *jus in bello*, demands justice in the means with which the war is fought. This second element is in many ways the more important of the two. For while it is fairly easy to think of wars fought in a just cause, few even of these – and most wars are simply unjust, full stop, struggles between two sets of swine in which one's moral sympathies belong with those wars' victims rather with either belligerent – have been fought justly.

For this, Catholic Just War Theory sets a very high threshold for what qualifies. To begin with, in practice if not altogether in theory, only defensive wars are justifiable, which means, to take an extreme case, that a war fought to abolish slavery in another country would probably not be considered just even if waged with the noblest of intentions. There is also an obligation that all realistic peace efforts have been exhausted and that there is no outside power that can protect a country from aggression. In other words, war must always be a last recourse. And even if these criteria are met, a war's moral legitimacy depends on other stringent conditions. As laid out in the Catechism, these are: first, that "the damage inflicted by the aggressor on the nation or community of nations must be lasting, grave, and certain"; second, that "all other means of putting an end to it must have been shown to be impractical or ineffective"; third, that "there must be a serious prospect of success"; and fourth, that "the use of arms must not produce evils or disorders greater than the evil to be eliminated".

This final point is crucial, both in its moral vindication of certain wars and in the stringent standards it sets for such vindication. For any moral justification of war that does not concede from the outset that war is evil is not worth taking seriously. That is because even the most just of wars fought with the most stringent effort to avoid the slaughter of innocents is inevitably going to cause the slaughter of innocents. It is because such slaughter is not a possible but rather an inevitable consequence of all wars, just and unjust alike, that gives Pacifist arguments their moral force. But if one is not a Pacifist, it imposes on those of us who are not Pacifists to justify why those few wars that one believes are being waged in a just cause qualify as just wars.

And by this yardstick, few turn out to qualify. The obvious example at this moment is the Gaza War. There are many arguments that can be made both by those who support Palestine and those who support Israel that their respective causes are just. But it is almost impossible to make a serious case that either side is fighting the war justly. But neither is it possible to seriously claim that those waging a just war will not do evil things, and Catholic Just War Theory makes no demand, only insisting the evil and disorder wrought by the just must not be greater that the evil being resisted. And self-evidently, the determination is anything but a simple one. The classic case of this is the

US decision to drop the nuclear bombs that in 1945 obliterated the Japanese cities of Hiroshima and Nagasaki. Those who justified the action did so by saying it would bring the war to an end, and thus save more lives than it would extinguish. Those who abhor the decision claim that it created a greater evil than the one it sought to eliminate.

I have been lucky enough not to face such an ethical dilemma. For both in the case of Bosnia between 1992 and 1995, and that of Ukraine since the beginning of the full scale invasion on 24 February 2022, those defending those beleaguered countries have both been morally in the right to do so and have done so in a way that has been as honorable as that of their enemies have been dishonorable. Again, to say this is not to make either the Bosnians or the Ukrainians out to be saints, although there have been many times, as in the case of those Serb concentration camps in Northern Bosnia or the torture mills the Russians established in Bucha during the time they occupied that martyred town, when the monstrousness of the Serbs and Russians seeking to destroy them has seemed inescapable.

For all the rigors of trying to bear witness in Bosnia then and Ukraine today, in moral terms it is an easy assignment. In thirty-two years, I have seen many wars as a journalist and as a writer and most confirm the humanitarian and "human rightsist" understanding of the world, which is to say that the wars in question should never have happened, those who caused them would in a better world be thought of not as leaders but as enemies of the human race, and solidarity should be offered only to the victims. But the sad truth, proven over and over and over again, from Sudan to Myanmar, Kyiv to Gaza, DRC to Yemen, is that while I wish that my friends in the human rights world had been correct in saying that, albeit painfully and infuriatingly slowly, we had shifted from the Westphalian order of nation states and realpolitik to a new international order of rights, instead the reality is that these ideas based on a functioning international community of functioning institutions and shared moral values now lie buried under the rubble of half a century's hopes.

But the fact that most wars are unjust, and that even other wars fought in the name of just causes are fought unjustly and, speaking for myself, seem to defy any effort to choose sides, does not mean that there are no just wars. And in our time Ukraine is that just war, just as, in my view the independence of Bangladesh was in the 1970s and the military struggle of the ANC was in the 1980s. In the case of Ukraine, the elements demanded by the Catechism in order to be able to call a war just have been entirely met. The first, that the damage the invader seeks to cause is "lasting, grave, and certain" is not open to question. The Russians deny even the existence of Ukraine as a nation ("so-called Ukraine" is the way the country is referred to on Russian television), as a culture (i.e. Ukrainian culture is just a junior part of Russian culture, and of *Russkiy Mir*, "The Russian World"), and as an identity ("Ukrainians are bewitched Russians" is the way one popular Russian commentator often formulates it).

To put it starkly, for Ukraine to exist, it must resist.

Hence Catholic Just War Theory's requirement that the damage done by the aggressor be "lasting, grave, and certain" is being demonstrated every day in Ukraine. The Russian way of war is to destroy everything in its path. That was what Putin's army did to Grozny in 2001, destruction that two years later led the United Nations to designate the Chechen capital as "the most destroyed city on earth". It was what that same army did to Aleppo in 2016. And it is what Russia did to the Ukrainian city of Mariupol in 2022. If sufficient air defenses do not reach the Ukrainians in time, there is no reason to suppose that Kharkiv, Ukraine's second largest city after Kyiv, will not eventually suffer the same fate. This is what the firebrands on Russian Television call for nightly, and as, in the past, this is what Russia has done elsewhere, only a fool would not take them at their word.

Another requirement of Catholic Just War Theory is that all other options than war have been tried and proven ineffective. And there are those who argue that Ukraine could have offered Russia more concessions in negotiations in the run-up to the full-scale invasion. But the concessions in question were basically that Ukraine accept recolonization by Russia, or, more precisely reabsorption into *Russkiy Mir*. Anyone doubting this should read Vladimir Putin's essay, "On The Historical Unity Of Russians And Ukrainians", which he published in July of 2021. Ukraine and Russia, he writes, are essential "parts of the same historical and spiritual space", and Ukrainian nationalism is nothing more than an effort to "sow discord among people, the overarching goal being to divide and then to pit the parts of a single people one against the other."

Those who believe that Ukraine should have been more conciliatory toward Russia are guilty of what, in first year philosophy, is called a category mistake. For the fundamental issue was never Russia's anxieties about NATO expansion, let alone the rights of Russian-speakers in Ukraine. It was Ukraine's right to exist. For as far as Putin is concerned, Ukrainian nationhood is by definition an anti-Russian project. And you cannot negotiate with an adversary who denies your existence, the legitimacy of your national project, and the validity of your cultural identity. It is true that between Ukraine's formal independence in 1991 and what Ukrainians call the Revolution of Dignity in 2014, Russia was willing to accept the existence of a Ukraine that was formally independent as long as its subservience to Russia was understood. But the moment the Ukrainians chose real independence, which is what the 2014 revolution in the Maidan was all about, Russia chose war, first a limited war in the east, then the annexation of Crimea. And when Ukraine did not bend, Putin opted for the full scale invasion of February 2022.

Against this invasion, Ukraine's resistance has been heroic; it has surprised the world, perhaps including the Ukrainians themselves. But can that resistance be sustained? The honest answer is that, at this point, it is impossible to know. For we are still deep in Clausewitz proverbial "fog of war". But as far as fulfilling the final requirement of Catholic Just War Theory goes, which is that for a war to be just, the just side must have a reasonable chance of prevailing, there is no longer any question. Ukraine has proved that it can win, providing it gets the armaments it needs to do so. In short, if any modern war can be called just, it is Ukraine's fight against Vladimir Putin's determination to make an example of their country as he continues his project of restoring the Russian Empire. The bitter irony is that while the case of Ukraine validated Catholic Just War Theory, the Catholic Church itself seems bent on repudiating it.

To be sure, Just War Theory remains part of the Catechism, and thus is still doctrinally authoritative. But Church leaders beginning with Pius XII in the 1940s and 1950s, continuing with John XXIII in his encyclical *Pacem in Terris* in 1963, and now and most explicitly and frontally with Pope Francis' comments on the Russian war on Ukraine, have questioned its relevance. It was Pius XII, in 1953, who affirmed that although in principle nations had the right to go to war to defend themselves against unjust aggression, the development of nuclear weapons meant that the harms wrought by war could be so great that they would no longer be comparable to that caused by tolerating injustice. In such a case, he insisted, "We may be obliged to suffer injustice." Francis has gone much further. "We can no longer think of war as a solution", he insisted in response to calls for him to support the cause of Ukraine against Russia, "because its risks will probably always be greater than it supposed benefits. In light of this, it is very difficult nowadays to invoke the rational criteria elaborated in earlier centuries to speak of the possibility of a 'just war'" (the symbolically resonant quotation marks are Francis' own). Instead, Francis demanded, "Never again war!"

How much of a role Francis' own leftwing Argentine Peronist worldview, with its ingrained anti-Americanism and its resulting indulgence toward anti-American regimes including that of Putin's Russia, played in his stance is impossible to know. But at least Pius XII's opposition to Just War Theory faced up to the injustice discarding it would produce. Francis has shown none of this willingness to accept the consequences of his position. To simply say "Never again war" when, precisely, across the world, from Ukraine to Sudan and Gaza to Myanmar, ploughshares are being beaten into swords at Mach 2, while Ukraine is being destroyed piece by piece, coldly and deliberately by the armed forces of the Russian Federation, is not a principled position but rather one that in its willful refusal to acknowledge the here and now is little more than utopian hot air, whether or not it conceals a more odious agenda, as Ukrainians tend to believe – a view I largely share.

When I went to Bosnia in 1992, I intended to stay for two weeks, and ended up staying for the better part of three years. I remained because, although then, as I have said, I was still ignorant of Catholic Just War Theory, it seemed to me that the Bosnian cause was just. Since then, I have reported on many wars: Rwanda, Sierra Leone, Sudan, Israel-Palestine, Iraq, and Afghanistan, to name only some of them. In the end, old age caught up with me, and when I realized that I could no longer run, I threw off the motley of the war correspondent. The last thing I want is for some 22-year-old to get shot in the lung because I am too arthritic to clamber out of a trench, or scamper across a field. But then along came Ukraine. Like Bosnia had been for me, Ukraine seems morally pristine, even though of course I know that in war even the just side will do terrible things. And so I am back in the world of war, risking my now very arthritic neck in Ukraine's cause, and hoping that I am more useful to Ukrainians than I am a burden to them.

One does what one is good at. There is no better feeling, at least not one that I know. Yes, of course, I'm too old for my life. But in a sense that makes it all the more precious. And old age is here, which means that death is around the corner anyway. People in Ukraine often say to me, "Why do you come here?" To which the answer is that it is a privilege.

David Rieff (born 1952) is an American nonfiction writer and policy analyst, whose books have focused on issues of immigration, international conflict, and humanitarianism. Rieff was a senior editor at Farrar, Straus and Giroux from 1978 to 1989, and has at various times been a senior fellow at the World Policy Institute at the New School for Social Research, a fellow at the New York Institute for the Humanities at New York University, a board member of the Arms Division of Human Rights Watch, of the Central Eurasia Project of the Open Society Institute, and of Independent Diplomat.

He is the author of 15 books, including Slaughterhouse: Bosnia and the Failure of the West *(1995),* A Bed for the Night: Humanitarianism in Crisis *(2003), and, more recently,* The Reproach of Hunger *(2015) and* In Praise of Forgetting *(2016). He is the editor of* On Women *(2023), a new collection of feminist essays from the influential writer, activist and critic, Susan Sontag.*

FINAL REPORT:
4 January 1943

—

Unnamed Gestapo Officer

Swiftly despatched.

One Krsto Grbin was arrested in his apartment during an action, since according to prisoner statements from the Homolje Oblast, he had recruited persons to illegal Četnik units. G. admits that he sent refugees from Croatia to one Captain Todorović – of the SDS – in Petrovac, who were allegedly to be received into Todorović's unit. However, G. denies that it was known to him that T. was a follower of D.M., or that he directed refugees to illegal Četnik units. Todorović is already arrested, and is now in Germany. A confrontation with the followers of D.M. whom Grbin recruited to the D.M. organisation is not possible, since these detainees are already transported. The attached note, as well as the partial confession, undeniably prove that G. recruited people for the illegal Četniks. Furthermore, a certain list was found at Grbin's residence, in which many persons who had allegedly killed Serbs in Croatia were listed (attachments 1 and 2). Without doubt it is Grbin who assembled this list, in order to take revenge against those persons on it. Regarding this matter, G. gives uncredible statements. Furthermore, at G.'s residence, one other letter was found, which seems to come from a certain man in the forest. And this G. denies. Grbin is a refugee from Croatia, and due to his insults against the Poglavnik [see translator's note], he was chased out by the Ustaše [ditto] and had his property confiscated.

Grbin was arrested simultaneously with the Lalić and Jovanović families from Kumanovska Street, no. 13. It could in no way be established what connection Grbin had with the events at Kumanovska no. 13, since he had known neither the Lalić nor Jovanović families beforehand, rather had only become acquainted with them in the camp at Dedinje. The Lalić and Jovanović families also stated that they had not had any earlier connections whatsoever with Grbin.

Grbin, despite intensified interrogation, did not confess to anything. He gives the impression of an ardent enemy of Germans, lying obstinately; and on the basis of the existing proven material, it can be assumed with absolute certainty that Grbin occupied a leading role in the D.M. organisation, and that in this role he was very active. Accordingly, he is recommended for EXECUTION.

Translated, from the Serbian (itself a translation of the original German), by Jacob Agee.

TRANSLATOR'S NOTE

Krsto Grbin was born in 1903 on the island of Korčula, modern-day Croatia, but then a part of the Austrian Crown Lands of the Austro-Hungarian Dual Monarchy. He was born a Roman Catholic (Slav) Croat under Germanic rule. Following the dissolution of Austria-Hungary in 1918-1919, Korčula, along with other predominantly Slav parts of Dalmatia and Istria, found itself under Italian rule rather than a part of the newly-formed Kingdom of Serbs, Croats and Slovenes (renamed Yugoslavia in 1929), despite its ethnic Croat majority. This was due to the terms of the secret Treaty of London (1915), whereby Italy was persuaded to join the Entente forces and declare war on Austria-Hungary, Germany and the Porte in exchange for territorial aggrandisement at the expense of those powers once defeated. These lands promised Italy included Korčula. As a result, in the aftermath years of the Great War, in the Italian-controlled Croatian and Slovenian territories, a strong political tradition developed of Pan-Slavism and support for incorporation into the Yugoslav state under the Serbian Monarchy. This contrasted with the dominant politics of Croats in the interwar period, which became increasing disillusioned with the new state due to discriminatory practices against non-Serbs from the dominant Serbian nationalists. While Croats who supported autonomy or federalism within Yugoslavia may have accepted the Serbian monarch as head of state, active monarchism was generally synonymous with Serbian nationalism.

Hence, a Catholic Croat who initially may have been an active supporter of the Draža Mihailović (D.M.) Movement, better known as the Četniks or the Ravno Gora movement, was relatively paradoxical, as this movement was devoutly Monarchist, though at the beginning not officially Serb ethnic nationalist as opposed to patriotically Yugoslav. In practice, however, the organisation was a virulently Serbian nationalist organisation that, as the war progressed, committed ever-larger atrocities against non-Serbs, especially Bosnian Muslims and Catholic Croats. As the war progressed, it also moved from a resistance organisation towards a policy of de-facto collaboration with the Axis powers, first the Italians and eventually the Germans too. The story of Kršto Grbin, a Korčula-born anti-fascist Catholic Croat and Pan-Yugoslavist who may have had some involvement with the Chetnik movement while it was still possible for non-Serbs, is thus a story that stands out against the cleavages of ethnic essentialism that have defined not only the Balkan present, but have also redefined the Balkan past.

PORTFOLIO

——

Don't Close Your Eyes

The week before the full-scale war in Ukraine began, I had been working on images for a children's book. In absolute disbelief of the invasion, I, like most of the world, asked myself: how can this be happening in the twenty-first century? As the war unfolded, the images in my mind's eye shifted from colorful representations of a child's world to troubling depictions of tanks, missiles, refugees, and mass graves. I began a series of drawings in reaction to the war. I also came across the works of like-minded artists in Ukraine, responding to the war with powerful imagery. These images were being exhibited in Ukraine and parts of Europe. I had a vision of bringing them to the US, so I struck up a partnership with Halyna Andrusenko, an artist from Kyiv. With her help, we sought artists whose works resonated for us in terms of the images they were making in response to the horrific violence and destruction that the war was bringing to a peaceful country. Many of the artists chosen were producing small drawings, and working on larger pieces. We decided, for practical reasons, to focus on bringing some of these smaller works on paper to the US.

When faced with the horrors of war, artists can continue to create as they always have; alternatively, they might be forced to respond to the changes in the world around them. In the exhibition *Don't Close Your Eyes*, the artists do not hesitate to create feelings of discomfort as they show you the reality Putin has brought to the people of Ukraine. We cannot ignore the trauma, death, and destruction wrought by the war and the fact that lives that have been permanently changed. The artists in this exhibition were forced to transform themselves into political artists. No longer are beautiful images accessible; they continue to be visionaries, but are now also archivists, emotional and visual, recording the destruction of their homeland.

In her book, *Depiction and Interpretation: The Influence of the Holocaust on the Visual Arts* (1993), Ziva Amishai-Maisels writes: "Art and the Holocaust are concepts that seem to be mutually exclusive; they belong to two entirely different spheres which appear to be separated by an unbridgeable gap." Yet, artists are capable of bridging this gap. Artists are emotional beings that will respond both to the beauty and the ugliness of our existence. They make this art out of necessity. In her book, *War and Art: A Visual History of Modern Conflict*, Joanna Burke writes:

> But even when not explicitly depicting the human body in its abject or mortal states, war art involves the cultural contemplation of violence. The victors and the defeated, the landscapes in which they moved, and imagined pasts, presents and futures are refracted through the creative energies of artists. The dead also live on in the hand of the artist and the eye of the witness. Loss is there for all to see. Audiences as well as artists celebrate an aesthetic of responsibility; looking closely rather than looking away.

How do artists depict war? It is one thing to photograph the scene before you, but another to sift through information at a distance, the brutal irrationality of violence and destruction. How does one convey the massacre in Bucha through a drawing that impacts the audience? What forms, colors and images does the artist use? Some of the artists represented in this room, such as Inga Levi, have been documentarians of the daily events that come with war. Inga, who worked on/created comic books, adapted the specialized style to her depictions of the war, as her complex, layered compositions evoke curiosity in the viewer. Halyna Andrusenko has turned to a meditative depiction of monuments in Lviv, which are draped in cloth to be protected from falling bombs. Halyna also created a video in which she wraps her parents in cloth as an act of protection. Vladyslav Riaboshtan bases his spontaneous graphite drawings on the instruments of war and the scenes of battlefields by referencing photographs of the conflict. Danylo Movchan, an icon painter by practice, juxtaposes vibrant colors with tragic imagery to create the conflict of emotions evoked when listening to Chopin's Prelude in D-flat Major, Op 23: No 15 "Raindrop." Ilya Yarovoy's painting of a destroyed vocational and technical school in Sumy, Ukraine is set against a brilliant blue sky with the sparkling yellow leaves of fall seducing us briefly with their beauty until the eye sees the falling building and all that that implies. It is difficult to not react to the raw emotion of Valeriia "T" Rybchenko's self-portrait "Loud," swallowing a tank. Ksenia Datsiuk uses her body and face to portray the heavy emotions and anxiety that settles into our beings/bodies when we think about the war. Evgen Klimenko captures the immediate shock of viewing destroyed building in his sketches. Olga Zaremba's "Mutilated" depicts a pink deer that is wounded and looking at us with helpless dark eyes. Rostyslav Luzhetskyy's pinkish red painting "Anxious City" conveys a feeling of wounded flesh, with dark gashes reminding us of all the suffering people have endured during the war. Olena Shtepura's weeping women transform classical paintings into dissolving images that change before our eyes into sorrowful images. Natalia Kursonova's series of "vytinanki" (cutouts) are inspired by traditional Ukrainian paper cutting folk art. At the beginning of the war, she started making "vytynanky firanky" (cutout curtains) because the artist said she "could no longer draw – just cut – due to the constant bombing all over Ukraine."

Artists present to us their view of reality, which is necessarily different from what soldiers and other victims of war have experienced. Each artist's perspective and method of artistic communication is unique. Each piece tells its own story. Each is an attempt by the artist to touch viewers like you, thousands of miles from where these events continue to unfold. They are asking you to stand with them. In return, they promise to stand with you.

Hanna Melnyczuk, Co-curator

Hanna Melnyczuk received an MFA from Massachusetts College of Art. Her work has appeared at Art Space in Maynard, Massachusetts; University of Massachusetts Lowell Mahoney Gallery; The Gallery at the Piano Factory; The Danforth Museum; Tufts Gallery; Brush Gallery; Fountain Street Gallery: New Art Center; and more. She has curated two art exhibitions: Agni Magazine *of Emerging Artists (published by Agni Press as "Agni 37: Standing on the Verge: Emerging Poets & Artists"); the other, a travelling exhibition of Ukrainian artists' works, "Don't Close Your Eyes", responding to the current war. Hanna teaches Drawing and 2D Design at University of Massachusetts Lowell, and lives in Groton, Massachusetts.*

Where I End (2022) by Nastya Didenko

—

Acrylic on cardboard

"The Rule of Two Walls" is a series of paintings and objects created after the full-scale war in Ukraine started. The safest part of a building during a bombardment is considered to be any space where there are no windows and at least two walls between the person and the street. This is called the "rule of two walls."

The paintings in the series illustrate the image of "home" as linearly depicted buildings on an abstract landscape that resemble the "ghosts" of buildings that no longer exist, and as a child's familiar drawing of a house. In childhood, everyone drew a house with straight simple lines, a square, a triangular roof, and a window; an image that is familiar and recognizable to everyone. Didenko takes this formal method of depicting the "home" and transforms it into something horrifying – for many Ukrainians, their homes have become death traps or have been lost entirely.

The objects (houses) in the series are considered by Didenko to be like living entities. The ochre colors are a reference to the human body. The houses have retained their monolithic form, but they are wounded and bleeding. The wounds will remain after the victory and will never heal.

Sketches of the War (2022) by Evgen Klimenko

———

Pencil on paper

My drawings are a direct response to the early days of the war. I drew them on site in Kyiv and Dnipro. I wanted the world to see what was happening in Ukraine, so instead of a photograph, I went to the checkpoints and drew them. These drawings were a direct response to the terrible destruction of my country.

Scythe (2022) by Ave Libertatemaveamor

——

Paper, liner, marker

These works are a reaction to the full-scale invasion by the Russian Federation. This is a conditional diary: therapy. I have always been addicted to drawing — it is my way of expression, the process of calming down and documenting the search for answers to questions. This is not a documentation of personal searches, but an attempt to understand the new reality, to give it a form. The context of the war imposed a black and white filter on the optics of today. Color breaks through as he strives for a spectrum of experiences; yet, he is suppressed by monochrome reality.

City of Anxiety (2022) by Rostyslav Luzhetsky

———

Acrylic on canvas, author's technique

"Hypoglycemia" is a series of works by Rostyslav Luzhetsky, based on his personal experience while in this physical condition. At the same time, thanks to the artistic re-interpretation, this experience easily goes beyond a specific personal experience and offers – through contemplation – a kind of recipe for overcoming a critical condition for a person: his physical or emotional exhaustion, living in a disaster, war, family drama, loss and lostness.

Wires, Anticipation (2021) by Oleksii Revika

———

Paper, ballpoint pen

The exhibited works are part of the series "Premonition." All the works are from different series, but they are united by a single theme – the premonition of war. The present war in Ukraine began as far back as 2014 with the Russian occupation of the Crimean Peninsula. This evoked in me a premonition – a feeling of threat that would not leave me – through the subsequent invasion of Ukraine on 24.02.2022. I understand that this was a subjective feeling, but it evolved from my observation of the aggressive behavior of Russia towards Ukraine.

In my works leading up to the invasion, I tried to visualize: to give greater material features to this anxiety, fear, and a sense of danger. Focusing on the plots of the landscape – different, strange, funny, melancholic – I tried to add something extra, something completely dissonant and contrasting that provokes questions. For example, in "Wire" – comprising a sandy shore with a pole and broken wires, seashells flying over the sea of sand – one sees a story about broken connections, the loss of causal chains, acclimating to existing threats, and adapting to life in permanent danger. People get used to the hybrid course of war and can act inappropriately. In the artistic images I present for this exhibition, my goal was to combine different contexts of reality such as peace and war in the same space and time. I did so without seeking to cause disharmony in the viewer, at least at first glance; thus, I create each artistic image in terms of content and composition.

Through the Looking Glass (2023) by Ilya Yarovoy

———

Watercolor on paper

My works are my personal path, personal experience and reaction to events, as well as historical evidence and a tool of struggle. A very active impetus for me was my own experience gained during my stay in the occupation in Bucha. When I worked on my first pieces, it was very dangerous; however, it is not fair to remain silent. The occupation gave me a deep understanding of the problems of war – the real war as it is. My painting of a destroyed vocational and technical school in Sumy, Ukraine is set against a brilliant blue sky with the sparkling yellow leaves of fall seducing us briefly with their beauty until the eye sees the falling building and all that this implies; where each person is on the verge of choosing who they really are. The main thing in these works is not technique or skill, but an idea – an idea that makes the viewer think and feel. It is the concept that is the tool of struggle. I am one of the bees of the great swarm of resistance of the Ukrainian People. Together and only together we will win. *Glory to Ukraine!*

Mariupol 3 (2022) by Anton Logov

———

Acrylic on paper

Logov's early works focused on themes of social consciousness. His more recent works revolve around ideas and concepts of abstraction and notions of the avant-garde.

DISPATCHES

———

Artem Chekh

Acid bomb.

Untitled town in eastern or southern Ukraine
3 April 2022

"Please, just don't shoot our dogs."

"Good God! We would never!"

"The orcs also promised they wouldn't shoot them, but they killed almost all the dogs in the village. Two of mine. They just came into my yard and shot them. The white one got away – if you see a big white one, don't kill him."

Dog corpses, puddles of blood, burnt-out cars, destroyed houses: who'd be surprised by this scene now? The woods are full of presents, left behind for us: the IEDs may have been put up in haste, but there's a lot of them. Everything has been put through an iron mincer, and the towns are strewn with wreckage.

Black-and-white photographs lie on the ground: someone's memories from the seventies or early eighties. I want to gather them all up and return them to their owner. But there is no time now – besides, where could I find their owner? There's little left of their building; only these photographs skittering down the street.

The yards here are ruined and naked, like an acid wasteland. You walk past and unashamedly gawp at the remnants of someone's ruined home, their refuge. There's no home left. There's nothing left. Everything's dead. Everything's evaporated. Everywhere is dark.

A glowering anger is in the eyes of those who stayed behind. They leave their wooden homesteads to tell their stories. They really want to tell us what happened. But there's no time to listen.

The older ladies start crying as soon as they start talking. The fuck, I'm also crying, and my glasses start steaming up straightaway. I turn aside so my boys can't see me.

I recognise some of the houses here since we've passed through so many times. But everything's changed. Now people will recognise this landscape by its battle scars. Our toponymy will change: "next to the tank over there, behind the Russian trenches, where old lady Nina's house used to be ..."

I used to think that I was too callous for this war. Now I think I'm too sensitive.

What not to eat on duty
6 July 2022

I took this photo after a night of seven hours spent lying in the sniper's nest. The guy here before me had been eating smoked fish, and the sleeves of my fleece reeked of this insufferable smell, a smell I associate with red, unwashed necks and swollen yellow fingers.

Before taking it, I killed approximately one-and-a-half-thousand midges. It took me 15 minutes to count the number of casualties and I arrived at that number. An eagle was flying overhead, bronzed-brunette beavers bobbed and grubbed around nearby, and a brood of ferrets scurried about. Khudya sat a metre away from me. He couldn't see the ferrets, because I was the one looking through the thermal imager, so long that my eye started hurting.

Then dawn broke, and I took this photo. And then another half an hour later the sun came out, and I shuffled off to sleep. True, before that I washed my hands thoroughly. It seemed the smell of smoked fish became one with the smell of my body; and that my neck had become red and dirty, and my fingers swollen and yellow. But no, it's just the fleece – it's going straight in the wash!

For breakfast I ate buckwheat, hummus, cheese, olives, and tomatoes. One must always have cheese and olives. One must always have a strategic supply of cheese and olives. Especially cheese: Brie, chèvre, aged goat Gouda, Cambozola, Lithuanian Džiugas and even plain old hard cheese ... You can match cheese with any food.

Later I went back on sentry duty. Bossa nova played on low volume, and a storm threatened. I sent my wife the photo that I took after a night of seven hours spent in the sniper's nest. She replied: "That's some otherworldly beauty!"

It's because she couldn't smell the smoked neck and swollen yellow fish.

Wartime etiquette
27 October 2022

"Dear Artem, good afternoon", she writes to me. "I would like to ask – as I know they're difficult to come by in the army – if you would mind if I sent you some nudes?"

"Hello there." I answer as tactfully as I can: "I, of course, do love beautiful things, but I already have some and right now I'm not in any severe need. Though some of the lads in my unit are not adequately provided for. I could act as an intermediary and pass them along, and you could send them directly to me."

"Are you trying to be funny?" she replied, offended.

Then she blocked me.

Still, I'm glad she didn't write "Dear Anton".

Thank you for blocking me. Otherwise, I wouldn't have written this post, out of respect for good intentions, no matter where the road paved with them leads.

But afterwards I sat there and got kinda sad. I regretted offending her. Yeah, I hadn't slept enough, we were out of electricity, so I hadn't drunk my morning coffee or had breakfast, and there was no time to cook something over the fire since I had to go out on duty. As a result, like a hungry kitten I was in the mood for play, with lots of banter, ironic jokes, and sarcastic excursions during conversation.

Once I'd arrived at my position, I wanted to write something to cheer her up, to apologise. Which is when I saw she'd blocked me. I should have just not replied, like I usually do. Now I see that I'd managed to both offend the girl and sell the boys short as well.

Then again, sharing nudes that have been sent to you personally is not just bad form, it's a violation of wartime etiquette.

Screaming in pixel
6 August

I feel like my life has a shitload of pixel in it. Too much.

This unforgiving and unrelenting camouflage pattern has followed my tracks for so many years now. It has been close at hand the whole time, even during my personal interwar period. An old field jacket that Tsilyk would wear at our dacha when it rained (which I now wear once more); some army caps and sun hats which used to sprawl like dead rats in the corners of the same dacha; a worn-out smock that journeyed from one flat to another in a bag full of unused stuff; chance pixel smudges popping up on Kyiv's Solomyanka Street, in the metro or on Facebook pages … Now it's everywhere. Around me, on me, in me. Lads from construction battalions, rifle units, tank platoons, air defence, artillery, fire support, volunteer support, holy spirit support and forest spirit support: they're all in pixel uniform. The sky above me is also cammed up in pixel. It seems the time is nigh when my own skin will also become pixelated.

For me, all this is associated with pride, love, fatigue, and being broken. With misery, smoke, and crude jokes.

I am a sceptic, a pessimist, and a difficult person. I know I am hard to put up with, and harder to love. Yesterday I also found out that I can be a fucking pain in the arse. I can be such an annoying pain in the arse that people lose it and scream at me in rage. I guess I will also come to associate pixel camo with these screams.

I can also shout, but I do so silently. I wear my pixel uniform and I shout, silently. But so loudly that I piss off everyone around me.

"Anyone want an acid bomb?" the commander asks my lads while they're setting up their positions.

The commander fetches me and brings me to them. That's me: I'm the acid bomb, the sour puss who's liable to explode. I don't deny it. Now and then, of course, I exhale and come back to earth.

A whole day and a night on stag duty. I started nodding off. The sun rises and starts to scorch the clearing. I meet Shura at the crossroads and give her a big hug through the window.

"Take me away from here", I say.

Shura smiles, says something nice and drives off. And I keep screaming. I'm wearing pixel, like the rest of my lads. It's clear that some of them are screaming in silence as well. Actually, they're all probably screaming. Even the ones wearing multicam. The ones wearing multicam are probably screaming even louder than we are. It's just we can't hear them.

(Swiss)-Russian solidarity
23 November

"Have you already been to the building Lenin used to live in?"

"Uhhh ..."

"There's also a church here where this scientist brought together a famous collection on physiognomy. And do you know who helped him? Karamzin!"

So, Karamzin helped him then. And Lenin lived here too. Fucking wonderful. The writer Mikhail Shishkin is also hanging out here somewhere, keeping up his woke status as a "good (Swiss) Russian".

On my sleeves I wear a patch from my brigade, an army chevron featuring the Ukrainian trident, and two Ukrainian flags ("Oh lord, look, a Ukrainian flag!" I hear, "Ukrainian" pronounced in a Russian accent, of course).

I imagine myself going to the building Lenin lived in, tracing my quivering hand over the stone walls, looking around in search of the taverns and kellers where dear old Vlad would pass the time; I imagine breathing in the fragrance of revolution and arsenic, crying tears as pure as vodka.

Here, I was confronted by many questions about my upbringing in a Russian-speaking family, about my first texts that were written in Russian:

"Is that true? Oh, that's how it was? See, it's not all that bad!"

They clutch at something, perhaps their last chance to see something human in me, something understandable, like Karamzin; a shared cultural space, a shared history, that it's a temporary misunderstanding but with imminent reconciliation. A stubborn search for common points of intersection:

"There are Russians who don't like Putin after all. I actually know one! Isn't that funny! Why don't I introduce you to him! We'll sit at the negotiating table; culture unites us, culture does us all good, culture heals all wounds. You used to write in Russian, after all. You used to speak Russian. You used to be a part of Russia. Everything was great, we didn't get muddled up in these national separatisms of yours. Do you remember that Pet Shop Boys song? 'Go west in the open air!' It's about all of you, about your freedom, about our hope for your freedom, about love and forgiveness, unification, about not having to lower the thermostat in our apartments by three degrees or save on energy resources. You are in this together, we are in this together; you are part of a great culture, a part of Russia; you, bei Gott, are Russia!"

"Oh, ha-ha, no, of course not! Artem, sorry, I didn't mean to. I went overboard, mea culpa! Ha-ha! It's just my Swiss bluntness. Of course, it's all that crazy Putin. It's all him. Your people are very stoic. We are all for your freedom;

we are all rooting for you. Thank you for coming and gifting us the possibility of finding out more about your culture, about you, about this war. Oh, Putin is mad! We saw those horrible shots of dead soldiers from both armies. What a bloody war. You're a tough, stoic people; but you'll get to trade with Russia again, as in, you'll get peace, as in... damn! What can I say without you getting offended? Victory? Ok, we support you – here's to victory! *Buchmo!* Cheers!"

"Lenin's house is on the Spiegelgasse. You should definitely go. Everything there is literally soaked in the spirit of your country's history. Well, not your country, or not a country either, well, it was a country, but another one, where these real misunderstandings, well, a conflict, well, a war, happened. Is that not the spirit of the age, Der Zeitgeist? What a heavy, muscular spirit! Oh, Russian missiles, Iranian drones, Buryat tank crews, Kalmyk horsemen, Udmurt archers and Kalugan convicts? It's hard to understand, but you are opening our eyes, eyes full of tears pure as vodka."

"Alright, you go and figure it out then, if we don't understand anything. It's like one street against another street, region against region, canton against canton! Capitulate! Surrender! Bless you!"

Or they say some flaccid phrase, like:
"¡No pasarán!
¡Viva la Libertad !
All you need is love!
Stand with Ukraine!"

O, Karamzin! O, my state of Denmark! O, my dear Ukraïna!

Not all military branches are equal
20 October

Yesterday, some of the lads from air defence who'd just shot down a missile came by, and I saw their joyous little mugs (ok, faces). After they sat and waited, and waited, and waited some more – bam, they blatted that little cunt out of the sky and saved someone's life.

And here I think: what should someone who's just saved dozens of lives feel like? The AD lads obviously have to treat their work like work, but there's obviously another side to it: a conscious understanding of their mission, of their usefulness. Maybe, even, of their life's greatest undertaking.

Let's compare them to the infantry, shall we: with its close-quarters-battle that tends to be not that close-quarters; rifles; grenade launchers; where you maybe get a fucking BMP in and shred some enemy fortifications; where lads cut about doing tank stalks with NLAWs, call in a little artillery strike and blast a square full of enemy manpower. Basically, the aim's clear – to kill as many orcs as possible, advance, hold, repel enemy attack, and build up your positions. In a way you're also saving someone's life but from this sort of hazy perspective, so the chain of events may take place in different ways. For this is just a battle, war in the here and now, and what comes next isn't often clear. And if you fuck up the operation, you can always get your artillery or even your air corps in to support you.

But if you don't shoot down that missile, death and destruction are guaranteed to follow. Your mortars can't cover you. Your artillery can't help.

And then these satisfied faces (I just want to call them mugs) arrive and we know they've shot something down. It's like the day gains more colour, as does your mood. The surrounding nature is more hospitable, and even food tastes better.

From the other side your work seems insignificant and boring in comparison. You spend a sober evening staring into the windy blackness, holding your body armour up with your hands because your back can barely hold out any longer, and you think about the baklava you bought that day and about your Chinese cabbage, avocado and gorgonzola salad. Or you think about how you are unequivocally saving someone's life, even if the result isn't obvious. Or maybe you've already saved someone's life, only you don't know it yet. And you comfort yourself with this self-deception, happy as Larry.

You also think about how your face is no longer a face, but a mug, and that to make it a face again you'll have to shave.

But the trimmer is still at the post office. I must get it sometime.

Oh, I will.

"Kill!"
10 March

These days I often think back to Ilya Ehrenburg and his anti-German pamphlet, *"Kill!"* Despite its declamatory rhetoric and sturdy propagandist stem, this text resonates with current sentiment among most Ukrainians. Once upon a time I couldn't even imagine what must be happening inside someone's soul for them to write such a thing: "KILL THE GERMAN! Kill!"

Well ... now we know what it is to truly hate.

But true hate is a terrifying thing, if you think about it. To hate enough to "KILL!" To kill without pity, without depersonalising the "target" (as happens only in wars of aggression, not liberation), to say clearly and tangibly, "Kill! Fucking kill him, otherwise he'll kill you". Despite the stupor, the despair, exhaustion, and pain – one must kill. This cry is so terrifying and strong, that one (or I) could never talk about this, mention or pronounce it on any leftie panel discussion.

"What did you feel like when you killed someone? Let's try working through your traumas through the prism of cultural initiatives and thereon enter a broad path of dialogue and reconciliation. How does a fee of four hundred euros sound to you?"

This "Kill!" is about survival, something animal, ferocious; something stripped bare. It's about how things shouldn't be so, but for some reason they are. It's about something that should have been left in the past, something that we love reading about in our comfy beds. Or that we used to love reading about.

But sure, that fee of four hundred euros suits me just fine.

Translated, from the Ukrainian, by Daisy Gibbons.

Born in 1985 in Cherkasy, central Ukraine, Artem Chekh is a writer, musician, journalist and soldier. Since 2007, he has written some 16 books, most recently Who Are You? *(2021), which have been translated into German, English, Polish, Czech and Russian. He served in the Armed Forces of Ukraine from May 2015 to July 2016 as a senior shooter and gun layer in an armoured personnel carrier in the War in Donbas. At the beginning of Russia's full-scale invasion of Ukraine in 2022, he returned to the ranks of the Ukrainian Armed Forces. In late May 2023 he sustained a concussion in the battle for the city of Bakhmut.*

See biographical note for Daisy Gibbons on p 135.

POEM

———

Iya Kiva

refugees. the theater

first night in safe city – as we call the country's west
you spend it on the theater floor like a prop
for a war you can watch for free
reflected in all the eyes of the terrified beasts

(you can still buy a front-row ticket to world war three –
wrote a famous western journalist on the eve of the great flood)

the light falls so well
that the world can see the dirt under your nails
and your hair (grown out since your trip to poland)
has split like the branches on your jewish family tree
when a righteous piece of chalk marks it with a cross

your nails are unpainted – eight years since your last manicure –
and when you read "for the bucha woman"
(will school teachers discuss this photo in class?)
posted beneath somebody's sleek cherry-orchard fingers
you ask the red nail polish: is the comparison embarrassing

but now we, like the daffodils old women sell at bus stops,
are never embarrassed to be and not to be
like the bitter bulbs of trees that grow on history's margins

this will be you in a couple of days, walking down freedom avenue
    (not a metaphor)
to leave all your prophetic dreams on the barbershop floor –
but this won't save you: for, like a madman with a razorblade
    of longing under his nails,
memory leads you across a dusty field of dead tubers
so vast that even in children's eyes you see soil

but for now you're lying on the theater floor like a prop
and you tremble with the rumbling trams –
those civilian singers in the chorus of aerial warfare
and you can't pull the wax from modern music lovers' ears

13.04.2022

Translated, from the Ukrainian, by Amelia Glaser and Yuliya Ilchuk.

See biographical notes for Amelia Glaser on p 202.

Iya Kiva is a poet and translator. She was born in 1984 in Donetsk, studied at Donetsk National University (philology and cultural studies) and later graphic design at another educational institution. In 2014 she was forced to move to Kyiv because of the first Russo-Ukrainian War. She is the author of three poetry collections – Further from Heaven *(2018),* The First Page of Winter *(2019), and* Laughter of an Extinguished Fire *(2023) – as well as a volume of interviews with Belarusian authors, entitled* We'll Wake Up Different: Conversations with Contemporary Belarusian Writers on the Past, Present and Future of Belarus *(2021), dedicated to the 2020-2021 protests in Belarus. Kiva's poems have been translated into more than 30 languages, including in books published in Bulgaria, Poland, Italy and Sweden. She herself translates Polish and Belarusian poetry, and children's books from English.*

TWO POEMS

—

Oksana Lutsyshyna

EASTERN EUROPE IS A PIT OF DEATH…

eastern europe is a pit of death and decaying plums
I hide from it in the body of america
but sooner or later I'll slip from this light
back down into that other
and will start talking about death because that is our national sport
talking about death
sad yet beautiful
hoping that the world will hear us and gasp at the beauty and sadness

my lover spreads my fingers with his own
he was educated in good old france
then america
he also studied buddhism and erotica somewhere near the borders
                                                        of thailand
it's good to drink wine with him and chat
but not about death or eastern europe
because the world's a shithole and it's worthwhile to learn only one art:
that of hopping from one pleasure islet to another
and not giving a damn about plague-infected continents with their
                                                        corpse-eating flies

he kisses me goodnight and disappears into his dream
as I lie in mine, full of summer sun and ephemeral sweetness
mitteleuropa zbigniew herbert whispers in my ear
middle europe enters a labyrinth without a single turn
a labyrinth of fate and freshly laid brick
it enters and doesn't exit
it endures and revives, small like newly seeded grass in the evening
strong like the grandchildren of those that survived the war
when, when will I die? – someone asks in my still childish voice

but I don't hear the answer because it suddenly becomes dark
in this death pit, where miklos radnoti is writing his last poem

WHO IS ON MY SIDE, YOU ASK

who is on my side, you ask
who is on my side? – this tree here,
as if it could be against you?
as if trees could be against people?

a whole park of trees
a whole forest, you could say – and all are on your side
all of them

and the cat? is the cat against you?
no, the cat is on your side
this cat and all in the world's cats
all – on your side, all – your army
nimble, yellow-eyed

and gods? yours and others – and everyone in the world?
wouldn't they help you?
of course, they would
they are on your side
how could they be – against you?

and that teacher that said – thoughts are everything?
what's his name – Swami Vishnudevananda
is he – against you?
why waste his time! of course,
he is on your side
on your side

and the sea? what – you think, the sea is against you?
all its waves and pebbles and beaches
visible and invisible
everything is for you, don't doubt it

everyday and every minute
do you hear – the sea roars?
it says to you: I
am on your side
on your side

and music? which of the notes is against you?
which of the melodies?
Mozart? rappers? pianists?
The Accademia Bizantina? Paul McCartney?
no, what are you thinking
everyone is on your side
on your side

and there is no one against you
and there will never be
and so love, keep on loving
don't be afraid

Translated, from the Ukrainian, by Olena Jennings.

See biographical note for Olena Jennings on p 127.

First published in Words for War: New Poems from Ukraine, *an anthology, eds. Oksana Maksymchuk and Max Rosochinsky. Boston: Academic Studies Press.*

Born in Uzhhorod, Western Ukraine in 1974, Oksana Lutsyshyna is a poet, scholar, and translator. Lutsyshyna earned a BA in English from Uzhhorod National University, an MA in French and Gender Studies from the University of South Florida, and a PhD in Comparative Literature from the University of Georgia. She is the author of four poetry collections, one of which has been translated into English: Persephone Blues *(2019). She has also published one collection of short stories and two novels, the most recent of which,* Ivan and Phoebe *(2023, translated by Nina Murray), won the Lviv City of Literature UNESCO Prize and Taras Shevchenko National Prize in Fiction. Her poetry and translations also appear in* Words for War: Poems from Ukraine, *an anthology of Ukrainian poetry in English responding to the first Russo-Ukrainian War in the eastern region of Donbas. She translates alone or in collaboration with Olena Jennings, Kevin Vaughn and Daniel Belgrad. Lutsyshyna lives in Austin, Texas, where she teaches Ukrainian and Eastern European Literature at the University of Texas.*

THE GIRLS WHO WERE BURIED
AND THE OLD MAN WHO WAS SAVED

———

Héctor Abad Faciolince

That last day.

"Stories have to save themselves whatever way they can, jump from
one near-dead body to another that is young and alive."

"Perhaps they were killed by a missile that fell upon their heads
purely by chance."

— Victoria Amelina, *Dom's Dream Kingdom*

Primo Levi, in the last book he published before taking his own life, *The
Drowned and the Saved*, sets out to reflect (in the form of an essay rather than a
testimony) on the intractable question of why some individuals in an extreme
situation – a campaign of extermination – have the good fortune to survive,
while others, perhaps the majority, have the misfortune to be dragged down,
devastated by blind hatred, the injustice of history, dictatorship, and the will
to power.

I've been asking myself this question since 19:23 on the evening of 27
June 2023, when a Russian, Iskander high-precision missile carrying seven
hundred kilos of explosives exploded above us in a pizzeria in Kramatorsk, just
21.6 kilometres from the front between free Ukraine and the area occupied
by the Russians.

In that hell that fell on us from the sky with the clear purpose of causing
the utmost harm, the highest number of deaths possible, the greatest amount
of pain and suffering possible, sixty people were seriously injured and twelve
died instantly, among them twin girls of fourteen, Yuliya and Anna Aksenchenko.

On the internet I find one of the last photographs taken of them, and I
look at the two adolescent faces with sadness and curiosity.

I have often observed in twins a touching, if fruitless, striving to be
different from each other. One of the girls clearly wears her hair up, like a

fountain spurting upwards towards the sky; the other, in contrast, wears her hair down, cascading towards the ground. They do this in order to warn others not to get them mixed up: if I'm Anna don't call me Yuliya, and if I'm Yuliya don't call me Anna. In that intimate connectedness that comes from being born with a clone, it is only natural that both twins seek to separate their fates, seek out their own identities. Different clothes, different smiles, even though each of them spent almost all her life seeing herself in the mirror of her sister's face. In the end, their fates were as indistinguishable in death as in their births. A few days after they died, I read they were buried in identical coffins, one beside the other, dressed in the same white bridal dresses, as is the custom in rural Ukraine when a young girl dies.

Their father, who had brought them for pizza as a reward for their high scores in school, and who sat facing his two little girls at the table, had the misfortune of surviving the Russian missile. He is one of the survivors and now he must attend the burial of his twin daughters. I do not know Mr Aksenchenko, but I have no doubt he would gladly swop his fate for theirs. I believe he would prefer to be dead and his daughters alive.

Again and again I have asked myself the same question, but I'm not so clear about it and I have no right to be hypocritical. I find myself unable to give the same obvious answer as this tragic father. I know how unjust it is, I know that it's an ugly thing to say or even think, but despite my age I am still governed by a selfish will to live. I also know that this would disappear completely if my two children were killed before my eyes.

———

In that same restaurant where the Aksenchenko twins died, not in the indoor dining-room (the site of all but one of the deaths caused by the attack), but outdoors on the terrace (where there were several minor injuries and one fatality), I was sitting with two old Colombian friends, a man and a woman, and two newly-made Ukrainian acquaintances, also a man and a woman. Dima, the Ukrainian man, was our *fixer*, chauffeur and translator. The Colombians were Sergio Jaramillo, ex-Colombian Commissioner for Peace, Catalina Gómez, war correspondent in the Middle East and Ukraine, and myself. The five of us had been travelling together for four days.

I can't say that our guide, the Ukrainian girl who sat amongst us, was a friend. I didn't call her Vika like her friends did. But I realised from the day I met her that she was a courageous and very brilliant young woman. Lucid, ironic, sad. She always wore black, like a widow, and had very pale skin, almost ghostly. More importantly and symbolically for me, she was the same age as my daughter. They were both born in 1986, the awful year of the Chernobyl disaster. She was called, is called, Victoria Amelina and she had left her job as an engineer to become a poet, essayist and writer.

That Tuesday 27th of June, we went to Pizza Ria as a way of saying goodbye to Donbas and to thank Victoria, our guide through that region devastated by the Russians, for her attentiveness, kindness and time. Pizza was her favourite food, and the Ria her favourite restaurant in Kramatorsk, a city she had visited several times. We were due to return to Kiev the following morning. The evidence of Russian terror we encountered there had made it a profoundly painful and emotional trip. We were aware of death's presence, but we hadn't felt it breathing down our necks. Whether that was ignorance on our part, or recklessness, at no time in those few days had we felt actual fear. A certain nervousness, yes, and perhaps the desire to get back to the safety of the West as soon as possible, but not fear.

———

The previous week, on the 24th of June, in the Arsenal Book Fair, Ukraine, Victoria had accompanied us to introduce the international campaign by Latin American intellectuals and writers in support of Ukraine's resistance to Putin's invasion: *Ukraine Stands Firm! (¡Aguanta Ukrania!)*. It was there I first met her and shook her hand. At the end of our presentation, perhaps because of the effects of two glasses of white wine, Victoria had agreed to come with us on our trip to the East of the country, to Donbas, where we wanted to record the war crimes of the Russian army.

In truth, that journey so close to the front wasn't in my plans either. It was the last-minute idea of the Director of the *Ukraine Stands Firm!* movement, Sergio Jaramillo, a highly cultured and subtle negotiator. I didn't want to go, I've always been a coward, but it's almost impossible not to be persuaded by an expert in negotiation. Victoria didn't want to go either, but she signed up at the last minute — she told us with a serious and sad smile — to show us some of the places where the Russians had carried out their acts of terror most brutally, and to say goodbye to the territory they had tried to take and then lost during the first weeks of the invasion.

This combination of circumstances, partly voluntary, partly fortuitous, led Victoria to accompany us (aliens from a distant country in South America) to see the destruction, death and horrors committed by Putin and his henchmen, the neo-Nazi mercenaries of the Wagner group, under the command of Prigozhin, who that very weekend had rebelled against the Czar and even dared to march on Moscow (an act of defiance he would pay for a few weeks later in an "accidental" explosion in the skies between Moscow and St Petersburg).

Victoria dreamed of a definitive victory by Ukraine over Russia. She was determined, too, that this anachronistic imperial power be stopped from exterminating, for the third or fourth time in history, a whole generation of thinkers, scientists, writers and intellectuals in independent Ukraine. For that reason, she had spent the previous year denouncing with meticulous detail Putin's crimes. She was immersed in the final stages of a book she had decided to write in English: *Diary of War and Justice: Looking at Women Looking at War*. A few weeks later she was due to travel to Paris with a bursary to spend a year polishing the manuscript in peace and quiet, accompanied by her twelve-year-old son and their white dog, Vovchystsia (wolf, in Ukrainian).

———

The last day that Victoria Amelina lived in a conscious state, on our way back from a training camp where we had met a charming, pacifist soldier, we saw a white dog roaming around the countryside. Victoria watched it with notable intensity and compassion. I didn't understand why the sight of the dog had moved her so deeply. The previous day we had all been in Kharkiv, a city recaptured by the Ukrainian forces and ruined during its occupation by Russian tanks in the winter of 2022, and again in spring that same year when, defeated and enraged, they were forced to abandon it. It was in Kharkiv that Victoria had introduced us to her friend Oksana, a young woman who rescued and cared for dogs that had lost their homes during the war, either because they had taken fright and bolted from artillery fire and the noise of machine-guns, or because their homes had been destroyed and their owners had died or were displaced by the war.

It was at that moment that another companion on our journey, a good friend of mine and Victoria's, the highly observant Catalina Gómez, explained this particular collateral damage of the Russian invasion: an infinite number of abandoned or lost animals in Ukraine, all searching for a home and owners who were probably not even alive.

———

Months after her tragic death, now that I've read some of Victoria Amelina's poems, several of her luminous essays and her second novel, *Dom's Dream Kingdom*, there are so many things I could talk to her about. I believe I would even ask her permission to call her Vika, like her friends did, rather than Victoria. Since she died I've become her friend. Since she died, I've also met her father, George Shalamay, in Toronto, a father who lost his eldest daughter, barely 37 years old. A father who has lived through something I could not bear, and who I wanted to tell in person the things I am telling you here in writing.

When we read writers we become their friends, sometimes almost intimate friends, because nothing resembles us more than what we leave in writing, and I believe no one resembles Vika more than the blind girl Marusia, the protagonist of *Dom's Dream Kingdom* which I read in Spanish, a novel with an ingenious technical feature: the story is narrated by a dog. A white dog called Dom.

At the end of the novel the dog-narrator says two things that really struck me. The first: "When you're a vagrant, you sleep very little and badly, and almost never have dreams. Except one. The one where you're looking for a home." And secondly: "Is my bad hearing getting worse?" There are occasions when we read books not only intensely but also superstitiously. As though there were something portentous in them, something almost prophetic.

It was my bad hearing that saved my life in Kramatorsk.

What I am about to say is something I would much rather be silent about, but it's the truth and therefore must be told. In that restaurant, Pizza Ria, at that rectangular table they (thankfully) led us to on the terrace, I sat down on a white sofa, to the left of Sergio Jaramillo, Colombian leader of the *Ukraine Stands Firm!* movement (*¡Aguanta Ucrania!*) who was sitting at the top of the table. As he sometimes speaks under his breath as though he were reciting mantras in Sanskrit, and I am half deaf in my right ear, I decided to move to a chair on the other side of the table, on Sergio's right side, so I could hear him with my good ear, the left one. Victoria took my place on the sofa, on his left, sitting opposite me. Catalina Gómez moved into Victoria's original place and Dima into Catalina's original place. Who could ever imagine that changing places at a table could have repercussions that would extend beyond etiquette or comfort? A waitress came with the drinks. Because of the war, Kramatorsk was a dry zone, so Victoria ordered an alcohol-free beer, and Catalina some sparkling water. I had gone to the bathroom and in my absence Sergio had ordered a glass of ice for me.

I found it odd that Sergio had ordered two glasses of ice, one for me and one for himself, but he quickly explained. It was our last night in Donbas, our last night with Catalina, Dima and Victoria, who were staying in Ukraine. We would ignore the ban on alcohol and raise a toast to our good health and to life itself. Jaramillo had brought a gift, a bottle of whisky hidden in his backpack. I remember which kind, Macallan 12-year-old, which I love, but that day I didn't get to taste a drop. Sergio surreptitiously bent down and poured it into my glass on the floor. He handed it to me, then ducked down again to pour his own. I looked at the amber liquid in my glass then looked and Victoria with some concern, saying "It's too obvious, they'll see what we're up to." Sergio was still leaning down, pouring. Catalina looked on with her habitual calm. Dim was already tucking into his food as he was ravenous. Victoria looked at me with that smile of hers, somewhere between ironic and sad, "You can say it's apple juice". I smiled back and raised my glass in a toast with her.

That was the moment when all hell descended from the sky. I fell to the floor, and when I got up again I was so stunned I didn't know if I was injured or not, but I felt my body and didn't have a scratch. I was unharmed, but I would never be the same. Victoria looked very pale, even paler than usual, with her head leaning gently back. She never recovered consciousness. Four days later, she died in a hospital in Dnipro, on the 1st of July, 2023.

Translated, from the Spanish by Lorna Shaughnessy.

Héctor Abad Faciolince (born 1958, in Medellin) is a Colombian novelist, essayist, journalist, and editor. Abad is considered one of the most talented post-"Latin American Boom Writers" in Latin American Literature. Abad is best known for his bestselling novel Angosta *(2004) and, more recently,* El Olvido que Seremos (Oblivion: A Memoir, *2006). In June 2023, he was injured when two Russian ballistic missiles struck a dining café in Kramatorsk, Ukraine where he was meeting Ukrainian writer Victoria Amelina, who later died as a result of her injuries. Abad is an atheist.*

Lorna Shaughnessy is a poet, translator and researcher. She has published four collections of poetry in translation from Spain and Mexico and co-edited a bilingual anthology of eco-poetry, as well as five poetry collections of her own. She is a co-founder of the Emily Anderson Centre for Translation Research and Practice at the University of Galway, and of the research group Crosswinds: Irish and Galician Poetry and Translation.

TWO POEMS

—

Halyna Kruk

THE STORY OF A FICUS, AS TOLD BY A HUMAN WHO PREFERS TO COMMUNICATE WITH PLANTS

half a year of war
an abandoned ficus registers the events from the window
dreams of leaving through the window frames,
long since empty,
but no
an abandoned ficus can't go anywhere, though the missile
gave it a glimmer of hope
and a sudden urge toward the outside world
few pages have survived from these chronicles of summer,
but if it rains, the ficus fills out
a person will enter the building, squeezing past the door,
that the shockwave unhinged:
not a home but an inn:
curtain rolled up by the wind, rooms filled with junk –
no clear way out
but the ficus below will survive and send out shoots
leave its broken pot
clasp the black lawn with thirsty roots
stand proud, grow, wait
for its old man's shuffling slippers, heart-to-hearts,
simple plantish pleasures

HUMAN WARMTH

choosing a thermal sensor or night-vision device,
you scroll, in wonder, through all these models,
designed for tracking animals,
and spotting shy birds in the wild,
and then, in horror, through those designed for hunting,
for neither beast, nor bird deserves this
not the elk, not the stiff carcass of a hare, not the delicate body of
    the roebuck
flashing past the thermal imager, confused and uncertain:
where to flee? who's in my rightful place?
a dog's hot body shows redder than a human's
how often did it warm you in the trenches, sheltering
from the roaring missiles
the gophers, weasels, moles are so small and unremarkable,
they don't count
taking aim, you must remember
human warmth is special –
it can kill

Translated, from the Ukrainian, by Amelia Glaser and Yulia Ilchuk.

See biographical notes for Amelia Glaser on p 202.

Halyna Kruk was born in 1974 in Lviv, Ukraine. She is the author of five books of poetry, a collection of short stories, and four children's books. She has received multiple awards for her writing, including the Bohdan Ihor Antonych Prize, the Polish Gaude Polonia Fellowship, the Bookforum Best Book Award, and the Kovaliv Foundation Prize for Prose. She has served as Vice President of the PEN Ukraine, holds a PhD in Ukrainian literature, and is Professor of European and Ukrainian baroque literature at the Ivan Franko National University in Lviv. Her latest collection of poetry, A Crash Course in Molotov Cocktails *(Arrowsmith Press, 2023, translated by Amelia Glaser and Yuliya Ilchuk) was shortlisted for the prestigious Griffin International Poetry Prize in 2024.*

POEM

———

Bruce Weigl

THE BODHISATTVA BLURRED
BY LILIES IN THE GARDEN

Let me tell you how the life inside a lie
feels, the immense jungle green
shattered by ambush in the evening.
Let me execute myself in peace, dear
strangers whom I love. The turning wheel is
a kind of lie too, unimaginable
photographs of disasters that shatter
into tiny pieces when you try to pick them
up, like history.
The world doesn't end or even
notice any of this lush blue orbit
flashing past, let alone my problems, or
yours, the Bodhisattva
blurred by lilies in the garden.

Bruce Weigl is an American poet whose work engages profoundly with experience of both Americans and Vietnamese during and after the Vietnam war. Weigl enlisted in the US Army shortly after his 18th birthday and spent three years in the military, serving in Vietnam from December 1967 to December 1968 and receiving the Bronze Star. Weigl is the author of more than a dozen books of poetry, most recently On the Shores of Welcome Home *(2019), as well as a memoir,* The Circle of Hanh *(2000). As he has remarked, "The paradox of my life as a writer is that the war ruined my life and in return gave me my voice." He lives in Lorain, Ohio, where he grew up.*

TWO "VIETNAM" POEMS

—

Marc Levy

FIRST WEEK

After the ambush
In monsoon rain we trudge to the wood line
A growling deuce and a half prowls behind.
Past no man's land,
Past the comforting sight of sand bag bunkers
We call out, hear the muted password reply,
See them step like deer from the green thicket.
Now, step back, see for yourselves the kindness
Of soldiers that I will never forget:
A sweated quartet, one man posted
To each loose limb,
See how gravity tugs at the flung back neck
The jolly flopping head. Drags the sad
Torso down, down. In the beating rain
Two lines form between the dead man –
The purring truck.
In the wordless muck we pass the warm corpse
Hand to hand, as if he were a fire brigade bucket.
Look at him:
Behold foul steam rising from jungle fatigues
Rain bitten, the large brown eyes unblinking.
See this handsome man, slender, black
Thrust into the truck, lugged back to base
His last day in Cambodia.

THE BEAUTIFUL BLACK SKY

Long past midnight slowly they crawl
Past the glinting wire,
En mass attack sleepy bunkers,
Hurl satchel charges, grenades,
Empty AKs into waking men,
Spangling sandbags red and red.

A man, not yet wounded
Keeps still as one walks past,
His gaunt face, long whiskers
Silhouetted by star light.
A sergeant grabs his rifle
Topples the enemy down,
Too late cradles Dawson
Who dies in his arms.
Too late, a screaming jet
Drops its lethal load.

Fire in the Hole!
The gun crew shout –
The soaring flare sparkling
Red the beautiful black sky.
Barrels low, the cannons
Fire directly into the wood line
The shells hurtling through jungle
Storming down trees, exploding
In loud metal bangs.

Everywhere, the wailing wounded
The machine guns' stuttering chatter.
In the free for all the captain
And Michael jump the berm
To hunt survivors down.
At dawn
We tour the beautiful wreckage

Inspect the army of porcelain dolls,
Behold their mute poses,
Silent weapons scattered like rice.
There, slumped on a bunker,
A toppled man shot in the face.
Elsewhere, dime-sized holes
Dimple the sleepy dead,
Who are tossed into bomb craters,
Salted with lime.

For no reason, it begins to rain.
The tropical drops pelt the black body bags
Which noisily flap in the back wash
As medevacs whisk them away.

From dawn to dusk
We tend to our brokeness
Then lay our rifles down.
One less day in the long march home –
Until it starts all over again.

Mark Levy is a poet living in Massachusetts. He is the author of three books of poems, most recently Dreams, Vietnam *(2017) and* Other Dreams *(2018). He was a medic with Delta 1/7 First Cavalry in Vietnam and Cambodia, 1969-1970. His decorations include the Combat Medic Badge, Silver Star, two Bronze Stars (with V), and Air Medal (Arcom). He has also edited* Medic in a Green Time: Writings from the Vietnam War and Its Aftermath *(2020).*

TWO POEMS

———

J.R. Solonche

THE HORSES

Eight million died in World War I.

They would have needed 8,000,000 men
for one man to apologize to one horse.

When the men did not do so to one another,
where would they have found men to apologize to the horses?

It would have taken 8,000,000 Picassos
to do justice to the death agony of 8,000,000 horses.

Of the 8,000,000 horses, how many had names?
The Germans in particular targeted the horses.

When a British soldier's was killed or died,
he was required to cut off a hoof from his horse

to prove to his commanding officer that they
had not simply been separated, he and his horse.

Too tired to lift their heads high enough to breathe,
they drowned in the deep mud, thousands of the horses.

Because they were used to draw the artillery,
the most losses were suffered by the Clydesdale horses.

For some countries, the largest commodity
shipped to the front was fodder for the horses.

Because sawdust was mixed with their food,
they starved to death, thousands of the horses.

Gasmasks were issued for the horses,
but they destroyed them, mistaking them for feed bags.

The better-bred horses suffered from shell shock
more than the less well-bred horses.

These learned to lie down at the sound of the guns.
They were sold to the French butchers, the surviving horses.

THE SHIELD OF HECTOR

The shield of Hector
was not much to see,
just bronze and leather,
so unlike that of Achilles,
the great masterpiece
Hephaestus made,
but Hector's stained shield
smelled of the sweat he shed
in battle, and was used to carry
his son, Astyanax, dead
from Troy,
and was the coffin
he was buried in.

J.R. Solonche received a BA from New York University and an MA from SUNY–New Paltz. He is the author of many books of poems, most recently Selected Poems: 2002-2022. *He is Professor Emeritus of English at SUNY, Orange County, New York.*

POEM

—

Gjertrud Schnackenberg

AUS LIEBE

> *Each of us must bear our part.*
> — Chris Zimmerman, The Bruderhof

I need a heart of bronze for hearing this,
And not the lost wax melting off
Beneath a molten pour of sound

When, out of love,
A solo flute appears —
Appears, whether or not I've grown

Sick of the world, sick of the things
That people do, sick of the ache, and in the end
What difference does it make

That *He has cast out every sickness,*
Given what has happened.
Given this —

Why summon from the air the oxygen
That's needed for a last
Outflowing breath

Above a slowing pulse? And what
Can flutes accomplish? What do
Flutes have the ability to do?

Why draw a breath
Not even deep enough
For blowing out a candle flame

That cleaves *aus liebe*
To the wick it carbonizes
As it writhes, why take

Repeated shallow sips of oxygen,
And why array
The fragile respirations of a flute's

Expiring *appoggiatura* sighs
Against the site of massive violence
And abandonment at Golgotha,

And why apply circular breathing
To a frail lament that seems
To breathe itself into existence

For my joy and pleasure,
While Thou must suffer –
Though it's true

That, lifted to the lips, Bach's flutes pursue
The anguish to its source,
With tongue-assisted embouchure,

The way a tongue will touch,
Draw back,
Then touch again

A welling gap of sudden blood
No gauze can stanch
After an aching truth

Is torn out by the roots –
I take a breath, and move
To turn the music off, but stop myself,

Relenting, giving up
Because it's clear it doesn't matter
Whether I concede

The miracle that flutes,
For all their frailty,
Can overflow with truth

When human beings are themselves
Incapable of saying it –
The truth that *each of us,*

However frail, must *bear our part* –
The truth that he has held
The lead weight of your heart,

And weightless notes are capable
Of weighing it
Before they vanish off

To go wherever music goes
When nobody
On earth is playing it.

Gjertrud Schnackenberg was born in 1953 and graduated from Mount Holyoke College, Massachusetts. She has published six books of poetry, most recently Heavenly Questions *(Farrar, Straus and Giroux, 2010), which won the 2011 International Griffin Prize. The poem "Aus Liebe" is taken from a sequence of poems about listening to the "St. Matthew Passion", which will be published in the Fall of 2024 by Arrowsmith Press.*

SUBSTACK COMPENDIUM

—

Timothy Snyder

BEWARE THE WEAK MAN

Time for a reckoning.

Thoughts from the Munich Security Conference.
22 February 2024

Who is the weak man? You shall know him by his itinerary. The weak man knows that Ukraine is what matters, so he goes to Texas. The weak man of Congress buys some casual clothes, has a staffer write a speech about the border, and recites it word-for-word. A real invasion is replaced by a pretend one. The weak man invites us to fear phantoms rather than face issues.

House Speaker Mike Johnson did this, as did other American legislators seeking excuses not to help Ukraine. While I was in Munich, Elon Musk put on a cowboy hat and took his turn. In fall 2022, when Ukraine might have won the war, Musk cut the Ukrainians off from Starlink. Rather than going to Ukraine and learning, he made a profoundly bad decision on the basis of personal fear.

The Munich Security Conference is a place where people get together to take action. Unlike Johnson and Musk, Senator J.D. Vance (author of *Hillbilly Elegy*) was at least present. But he was there to demotivate. Invited to meet Ukrainian president Volodymyr Zelens'kyi, Vance made his excuses. Rather than looking a courageous man in the eye, he retreated to his hotel room and searched for "dolphin" and "women" on the internet.

At a meeting I attended, Danish Prime Minister Mette Frederiksen announced that her country would donate its entire stock of artillery shells to Ukraine. Vance stood outside the building and said that we should give up. He told the leaders of a democracy (but not to their faces) to give up territory. If the Ukrainians followed his advice, the chain of events would be similar to what happened the last time fascism was appeased in Munich: the collapse of faith in order, and a world war.

Ukraine could win, if Americans would help; but our weak men have cut off the weapons. Musk spreads Russian propaganda. Vance amplifies Russian foreign policy. Trump follows Putin's wishes. Johnson maneuvers for months to block a vote on aid to Ukraine. And so the Ukrainians, fighting for their lives, run out of artillery shells, and must withdraw from losses from Avdiivka.

The weak man kills because he lacks the energy to act and consumes the energy of others. He scorns those who struggle with real danger, and wants them to fail and die.

The problem is not masculinity. Radek Sikorski, the foreign minister of Poland, is a man's man from central casting: good looks, deep voice, firm stare, bad jokes. When not in office, he was raising money for pickup trucks and driving them to the front. At Munich, plenty of competent men were at work: such as Czech President Petr Pavel, a former general, who has been searching the world for artillery shells to send to Ukraine. The problem is brittle masculinity, the male form of weakness that substitutes mendacious prattle for necessary action.

Instead of aiding Ukraine, the weak men of Congress have dedicated months to a long series of lies that have wasted the energy and good faith of others. First Johnson said that he wanted to protect the border and would pass aid for Ukraine if it was connected to a border bill; then, when presented with exactly this solution, he rejected it. When aid for Ukraine was then separated from the border issue in another bill, he rejected that too, on the grounds that the border was not mentioned. The weak men of Congress want inaction both at the border and in Ukraine. They only mention the one to explain why they are not acting on the other.

After this parade, Johnson called the House of Representatives to recess. But Johnson himself is not on vacation. He has to put on a tie to abase himself before Trump in Florida. In the photograph Johnson posted, Trump lacks the strength to raise his thumb. Trump submits to Putin, and encourages Russia to attack American allies.

And Putin, in his turn, is all fear. He kills opponents because he fears that a younger generation might do better. He attacks Ukraine because he cannot stand the thought of democracy in Russia. The submission chain that runs through Johnson and Trump to Putin ends in a vacuum.

The danger is that this vacuum will consume our democracy. The weak man runs from danger by running for office. Not strong enough to believe in law or to live by it, the weak man breaks laws and then tries to break law itself. Putin wants to die in his bed. And so we will soon have another fake

Russian presidential election. Trump wants to pardon himself or otherwise avoid prosecution for all the crimes he seems to know he has committed. For the weak man, fear is everything, and fear must also become everything for us.

On the first day of the Munich Security Conference, the news arrived that Alexei Navalny, the foremost Russian oppositionist, had been killed in Russian prison. Navalny was known for his courage. He had returned to Russia after Russian authorities poisoned him. After his poisoning, but before he returned to Russia, he telephoned the Russian secret police, impersonated one of its officers, and elicited the truth about what happened. He was also courageous enough to be a friend to his friends and a father to his children.

Weak men therefore find Navalny unbearable. Putin cannot say his name. Nor can Musk – and the social media platform he owns suspended the account of Navalny's widow. Trump claimed that Navalny died to show how much Trump suffers. Navalny committed no crimes, but drew attention to those of oligarchs. Trump is a wannabe oligarch who says that, should he become president again, he will round up and imprison his political opponents. He wants to be able to do with all Americans what Putin did to Navalny. And, like Putin, he will claim to be the victim as he does so. The weak man always says that he is the victim.

One way the weak man kills is by broadcasting his fears. Putin might or might not have given a direct order to kill Navalny. More likely it was an indirect suggestion, picked up by other weak men. On 6 January 2021, Trump used language other weak men understood. He now uses the internet to encourage violence against elected representatives, prosecutors, and judges. He prepares for a second coup attempt.

Munich is a city full of resonances for a historian. Hitler's first coup attempt took place here. After his second one, the one that succeeded after an election, he let others understand what he wanted done. Like Putin, and for that matter like Trump, he made his general wishes known, and let others turn them into fearful acts. And so institutions changed, and society altered, and life became fear.

Americans don't tend to learn from foreign examples or from the past. We don't recognize a politics of fear, which makes us vulnerable to it. We assume that any action they take from personal fear must be justified. And so we normalize fear, and spread it, and institutionalize it.

The Republican Party is becoming a party of fear, in which Republicans fear other Republicans, fear their constituents, and fear Trump, which means fearing Russia. Republicans enter the submission chain that binds them to

Trump, and to Putin, and then rationalize what they have done. From this position, actual cooperation with actual Russians no longer seems to be a problem, as we have just seen in the attempt to impeach Biden with the help of Russian lies, and for that matter in a series of events going back a decade.

Americans beyond the cult of MAGA submit in a different way. They decide that the weak man is the strong man, and thereby make it so. They instruct us, absurdly, that the war in Ukraine or the work of democracy makes us "fatigued". If we think that labor and courage are bad things, we are conceding the point – and our democracy – to the weak man. But the work itself is invigorating, as is the example of those doing the work.

American newspapers instruct us that Biden is old. If he's old (goes the thinking), he must be weak; and if he is weak, then we are permitted to give up. But Biden is not weak. He is not running away from prison, or from anything else. He does not act from fear. He gets work done. His record is one of the strongest in the history of the American presidency. And he went to Ukraine with zero military protection. That was courageous. No other president has ever done that.

In Munich I thought of the Ukrainian writer Stanislav Aseyev, whom I last saw in Kyiv. He survived a Russian torture camp, tracked down his own persecutor, and wrote a book about it. Aseyev is now at the front in the Ukrainian army. He doesn't like being in a bunker, because it reminds him of his cell. I saw another Ukrainian soldier I know at the conference. The last time I talked to him he had his right pants leg tied below the amputation. This time he had a prosthesis. He stood and spoke of the "spirit of freedom".

It is absurd, in such a world, where so much is at stake, where so much is to be won, to speak of our "fatigue" either with the struggle in Ukraine or the struggle for our own democracy. Doing so is the prologue to a story of weakness, which ends with the victory of the weak man. When we fall in line behind the fearful, when we forget the "spirit of freedom", we help the weak men create a politics of fear. When we obey in advance, we invite the weak man to take power over our souls, which then means power over our politics.

In 2024, a year of war and a year of elections, a year that will test decency and democracy, the weak man wants to see his fear in our eyes. We will need the courage to admire the courageous, and to say something that might feel risky. For example: we believe in our values, and we believe in our strength. Ukraine can win this war, Biden can win this election, and democracy can thrive.

THE APOCALYPSE WE CHOOSE

Submission chain.

Mike Johnson's Record as Speaker of the House
3 March 2024

In four months as Speaker of the House, Mike Johnson has given Russia a chance to win its war in Ukraine, and thereby turn the world towards tyranny.

Johnson's term of office consists of stratagems to avoid funding Ukraine. He and a minority of Trumpist Republicans have left Ukrainians without the means to defend themselves, and enabled Russian aggressors to retake Ukrainian territory. As a result, troops are killed and disabled every day.

Around the world, Johnson's behavior is seen as betrayal and weakness. We tend to focus on the details of Johnson's various excuses, rather than seeing the larger pattern. Johnson's success in making the war a story about him exemplifies the American propensity to miss the big picture.

Alive? Thank a Ukrainian. The great American capacity is to take others for granted, and our specific form of hubris blinds us to the great services others perform for us. The resistance of the Ukrainian armed forces and Ukrainian civil society is holding back every form of modern catastrophe. Ukrainians are preserving an order established after the Second World War, but also pointing the way towards a brighter future. Their tremendous daily efforts have pushed the world toward a set of better alternatives we would all lack without them. But they need us at their back.

An elementary form of apocalypse is genocide. Russia is making war on Ukraine with the genocidal goal of eliminating Ukrainian society as such. It consciously fights its war with its own national minorities, and takes every opportunity to spread racist propaganda (including about African-Americans). Russian occupiers deport Ukrainian children, rape Ukrainian women, castrate Ukrainian men, and murder Ukrainian cultural leaders with this purpose in mind. They keep children out of school and force families into emigration, all with the goal of putting an end to a nation. Ukrainian resistance, though, has put the backbone into "never again". Where Ukraine holds territory, and that is most of the country, people are saved. Ukrainians have shown that a genocide can be halted – with the right kind of help. When we cut off that help, as we have done, we enable genocide to proceed. This is not only a horror in itself, but a precedent.

A great fear of our age is nuclear war, and Russia has used nuclear blackmail against Ukraine. Russians want Ukraine (and the rest of us) to give up because Russia has nuclear weapons. Russian propaganda instructs that a nuclear power cannot lose a war. This is of course untrue. The US lost in Vietnam, the USSR lost in Afghanistan. Nuclear weapons did not hold the British and French empires together, or bring Israel victory in Lebanon. Had Ukraine submitted to Putin's nuclear blackmail, this would have incentivized every country to build nuclear weapons: some to intimidate, some to prevent intimidation. Ukrainian resistance has saved us from this scenario – thus far. Should America abandon Ukraine, we can expect nuclear proliferation and nuclear jeopardy.

Another traditional worry has been a Russian attack upon a European country that triggers the collective defense provision of the NATO alliance. For now, Ukraine is making this all but impossible. Ukraine has absorbed an attack by Russia. At horrible cost, Ukraine is fulfilling the entire mission of NATO, thereby sparing all other NATO members any risk of loss of territory or of life. The NATO economies are about two-hundred and fifty times as big as the Ukrainian economy. If they exploit a tiny fraction of their economic power, they could easily sustain the Ukrainian armed forces. Unfortunately the largest by far of these NATO members, the United States, is doing nothing. Should this continue, and should Russia win its war in Ukraine, then further war in Europe becomes not only possible, but likely.

For the past two decades, the main concern in Washington, D.C. has been a war with China in the Pacific over Taiwan. Never was this concern more pressing than in February 2022, when Russia began its full-scale invasion of Ukraine. Putin had just received China's blessing for his adventure. Had Ukraine fallen, as so many expected, it would have been a signal that other such adventures were possible. Ukraine's endurance has made clear that offensive operations are unpredictable and costly. Ukrainians are achieving what we could not, as Americans, achieve ourselves: sending a counsel of caution to China without in any way antagonizing the Chinese. Of course, should Ukraine be abandoned by its allies, and should Russia win, our earlier fears would return, and rightly so.

Russia is testing an international order. The basic assumption, since the Second World War, is that states exist and have borders that war cannot alter. When Russia attacked Ukraine, it was attacking this principle. Russia's rulers expected that a new age of chaos would begin, in which only lies and force would count. The consensus in Washington, we should remember, was the same. In the beginning, the American leadership expected the Ukrainian president to flee and for the country to fall in three days. Every day since the fourth day is one in which Ukrainian blood has bought for us a future that we ourselves did not think we had. After two years, too many of us take this for granted. But if we decide not to help the Ukrainians, disorder will ensue, and prosperity will collapse.

For the past half century, people have been rightly concerned about global warming. Whether we get through the next half century will depend upon a balance of power between those who make money from fossil fuels and lie about their consequences and those who tell the truth about science and seek alternative sources of energy. Vladimir Putin is the most important fossil fuel oligarch. Both his wealth and his power arise from natural gas and oil reserves. His war in Ukraine is a foretaste of the struggle for resources we will all face should Putin and other fossil fuel oligarchs get the upper hand. Precisely because Ukraine resisted, important economies have accelerated their green transition. Should Ukraine be abandoned and lose, it seems unlikely that there will be another chance to hold back fossil fuel oligarchy and save the climate. More broadly, Putin's idiotic notion that there is no Ukraine is an example of the kind of oligarchical fantasy which wastes time and destroys life as we try to confront the world's actual problems.

Global hunger is an important scenario for catastrophic global suffering in an age of drastic inequality and resource strife. Here no country is more important than Ukraine. For more than two thousand years, since the ancient Greeks, the fertile soil of Ukraine has fed neighboring lands and civilizations. Ukraine today is capable of feeding something like half a billion people. Russia's war against Ukraine has also been a hunger war. Russia has mined farms, flooded others by destroying a critical dam, targeted grain-storage facilities, and blockaded the Black Sea to prevent exports. In 2023, Ukraine was able to win an astonishing victory, clearing the western Black Sea of the Russian navy, and opening lanes for export of grain. Because the Ukrainians did this on their own, it has hardly been covered in our press. But it is a huge achievement. People in the Near East and Africa are being fed who might otherwise starve. If Ukraine is allowed to fall, all of this can be reversed, and suffering and war will spread to those vulnerable and critical areas.

From a different perspective, people fear that our world can end as a result of artificial intelligence, digital propaganda, and the collapse of the human contact needed for political decency. For a decade now, Russia has been in the forefront of digital manipulation. Its first invasion of Ukraine, in 2014, was successful chiefly as a hybrid war, in which it found vulnerable minds in the West and inserted useful memes – ones which are still in use today. And Russia does find backers today among the digital oligarchs, most notably Elon Musk, who has bent his personal account and indeed his entire platform to become an instrument of Russian propaganda. That said, the Ukrainians have, this time, shown how this can be resisted. Volodymyr Zelens'kyi and other Ukrainian leaders, by taking personal risks in time of danger, have reminded us that there is a real world. And Ukrainian civil society has this time taken a playful approach to new media, deconstructing Russian propaganda and reminding us of the human side – and the human stakes.

Perhaps the most insidious calamity we face is one of doubt: we cease to believe in ourselves, as human beings with values, who deserve to rule themselves in the system we call democracy. For most of this century, democracy has been in decline, and this decline has been accompanied by a discourse of passivity and a lack of resolve. Russia's attack on Ukraine – the rare event of an armed autocracy seeking to destroy a peaceful democracy by military force – was a turning point in this history. Which way we will all turn remains to be seen. By resisting on the battlefield, Ukraine has, for the time being anyway, preserved its own democracy, and given new hope to democracies in general. There is nothing automatic about democracy. People have to believe that they should rule. And this will always involve some risk. By taking great risks for the right values, Ukrainians can and do encourage others around the world. If Ukrainians are killed, maimed, and forced to retreat as a result of US policy, everyone is demoralized – including us.

If Americans let Ukrainians down, it will be a blow, perhaps a fatal one, to the "spirit of freedom", as a Ukrainian veteran put it in a speech I heard at the Munich Security Council. We need that spirit, in part to oppose those who lack it. The people who block aid for Ukraine today wish our own democracy ill. In the last few days and weeks we have witnessed, again and again, the overlap between Russian influence in American politics, opposition to aid to Ukraine, and hostility toward the American constitutional system. Putin knows that his only route to Kyiv passes through Washington, D.C., and he has acted accordingly.

The people working to assure the destruction of democracy in Ukraine also oppose democracy in America. We have just experienced a bogus impeachment proceeding against President Biden, where the chief accusation (long ago discredited by Ukrainian and other journalists, incidentally) arose from a Russian agent. Mike Johnson is in a submission chain that passes through Donald Trump to Vladimir Putin. Trump presents himself as an admirer of Putin and has been his client, in one form or another, for a decade. He has succeeded in conditioning the media by teaching his followers to shout "Russia hoax" whenever the subject comes up: but, all the same, Russia has backed him in every campaign and is backing him in this one. Johnson's 2018 congressional campaign, for that matter, took laundered funds from a Russian oligarch, and Johnson was one of the Congressmen most deeply implicated in Trump's attempted coup in 2021.

Ukraine should and can win this war. To do so, it needs arms and funds. The amount needed of both is tiny on an American scale, not anything we would even notice. It is the choices of certain Americans that have brought the Ukrainians to this cruel pass, and brought the world to the edge of multiple catastrophe. Should we fail to assist Ukraine, we will be inviting the worst of catastrophes. We will put the security of the world at risk, and betray what is best about ourselves. Americans can enable Ukrainian victory. If we fail to do so, we will face an apocalypse Americans have chosen. And, in particular, an apocalypse Mike Johnson has chosen.

Timothy Snyder is the Richard C. Levin Professor of History at Yale University and a permanent fellow at the Institute for Human Sciences in Vienna. He speaks five and reads ten European languages. His eight chief books are Nationalism, Marxism, and Modern Central Europe: A Biography of Kazimierz Kelles-Krauz *(1998);* The Reconstruction of Nations: Poland, Ukraine, Lithuania, Belarus, 1569-1999 *(2003);* Sketches from a Secret War: A Polish Artist's Mission to Liberate Soviet Ukraine *(2005);* The Red Prince: The Secret Lives of a Habsburg Archduke *(2008);* Bloodlands: Europe Between Hitler and Stalin *(2010);* Thinking the Twentieth Century *(with Tony Judt, 2012);* Black Earth: The Holocaust as History and Warning *(2015);* On Tyranny: Twenty Lessons from the Twentieth Century *(2017); and* The Road to Unfreedom: Russia, Europe, America *(2018). He has also co-edited three further books:* The Wall Around the West: State Borders and Immigration Controls in Europe and North America *(2001);* Stalin and Europe: Terror, War, Domination *(2013); and* The Balkans as Europe *(2018). His essays are collected in* Ukrainian History, Russian Politics, European Futures *(2014), and* The Politics of Life and Death *(2015).*

Snyder's work has appeared in forty languages and has received a number of prizes, including the Emerson Prize in the Humanities, the Literature Award of the American Academy of Arts and Letters, the Václav Havel Foundation Prize, the Foundation for Polish Science Prize in the Social Sciences, the Leipzig Award for European Understanding, the Dutch Auschwitz Committee award, and the Hannah Arendt Prize in Political Thought. Snyder was a Marshall Scholar at Oxford, has received the Carnegie and Guggenheim fellowships, and holds state orders from Estonia, Lithuania, and Poland. He has appeared in documentaries, on network television, and in major films. His books have inspired poster campaigns and exhibitions, films, sculpture, a punk rock song, a rap song, a play, and an opera. His words are quoted in political demonstrations around the world, most recently in Hong Kong. He is researching a family history of nationalism and finishing a philosophical book about freedom. He lives in New Haven, Connecticut.

DHÁ DÁNTA

Simon Ó Faoláin

War in the Latin.

DON PILIB AR LONG COGAIDH

Mar atáim faoi láthair ó thaobh glórtha —
Cicero nó Valla, ní chloisim ceachtar,
ach brilléis aisteach agus béarlagair
barbartha garbh na mairnéalach.

Tá glór gáifeach na ngunnaí móra
(gléas do cheapadh ag duine uafásach
éigin chun an cine daonna a mhilleadh)
mar thoirneach ag tormáil i mo chluasa.

Táim i mbun claímh seachas i mbun pinn,
is nach beag an líon gur féidir riamh
máistreacht a bhaint amach i gceann
den dís úd, gan trácht orthu araon.

Sliocht as litir Laidine go Patrick Synnott, c. 1615

CAOINEANN DON PILIB A THEAGHLACH

Deirtear go gcanann an eala i mbéal an bháis amhrán,
dá bhrí sin canaimse faoi bhás mo gaol ionúin
mo thuismitheoirí aontaithe ag ceangal rúin

do ghin mórsheisear agus deichniúr clainne,
sinne, comhartha a ngrá ab ea gach duine,
ach do théasc an bás deichniúr is triúr i mbláth a n-óige

tráth roimh léirscrios go raibh ár dtír fós slán.
An dís gan nead, deoraithe sa Spáinn,
níor fágadh acu ach ceathrar iar mbris is dán.

Dán Laidine a cuireadh lena leabhar an "Patritiana Decas"

AUTHOR'S NOTE

I have been writing some poems/versions closely based on the work of Don Philip
Ó Súilleabháin Bé, the Latin scholar, naturalist and Irish exile who, having fled his
home on Dursey Island before the massacre there during the Nine Years War, spent
the rest of his life in Galicia. He also spent time fighting in the Spanish navy against
the Algerian Corsairs. He is a fascinating person and the translations are a work in
progress.

The two short pieces above are in one case a translation of a Latin poem he
wrote lamenting the death of his family, and in the other a poem based on a Latin
letter he wrote to his Latin tutor from aboard a Spanish warship. The prose below
English translations are from Denis C. O'Sullivan's published translation of *The Natural History of Ireland*, part of Don Philip's larger work the *Zoilomastix*, and my Irish
versions are dense, short verses based on these.

DON PHILIP ON BOARD A WARSHIP

"As I am at present, I hear neither the eloquence of Cicero nor the elegances of Valla or Manutius but the strange and barbarous language of sailors. The sound of cannon, which some dreadful person invented for the destruction of the human race, is rattling in my ears. I am wielding the sword not the pen. How few are those that can excel in either, much less both."

DON PHILIP LAMENTS HIS FAMILY

"They say the dying swan sings a song. So I sing the sad death of my dear ones. My parents united by the ties of wedlock gave birth to seventeen children, dear tokens of love, but the dark day of death cut off thirteen in the flower of youth, when my country was still unharmed. My parents, exiles in Spain, beheld but four after the mournful fall of defeated Ireland."

Simon Ó Faoláin was born in Dublin and raised in the Corca Dhuibhne Gaeltacht in Co Kerry. He trained as an archaeologist and for many years worked in the academic and commercial spheres, authoring and co-authoring several academic books.

Now a full-time Irish-language writer and translator, he has published three books of poetry: Anam Mhadra (Dog's Soul, 2008), *As* Gaineamh (Out of Sand, 2011), *and* Fé Sholas Luaineach (By Unsteady Light, 2014), *all from Coiscéim, as well as an illustrated chapbook,* Baile do Bhí (A Home that Was, 2014, Púca Press). *Amongst the awards for his work are the Glen Dimplex Prize, The Strong Prize, The Walter Macken Prize, The Colm Cille Prize (twice) and The Foras na Gaeilge Prize (four times). His latest two books are translations:* An Corrmhíol (The Midge, Coiscéim), *an Irish translation of the Scottish Gaelic long poem* A' Mheanbhchuileag *by Fearghas Mac Fionnlaigh; and* An Fheadóg Fia (The Deer Whistle, Southword Imprints), *translations from the Chinese poet Jidi Majia. He is Director of An Fhéile Bheag Filíochta, an annual bilingual poetry and arts festival in Baile an Fheirtéaraigh, and Editor of the Irish language literary journal* Aneas. *He is also a noted sean-nós singer with a particular interest in the songs of the great West Kerry singer Seán de hÓra.*

TWO POEMS

———

Ben Keatinge

Silences.

THE EDGE OF THINGS
August, 1969

We've come this summer to the edge
of things, the calm of Cleggan,
Irish rain, sheep, an air of loitering,
unreachable, like Hull; the poet
Murphy, neither Englishman
nor Taig, writes of credal wars.

We left Belfast as soon as, decently,
we could, seeing the city out of joint,
inflamed. This coast is different,
islands – Inishbofin, Inishshark,
their wavelets rippling without need;
you feel what's happening underneath
the boat, huge buoyancy offshore,
the wide Atlantic, calm before the storm.

TALKING ABOUT THE WAR

Germany is different came a voice
echoing from childhood saying
you never talk about the war.

The girl from Banja Luka walked
through forests, paying gangs,
our lives for money, they took money.

Ferit in Prishtina, grizzled, grim,
spoke of the bombardment,
the Serbs, he said, *stole everything.*

The outrage at Kumanovo last weekend?
My neighbour, laughing, *that's a brawl,*
shooting for the cameras, a teacup-storm.

For a little while we spoke,
then said nothing, sitting,
looking eye to eye, listening

to a long, volcanic silence.

Benjamin Keatinge is a Visiting Research Fellow at the School of English, Trinity College, Dublin. His poems have been published in The Stony Thursday Book, Orbis, Eborakon, The Galway Review, Agenda, Cassandra Voices, Flare *and in* Writing Home: The "New Irish" Poets *(The Dedalus Press, 2019). He taught English literature for nine years at South East European University, North Macedonia and he has travelled widely in the Balkans. He is the editor of* Making Integral: Critical Essays on Richard Murphy *(Cork University Press, 2019).*

PORTRAIT WITH NO MODEL

Marjana Savka

After happiness?

What were the chances that the first time they had sex, they discovered they had both lost their virginity at the same small hotel in Rusanivka. Obviously in different years. He actually stopped and laughed out loud. It was unexpectedly nice to have similar first-time stories. Especially since neither of them lived in Kyiv. Maybe it was the cheapest hotel in the city, who knows? It was so long ago. He said they should find that hotel and make love there, though it was probably long gone.

"Should we take a walk down memory lane: with whom and when?" she said, rolling over onto her belly and sweetly snuggling down into the sheets.

"No, I haven't finished what I started and I don't want to think about anyone else. I don't know why, but with you I can fuck and talk at the same time. And that turns me on even more."

He said this while flipping her onto her back and thrusting deep inside her. Now he was moving slowly, stretching out the pleasure and exciting her with his touches, only to then speed up and vibrate. She could barely breathe or signal her pleasure, ultimately coming five seconds before him. At that moment, he emerged from her like he was bursting to the surface for air, and came on her belly, blue in the light of the Christmas tree. It was such simultaneous and magical release from all the restraints of the body and mind that a deep, weightless sleep immediately overtook them.

In her sleep, she felt the weight of his arm on her arm, and breathed in his perfect smell. This was exactly how her husband was supposed to smell. She seemed to have a dream about his smell, though it was probably less of a dream and more of an endless cascade of falling asleep and waking up, as though her brain were constantly checking to be sure this man didn't go anywhere or the pressure of his arm on hers didn't lessen. He breathed silently. Every time she woke up, she listened for his heartbeat.

Ultimately, deep sleep swallowed her completely and turned off this unconscious control.

Simultaneous alarms from both their iPhones announced morning. The total darkness looked little like the start of a new day. The battery on the Christmas lights had died and the power wasn't back on yet.

She thought that was even better – it removed the anxiety that his body wouldn't be as beautiful in the light. That something would ruin the night's corporeal idyll. That she'd discover he had an ugly foot or kneecap. When they'd entered the apartment the night before in total darkness and started frantically ripping their clothes off, there was no chance to get a good look at each another.

This had always been important to her. She spent all day long in her cold studio, watching her students do anatomical sketches. She was daily persecuted by drawings of wrists, shins, torsos, and buttocks. Even now during the war she managed to hire nude models to keep her students' education going, despite the cold in the classrooms. The academy was alive and working. They were volunteering and even taking exams. Her students adored her. She devoted more and more of herself to them and spent less time on her own art. She needed a reason and motivation to paint.

He turned on a pocket flashlight to look for his scattered socks. As he was about to put them on, she noticed the noble shape of his narrow foot, the beautiful vault of his arch, properly formed, his nimble, perfect toes, and a hot wave of tenderness swept over her. She sat on the floor near the bed and kissed these feet. Caught by surprise, he pulled her up by her elbows, literally wrapping her in his arms, and ran his fingers through her mussed hair. She found his lips and fell to them as if he were the only air in an oxygenless environment. She realized that the whole night of sex and sleep was just a long prelude to what was happening now when their time together was practically up and he had to leave. But he held her so tightly they became a single body, a single substance. His skin entered her skin, his blood her blood, his lymph hers. His tattoos appeared on her body and the constellation of birthmarks beneath her breasts showed up on his skin.

———

They got ready in a hurry. His phone kept blowing up with new texts. He dressed quickly and efficiently – obviously a soldier.

"I'm sorry, but I have to go."

"Listen, don't apologize."

"I don't want to leave you, but I have to."

"Thank you, just … thank you."

His backpack barely squeezed through the small front door.

"Wait!"

He turned to look at her, flashing his light. Both of their eyes sparkled.

"Promise me", she took his hand, "promise me you'll come back soon and I'll draw you. You'll be my model."

"Yeah", he smiled, "that'll do wonders for my career."

"We'll sell it for millions", she tried to joke.

"Just don't forget my cut", he touched his lips to her nose and ran down the stairs. She rushed to the window. Outside it was just starting to get light. A jeep flashed its headlights and sped away.

———

She had to clear out of this apartment – which she hadn't even glanced around – by eleven. She collapsed back onto the pillows and fell asleep. An hour later she woke up like a shot as if ice water had been dumped on her head: they hadn't exchanged numbers. She got to her lecture forty minutes late and only eight students remained out of thirty. She should have told the TA she was sick and not tried to come in. It wasn't that far from the truth – her throat had swollen shut, her head was pounding from lack of sleep, and her eyes were watering. She gave them a list of books to read and dismissed them. She had ten missed calls from her mom.

This moment was always painful and unpleasant. Calling her mom after a prolonged break was like taking a deep breath and jumping into a cold April ocean.

"Where are you?" her mom didn't consider it necessary to use any greetings.

Reeling on the inside as if she'd been hit, she exhaled, "At work. Where else?"

"You didn't sleep at home, you don't know how to keep a house, your kid is running around fatherless, motherless, who knows where!"

This was too much.

———

"My son is not 'who knows where,' but with his father as you very well know. And I'm not fifteen years old. I don't have to report where I spend the night. I said I wouldn't be home."

"Don't hang up on me. Get some bread, bread and some of my heart pills. You didn't even ask me how my blood pressure was today."

She could hear noise, coughing, and a sob on the other end. She hung up.

December wasn't her month. They had sun even less often than power. It was gray and chilly. It was too early to go home; Yarchyk wasn't back yet. He alone, her son, her golden child, illuminated all the shadows of her lonely life. Sometimes it seemed like she didn't deserve him, that's how much love he offered her, forgiving all the shortcomings of her less-than-ideal mothering.

The coffeeshop on the corner was where   she went for her favorite flat white. At other places, they couldn't get the milky coffee just right. While she waited for Ustia, she could sit in the windowsill with her coffee, getting cozy in the cushions, close her eyes, and try to go back to the night, to remember every touch and the scent of his body.

Ustia was right on time, damn it, so she had to snap out of her sweet reveries.

"Hi, are you … sick? Your face is on fire."

Ustia was extremely observant. Nothing got past her. She'd check a hundred times to make sure she got the loose hair off her jacket, that her button wasn't loose, that her eyeliner wasn't smudged. It would have been weird if she *hadn't* noticed a change in her face.

"Well, if love is a disease, then there's a chance I'm sick."

"Come on. Straight to love?" Ustia looked her in the eyes. "I saw you on Wednesday. Today's only Friday."

She didn't say anything, but her lips quivered.

"Tinder?" Ustia guessed.

"No." She paused. "The Garrison Church."

"Alina!"

"What? Do you really think you can find love on Tinder? It's just one-night stands, and even that's not guaranteed."

"Okay", Ustyna took a sip of her latte. "So, it's not about sex."

"Or is it? It was my first time during this whole war. I was about to go crazy. I thought that I'd never get laid and I'd have to wear a chastity belt until the very last Russian died. But this is more than that!"

"Yeah, yeah, yeah" her friend stopped her. "I hear ya. What's his name?"

"Artem."

"Easterner?"

"From Dnipro."

She had never been to Dnipro. Actually, she hadn't been many places at all. After the war, she definitely wanted to visit the cities she hadn't seen before. Some of them she'd never get to. Once she had the opportunity to go to Mariupol with her husband on a work trip, but she didn't. Now it's hard to even remember why. It's scary to think that the former reality no longer exists, that some cities have simply been erased from the face of the earth. Yesterday she was in the Garrison Church – she had either gone in because she was cold or because some force pulled her in. The sharp smell of candles and incense slapped her in the face. It was full of people – mostly in uniform and barely squeezing into the chapel. In front of the altar were four closed caskets draped with yellow-and-blue and red-and-black flags. Young, armed soldiers stood in an honor guard. "Eternal Memory" in the chaplain's beautiful baritone cut through the heavy air and the men's choir took it up so powerfully that she got dizzy. She felt hundreds of needles tingling the back of her neck and she was certain she was falling through space. But she didn't actually fall because someone strong scooped her up from behind. She was afraid to breathe. She remained in this stranger's embrace for a few minutes, feeling supported. Her head was spinning. The man behind her must have sensed she needed to go outside because he turned her around, took her by the hand, and led her into the fresh air. He stayed beside her, tightly squeezing her hand. She finally dared look up and was met by his gray-blue eyes. She could tell by the patches on his jacket that he was a special forces officer. He was tanned, not very tall, with a trim, barely salt-and-pepper beard, and piercing eyes. A few minutes later they were sitting in a cafe together. He ordered chicken soup and a warm slice of quiche Lorraine for her, saying she was white as a lily and it was his responsibility to put some color back in her cheeks. There was a strange sense of recognition in everything that was happening. The man next to her couldn't have been a stranger. For the first time in the whole war, she felt completely safe. She was drawn to him. She wanted to accidentally brush his hand, scoot closer, feel the infrared waves of his warmth. It was getting dark outside when they exited the cafe into the cold of early evening and walked all the streets around the market. They ended up in front of the building where he had rented an apartment. He had to leave the city the next day. Going in to warm up was just a pretext for hiding from peering eyes. As soon as they crossed the threshold, all the power in the whole block went out. His hands were taking off her coat, unzipping her jeans, tearing off her t-shirt.

"Where is he now?" Ustia jerked her back from her memories of the day before.

"He left."

"What do you know about him?"

"I know that I have to draw him."

"That much? Well, you can find him online. What's his last name?"

"I don't know …"

"Eh, you can look him up by his phone number."

"Phone number?" despair flashed in her eyes. "I don't have his number."

———

When she got home, Yarchyk was doing his math homework at the kitchen table by the light of two flashlights, his head bent low over his notebook. Her mother said nothing. Buckwheat was boiling away in the kitchen, filling the apartment with the smell of her childhood when there was never enough of anything except for the fragrant warmth of home. Her father had the wonderful habit of putzing around the kitchen, forever making buckwheat. She steeped some tea in the darkness. She felt a pain settling into her body that couldn't be compared to anything else. How was she to go on living without this man who flashed like a star and then disappeared, went back to his war, offering her no hope they'd ever meet again? The realization that this was their only encounter was eating away at her heart. What she had experienced with him in their half a day together wasn't typical for her. It wasn't something she'd normally do. They took no selfies; they said nothing about their families or social standing. All they talked about was how important it was for soldiers to have a warm place to live and hot food, whether you could believe the official reports on casualties, how and where they each lost their virginity, how a weapon is not a woman to love, how painting is like speaking when you've run out of words, how adulthood is the time after happiness.

———

When she put Yarchyk down, she called Ustia.

"I can't sleep."

"Are you crying?"

"Uh-huh."

"How serious is it?"

"I don't know. It just hurts. Okay, fine, I didn't think to write down his number because I was on such an emotional high, but what about him?"

"Maybe he felt that way too."

"Who knows. Maybe it was all too ordinary for him – come into the city, sleep with the first broad he comes across, go on his way."

"No. Not the first broad."

"Yeah, and he wasn't for me either. He was special."

"Draw him."

She liked Ustia's suggestion. Besides, it was basically the only thing she could do anyway.

She got out some watercolor paper and a pencil, gave herself a little more light by lighting two candles, and attempted to recall his features. To no avail. Over and over she made sketches. She had to close her eyes to see his face, the line of his brow, his cheekbones, eyes, lips ... His lips. Yes, there was something special about them, a wandering laughter in the corners of his mouth that disappeared into his mustache. A smile suddenly appeared on the paper, one that determined the rest of the portrait. After that the cheekbones, radial waves from his eyes, his nose, forehead, short hair, and trim beard practically drew themselves. It was him, Artem. She looked at the drawing and smiled. Way to go, Alina, you could be a forensic sketch artist. She laughed at herself.

She took a picture of the drawing and texted it to Ustia. "What a hottie!" her girlfriend wrote back. But now what? Should she post it to Facebook with the caption "Help me find Artem because I can't live without him?" Her colleagues especially would get a kick out of that. She tucked the portrait into her sketchbook and put it in her backpack. Every time she walked past the Garrison Church she checked to see if her friend in camouflage was there.

The air raid sirens and shelling picked up in late December. She would go into the bomb shelters together with her students. But it wasn't scary. What scared her was the feeling that she'd never see Artem again. Christmas was getting nearer and this year they'd be celebrating on the twenty-fifth with the rest of the West. One morning Symon ran into the department all out of breath. All the artists in the academy considered him opportunistic and spoiled by fame, but she liked him because he wasn't interested in copying the living classics who stank of naphthalene and embalming fluid.

"Listen, sweetheart, I'm putting together a Christmas exhibition at Hrushka Gallery. If you've got anything, let me know. But right away. Christmas is coming sooner this year – well, you know that."

Symon slammed the door behind him, causing the window panes to ring. There were only three days until the birth of the Lord Jesus. It was raining.

—

Her ex-husband wanted to take Yarchyk to his parents' for almost an entire week. She couldn't say no since they had a big house outside the city with a fireplace and a black lab and, anyway, her son needed to spend time with his father. From time to time, their year-old divorce was still triggering for her. Especially when he wanted to introduce Yarchyk to his current flame. But she couldn't imagine taking him back. He was a complete stranger, a cold person she'd rather forget. But actually doing so was difficult. Her ex had recently entered the flowers-and-chocolate phase and often posted pictures with the "girl of his dreams" on Instagram. The girl was cute enough, even if her eyes bulged a little. Anyway, it wasn't about the bug eyes of this unknown woman who was sleeping with her ex-husband, but about the fact that he found her replacement so fast. She wasn't really looking. "I wonder how Artem is", she'd torture herself. "Is he alive? One night of happiness and that's it?"

—

Her mom wanted to visit her sister for Christmas. She couldn't remember the last time she'd had the chance to be alone. It made no difference to her that she was missing the holidays. What was there to celebrate? Not the love she lost thanks to her foolishness. Rather than buying a bunch of rich food, she picked up a large canvas and a few new brushes at the art supply store. She couldn't shake Symon's offer. Surprisingly the power was still on, so she had no difficulty getting her workspace ready. She stretched the canvas and set it up on her easel, laid out her tubes of acrylic paint. Artem's face appeared before her, his bright eyes and those clandestine corners of his mouth. She painted two wide stripes with a distinct line of demarcation: carolers walking through snow drifts on the horizon. Some carried weapons, others bells and they were being followed by transparent angels whose wings brushed the snow clouds above. In the middle of the snowy steppe stood a figure – a soldier? an archangel? her Artem? – holding the *vertep* Christmas star by its handle. Its rays cut through the snowy haze.

It was 2:00 a.m. when she finished. Tiny snowflakes twirled outside her window, each one unique. No one was coughing; no one was tossing in their sleep. The house was unusually quiet. She stepped back from the painting and stared into the face on the canvas. It was him. At least how she remembered him. This was why she liked acrylics – she could paint fine detail with her brush and also work with a palette knife to create texture. The man in the painting looked like he was about to step off the canvas into the room.

———

Symon was a master at organizing exhibitions. Hrushka Gallery was so crowded there was no room to breathe. There was a little of everything: the art scene, some officials, a few socialites, professors and students from the academy, journalists, poets, and onlookers who came in for the warmth and modest reception. Her painting was practically at the center of the show. The light of lamps fell on the *vertep* star, highlighting its rays even more. Symon invited the artists to take turns speaking about their pieces. Now she had everyone's attention. She felt awkward talking about herself and would have preferred if others did it. But Symon was already asking her what she wanted to convey with this painting.

She blabbered something about the Star of Bethlehem that was now in the hands of Ukraine's defenders and did her best not to let her voice shake. When everyone was finally standing around holding their glasses of Prosecco, a young blonde boy in civilian dress approached her.

"May I ask you something? This man in the drawing ... Did you maybe paint our commander?"

"What's your commander's name?" she asked, feeling her insides shrinking.

"Artem Kovalenko."

"He's alive? Artem is alive?"

"Of course. Not far from Soledar. I'm going back to my unit tomorrow. I had three days' leave. My sister dragged me out to this exhibition, but I'm glad. It's nice here. Well, can I get a picture with you and my commander? Alina?"

"Yes", her voice belonged to someone else. Her hands trembled. The guy stretched out his arm and pointed his phone camera at her.

"I'll show my commander."

She gathered her courage and quickly said, "Could you possibly give him my number? Here." And she quickly wrote her digits on the back of the pamphlet.

"Yeah, actually I've got his number. Write this down. But yeah, I'll give him yours. Download Signal. I don't think he uses anything else."

———

She had his number. Her hands clutched her phone; it was difficult to resist dialing right away. She grabbed her coat and went out into the cold evening. Generators were humming outside, providing power to the exhibition and the neighboring shops. "That's what light sounds like", she thought, taking a deep breath of cold air. She downloaded the app but couldn't bring herself to write anything. It was too scary to get a response, or not, or something like "thank you for the nice evening". She had to get home because her ex was bringing their son back from winter break. She missed Yarchyk so much she wasn't sure she'd let him go for so long the next time.

Artem's message came two days later.

"Alina, I knew we'd find each other. You can't just disappear from my life like that. Even if I was so caught up in my emotions that I forgot to get your number. I would have found you somehow – I know where you work :) But right now I can't get out of here. So, you beat me to it. Turns out you can draw me even without a model? How'd you do it? I can't believe it's really me. Though, I've never actually carried the *vertep* star. I guess there's more to come. Including seeing you again. And everything you've ever dreamed of. Will you let me make your dreams come true? I'd really like to. Because I think about you all the time. And love you."

Translated, from the Ukrainian, by Ali Kinsella.

Marjana Savka was born in 1973 in Kopychyntsi, Ukraine, and holds a degree in Ukrainian Studies from the Ivan Franko National University of Lviv. She is the author of 10 volumes of poems and six children's books, a number of which have been translated into English, Russian and Polish. She is also a composer and singer, and works as a translator.

POEM

———

Alhierd Bacharevič

Bloodlands.

ANAEMIA PATRIOTAE

Sometimes, I ransack myself for
blood.
For Polish blood,
for Jewish blood.
For Lithuanian blood,
for Latvian blood.
Slumped over the laptop at night,
I ransack myself for blood until
I pass out.
I try every spelling
of my family name:
with a z, Latinized, adding a squiggle.
Yet, the blood won't
come.
If only I woke up in a pool
of good blood.
With a passport of a free country.
Yes, sometimes I enjoy
thinking about blood.
I imagine myself
in the office of some consul:
Look what I have for you here!
What is this?
It's my blood.
My blood, same as your blood.
Here, lick it.
Lick it and give me a passport.
Look, your tie is now splashed

with that very blood that you list
on your website.
Now you and I are of the same blood.
Like brothers.
One word and I'll splash this whole bloody place.
I exchange blood for citizenship.
If a passport were blood sausage,
how much can you stuff into yourself
without bread?
My grandmother ate bread with every dish.
Even with pasta.
She'd sprinkle white Soviet bread with sugar
and say: nothing
in this world tastes better.
I did not believe her.
Under Polish rule,
she lived
in a village near Valozhyn Town.
And my grandfather lived there.
And my father's mother lived near the Navahradak Town
in the village where flies were swimming in milk.
Everyone I know
ate bread, if lucky,
and dreamed of sugar
on these bloodlands.
My family name, is it
that common
in this bloodless land?
And how many people have my last name
beyond the northern borders?
Nah,
I stake my last hope on the grandmother.
On my last name.
On the Jews.
On the Polish-Lithuanian Commonwealth.
On the Grand Duchy of Lithuania.
On God.
On hell.

I must have at least
some blood
recognized by the international community.
No blood found,
the search engine reports.
Please contact the archives.
Contacting the archives comes with a fee.
But here's the free truth:
you got neither kith nor kin.
I pass out
with nothing.
I fall asleep like a scientist
in an empty lab.
From the photos on the walls
my ancestors watch
and whisper:
our descendant is lost,
our great-grandson,
our pumpkin,
he has completely lost it
with this foreign blood.
We must have died too soon.
We need to dig ourselves from under the ground
and fill out his documents:
that our blood is that cursed blood, once upon a time
shed to the last drop.
To the last drop of that blood, that
blood was shed into this land,
and they called it
Belarussian blood.

Translated, from the Belarusian, by Valzhyna Mort.

Alhierd Bacharevič was born in Minsk, Belarus, in 1975. He is an author of several novels and collections of short stories and essays. His 900-page novel Dogs of Europe *(2019) received the Book of the Year Prize, the independent Reader's Prize and the Second Jerzy Gedroyc Prize in Belarus. His novel* Alindarka's Children *(New Directions, 2014) won the PEN Translates*

Award for the translation of the book. Having begun as a poet, he published a volume of poetry in 2023, Poems, *in which the above poem appears. He lives in exile in Austria.*

Valzhyna Mort is a poet, essayist and translator born in 1981 in Minsk, Belarus. She is the author of five poetry collections, the first three of which were written in Belarusian. Her fourth, Collected Body *(Copper Canyon Press, 2011) was the first composed entirely in English. This was followed by* Music for the Dead and Resurrected *(Farrar, Straus, Giroux, 2020), named one of the best poetry books of 2020 by* The New York Times, *and subsequently awarded the 2020 International Griffin Poetry Prize and the 2022 UNT Rilke Prize. She is recipient of many other prizes and fellowships, and her poetry is translated into a dozen languages, including full collections in German, Swedish and Ukrainian. With Ilya Kaminsky and Katie Farris, Mort co-edited* Gossip and Metaphysics: Russian Modernist Poems and Prose *(Tupelo Press 2014). She is also the editor of* Something Indecent: Poems Recommended by Eastern European Poets *(Red Hen Press, 2013). She teaches Creative Writing at Cornell University, in Ithaca, New York.*